Praise For This Bo

The authors have obviously explored the paths toward a. architecture. There is value in learning from their experience. If you have responsibility for or influence over how your organization uses artificial intelligence you will find *Smarter Data Science* an invaluable read. It is noteworthy that the book is written with a sense of scope that lends to its credibility. So much written about AI technologies today seems to assume a technical vacuum. We are not all working in startups! We have legacy technology that needs to be considered. The authors have created an excellent resource that acknowledges that enterprise context is a nuanced and important problem. The ideas are presented in a logical and clear format that is suitable to the technologist as well as the businessperson.

Christopher Smith, Chief Knowledge Management and
Innovation Officer, Sullivan & Cromwell, LLC

It has been always been a pleasure to learn from Neal. The stories and examples that urge every business to stay "relevant" served to provide my own source of motivation. The concepts presented in this book helped to resolve issues that I have been having to address. This book teaches almost all aspects of the data industry. The experiences, patterns, and anti-patterns, are thoroughly explained. This work provides benefit to a variety of roles, including architects, developers, product owners, and business executives. For organizations exploring AI, this book is the cornerstone to becoming successful.

Harry Xuegang Huang Ph.D., External Consultant,
A.P. Moller – Maersk (Denmark)

This is by far one of the best and most refreshing books on AI and data science that I have come across. The authors seek and speak the truth and they penetrate into the core of the challenge most organizations face in finding value in their data: moving focus away from a tendency to connect the winning dots by 'magical' technologies and overly simplified methods. The book is laid out in a well-considered and mature approach that is grounded in deliberation, pragmatism, and respect for information. By following the authors' advice, you will unlock true and long-term value and avoid the many pitfalls that fashionistas and false prophets have come to dominate the narrative in AI.

Jan Gravesen, M.Sc., IBM Distinguished Engineer,
Director and Chief Technology Officer, IBM

Most of the books on data analytics and data science focus on tools and techniques of the discipline and do not provide the reader with a complete framework to plan and implement projects that solve business problems and foster competitive advantage. Just because machine learning and new methodologies learn from data and do not require a preconceived model for analysis does not eliminate the need for a robust information management program and required processes. In *Smarter Data Science*, the authors present a holistic model that emphasizes how critical data and data management are in implementing successful value-driven data analytics and AI solutions. The book presents an elegant and novel approach to data management and explores its various layers and dimensions (from data creation/ownership and governance to quality and trust) as a key component of a well-integrated methodology for value-adding data sciences and AI. The book covers the components of an agile approach to data management and information architecture that fosters business innovation and can adapt to ever changing requirements and priorities. The many examples of recent data challenges facing diverse businesses make the book extremely readable and relevant for practical applications. This is an excellent book for both data officers and data scientists to gain deep insights into the fundamental relationship between data management, analytics, machine learning, and AI.

Ali Farahani, Ph.D., Former Chief Data Officer,
County of Los Angeles; Adjunct Associate Professor, USC

There are many different approaches to gaining insights with data given the new advances in technology today. This book encompasses more than the technology that makes AI and machine learning possible, but truly depicts the process and foundation needed to prepare that data to make AI consumable and actionable. I thoroughly enjoyed the section on data governance and the importance of accessible, accurate, curated, and organized data for any sort of analytics consumption. The significance and differences in zones and preparation of data also has some fantastic points that should be highly considered in any sort of analytics project. The authors' ability to describe best practices from a true journey of data within an organization in relation to business needs and information outcomes is spot on. I would highly recommend this book to anyone learning, playing, or working in the wonderful space of Data & AI.

Phil Black, VP of Client Services for Data and AI, TechD

The authors have pieced together data governance, data architecture, data topologies, and data science in a perfect way. Their observations and approach have paved the way towards achieving a flexible and sustainable environment for advanced analytics. I am adopting these techniques in building my own analytics platform for our company.

Svetlana Grigoryeva, Manager Data Services
and AI, Shearman and Sterling

This book is a delight to read and provides many thought-provoking ideas. This book is a great resource for data scientists, and everyone who is involved with large scale, enterprise-wide AI initiatives.

Simon Seow, Managing Director, Info Spec Sdn Bhd (Malaysia)

Having worked in IT as a Vice president at MasterCard and as a Global Director at GM, I learned long ago about the importance of finding and listening to the best people. Here, the authors have brought a unique and novel voice that resonates with verve about how to be successful with data science at an enterprise scale. With the explosive growth of big data, computer power, cheap sensor technology, and the awe-inspiring breakthroughs with AI, *Smarter Data Science* also instills in us that without a solid information architecture, we may fall short in our work with AI.

Glen Birrell, Executive IT Consultant

In the 21st century the ability to use metadata to empower cross-industry ecosystems and exploit a hierarchy of AI algorithms will be essential to maximize stakeholder value. Today's data science processes and systems simply don't offer enough speed, flexibility, quality or context to enable that. *Smarter Data Science* is a very useful book as it provides concrete steps towards wisdom within those intelligent enterprises.

Richard Hopkins, President, Academy of Technology, IBM (UK)

A must read for everyone who curates, manages, or makes decisions on data. Lifts a lot of the mystery and magical thinking out of "Data Science" to explain why we're underachieving on the promise of AI. Full of practical ideas for improving the practice of information architecture for modern analytical environments using AI or ML. Highly recommended.

Linda Nadeau, Information Architect, Metaphor Consulting LLC

In this book, the authors "unpack" the meaning of data as a natural resource for the modern corporation. Following on Neal's previous book that explored the role of data in enterprise transformation, the authors construct and lead the reader through a holistic approach to drive business value with data science. This book examines data, analytics, and the AI value chain across several industries describing specific use and business cases. This book is a must read for Chief Data Officers as well as accomplished or inspiring data scientists in any industry.

Boris Vishnevsky, Principal, Complex Solutions and Cyber Security, Slalom; Adjunct Professor, TJU

As an architect working with clients on highly complex projects, all of my new projects involve vast amounts of data, distributed sources of data, cloud-based technologies, and data science. This book is invaluable for my real-world enterprise scale practice. The anticipated risks, complexities, and the rewards of infusing AI is laid out in a well-organized manner that is easy to comprehend taking the reader out of the scholastic endeavor of fact-based learning and into the real world of data science. I would highly recommend this book to anyone wanting to be meaningfully involved with data science.

John Aviles, Federal CTO Technical Lead, IBM

I hold over 150 patents and work as a data scientist on creating some of the most complex AI business projects, and this book has been of immense value to me as a field guide. The authors have established the need as to why IA must be part of a systematic maturing approach to AI. I regard this book as a *"next generation AI guidebook"* that your organization can't afford to be without.

Gandhi Sivakumar, Chief Architect and
Master Inventor, IBM (Australia)

A seminal treatment for how enterprises must leverage AI. The authors provide a clear and understandable path forward for using AI across cloud, fog, and mist computing. A must read for any serious data scientist and data manager.

Raul Shneir, Director, Israel National Cyber Directorate (Israel)

As a professor at Wharton who teaches data science I often mention to my students about emerging new analytical tools such as AI that can provide valuable information to business decision makers. I also encourage them to keep abreast of such tools. *Smarter Data Science* will definitely make my recommended readings list. It articulates clearly how an organization can build a successful Information architecture, capitalizing on AI technologies benefits. The authors have captured many intricate themes that are relevant for my students to carry with them into the business world. Many of the ideas presented in this book will benefit those working directly in the field of data science or those that will be impacted by data science. The book also includes many critical thinking tools to ready the worker of tomorrow . . . and realistically, today.

Dr. Josh Eliashberg, Sebastian S. Kresge Professor of Marketing, Professor
of Operations, Information, and Decisions, The Wharton School

This is an excellent guide for the data-driven organization that must build a robust information architecture to continuously deliver greater value through data science or be relegated to the past. The book will enable organizations to complete their transformative journey to sustainably leverage AI technologies that incorporate cloud-based AI tools and dueling neural networks. The guiding principles that are laid out in the book should result in the democratization of data, a data literate workforce, and a transparent AI revolution.

Taarini Gupta, Behavioral Scientist/Data Scientist,
Mind Genomics Advisors

Smarter Data Science

Succeeding with Enterprise-Grade Data and AI Projects

Neal Fishman with Cole Stryker

WILEY

ATM4

About the Authors

Neal Fishman is an IBM Distinguished Engineer and is the CTO for Data-Based Pathology within IBM's Global Business Services organization. Neal is also an Open Group Certified Distinguished IT Architect. Neal has extensive experience working with IBM's clients across six continents on complex data and AI initiatives.

Neal has previously served as a board member for several different industry communities and was the technology editor for the BRCommunity webzine. Neal has been a distance learning instructor with the University of Washington and has recorded some of his other insights in *Viral Data in SOA: An Enterprise Pandemic* and *Enterprise Architecture Using the Zachman Framework*. Neal also holds several data-related patents.

You can connect with Neal on LinkedIn at `linkedin.com/in/neal-fishman-`.

Cole Stryker is an author and journalist based in Los Angeles. He is the author of *Epic Win for Anonymous*, the story of a global gang of hackers and trolls who took on big corporations and governments, and *Hacking the Future*, which charts the history of anonymity and makes a case for its future as a form of cultural and political expression. His writing has appeared in Newsweek, The Nation, NBC News, Salon, Vice, Boing Boing, The NY Observer, The Huffington Post, and elsewhere.

You can connect with Cole on LinkedIn at `linkedin.com/in/colestryker`.

Acknowledgments

I want to express my sincere gratitude to Jim Minatel at John Wiley & Sons for giving me this opportunity. I would also like to sincerely thank my editor, Tom Dinse, for his attention to detail and for his excellent suggestions in helping to improve this book. I am very appreciative of the input provided by Tarik El-Masri, Alex Baryudin, and Elis Gitin. I would also like to thank Matt Holt, Devon Lewis, Pete Gaughan, Kenyon Brown, Kathleen Wisor, Barath Kumar Rajasekaran, Steven Stansel, Josephine Schweiloch, and Betsy Schaefer.

During my career, there have been several notable giants with whom I have worked and upon whose shoulders I clearly stand. Without these people, my career would not have taken the right turns: John Zachman, Warren Selkow, Ronald Ross, David Hay, and the late John Hall. I would like to recognize the renowned Grady Booch for his graciousness and kindness to contribute the Foreword. Finally, I would like to acknowledge the efforts of Cole Stryker for helping take this book to the next level.

Neal Fishman

Thanks to Jim Minatel, Tom Dinse, and the rest of the team at Wiley for recognizing the need for this book and for enhancing its value with their editorial guidance. I'd also like to thank Elizabeth Schaefer for introducing me to Neal and giving me the opportunity to work with him. Thanks also to Jason Oberholtzer and the folks at Gather for enabling my work at IBM. Lastly, I'm grateful to Neal Fishman for sharing his vision and inviting me to contribute to this important book.

Cole Stryker

Contents at a Glance

Contents

Foreword for *Smarter Data Science*

There have been remarkable advances in artificial intelligence the past decade, owing to a perfect storm at the confluence of three important forces: the rise of big data, the exponential growth of computational power, and the discovery of key algorithms for deep learning. IBM's Deep Blue beat the world's best chess player, Watson bested every human on *Jeopardy*, and DeepMind's AlphaGo and AlphaZero have dominated the field of Go and videogames. On the one hand, these advances have proven useful in commerce and in science: AI has found an important role in manufacturing, banking, and medicine, to name a few domains. On the other hand, these advances raise some difficult questions, especially with regard to privacy and the conduct of war.

While discoveries in the science of artificial intelligence continue, the fruits of that science are now being put to work in the enterprise in very tangible ways, ways that are not only economically interesting but that also contribute to the human condition. As such, enterprises that want to leverage AI must turn their focus to engineering pragmatic systems of value that contain cognitive components.

That's where *Smarter Data Science* comes in.

As the authors explain, data is not an afterthought in building such systems; it is a forethought. To leverage AI for predicting, automating, and optimizing enterprise outcomes, the science of data must be made an intentional, measurable, repeatable, and agile part of the development pipeline. Here, you'll learn about best practices for collecting, organizing, analyzing, and infusing data in ways that make AI real for the enterprise. What I celebrate most about this book is that not only are the authors able to explain these best practices from a foundation of deep experience, they do so in a manner that is actionable.

Their emphasis on results-driven methodology that is agile yet enables a strong architectural framework is refreshing.

I'm not a data scientist; I'm a systems engineer, and increasingly I find myself working with data scientists. Believe me, this is a book that has taught me many things. I think you'll find it quite informative as well.

Grady Booch

ACM, IEEE, and IBM Fellow

Epigraph

"There is no AI without IA."

Seth Earley

IT Professional, vol. 18, no. 03, 2016.

(info.earley.com/hubfs/EIS_Assets/
ITPro-Reprint-No-AI-
without-IA.pdf)

In 2016, IT consultant and CEO Seth Earley wrote an article titled "There is no AI without IA" in an IEEE magazine called *IT Professional*. Earley put forth an argument that enterprises seeking to fully capitalize on the capabilities of artificial intelligence must first build out a supporting information architecture. *Smarter Data Science* provides a comprehensive response: an IA for AI.

Preamble

"What I'm trying to do is deliver results."
Lou Gerstner
Business Week

Why You Need This Book

*"No one would have believed in the last years of the
nineteenth century that this world was being watched keenly and closely. . ."*

So begins H. G. Wells' *The War of the Worlds*, 1898, Harper&Brothers. In the last years of the 20th century, such disbelief also prevailed. But unlike the fictional watchers from the 19th century, the late-20th century watchers were real, pioneering digitally enabled corporations. In *The War of the Worlds*, simple bacteria proved to be a defining weapon for both offense and defense. Today, the ultimate weapon is data. When misusing data, a corporate entity can implode. When data is used appropriately, a corporate entity can thrive.

Ever since the establishment of hieroglyphs and alphabets, data has been useful. The term *business intelligence* (BI) can be traced as far back as 1865 (`ia601409 .us.archive.org/25/items/cyclopaediacomm00devegoog`). However, it wasn't until Herman Hollerith, whose company would eventually become known as International Business Machines, developed the punched card that data could be harvested at scale. Hollerith initially developed his punched card–processing technology for the 1890 U.S. government census. Later in 1937, the U.S. government contracted IBM to use its punched card–reading machines for a new, massive bookkeeping project that involved 26 million Social Security numbers.

In 1965, the U.S. government built its first data center to store 742 million tax returns and 175 million sets of fingerprints on magnetic computer tape. With the advent of the Internet, and later mobile devices and IoT, it became possible for private companies to truly use data at scale, building massive stores of consumer data based on the growing number of touchpoints they now shared with their customers. Taken as an average, data is created at a rate of more than 1.7MB every second for every person (www.domo.com/solution/data-never-sleeps-6). That equates to approximately 154,000,000,000,000 punched cards. By coupling the volume of data with the capacity to meaningfully process that data, data can be used at scale for much more than simple record keeping.

Clearly, our world is firmly in the age of big data. Enterprises are scrambling to integrate capabilities that can address advanced analytics such as artificial intelligence and machine learning in order to best leverage their data. The need to draw out insights to improve business performance in the marketplace is nothing less than mandatory. Recent data management concepts such as the data lake have emerged to help guide enterprises in storing and managing data. In many ways, the data lake was a stark contrast to its forerunner, the enterprise data warehouse (EDW). Typically, the EDW accepted data that had already been deemed useful, and its content was organized in a highly systematic way.

When misused, a data lake serves as nothing more than a hoarding ground for terabytes and petabytes of unstructured and unprocessed data, much of it never to be used. However, a data lake can be meaningfully leveraged for the benefit of advanced analytics and machine learning models.

But, are data warehouses and data lakes serving their intended purpose? More succinctly, are enterprises realizing the business-side benefit of having a place to hoard data?

The global research and advisory firm Gartner has provided sobering analysis. It has estimated that more than half of the enterprise data warehouses that were attempted have been failures and that the new data lake has fared even worse. At one time, Gartner analysts projected that the failure rate of data lakes might reach as high as 60 percent (blogs.gartner.com/nick-heudecker/big-data-challenges-move-from-tech-to-the-organization). However, Gartner has now dismissed that number as being too conservative. Actual failure rates are thought to be much closer to 85 percent (www.infoworld.com/article/3393467/4-reasons-big-data-projects-failand-4-ways-to-succeed.html).

Why have initiatives such as the EDW and the data lake failed so spectacularly? The short answer is that developing a proper information architecture isn't simple.

For much the same reason that the EDW failed, many of the approaches taken by data scientists have failed to recognize the following considerations:

- The nature of the enterprise
- The business of the organization
- The stochastic and potentially gargantuan nature of change

- The importance of data quality
- How different techniques applied to schema design and information architecture can affect the organization's readiness for change

Analysis reveals that the higher failure rate for data lakes and big data initiatives has been attributed not to technology itself but, rather, to how the technologists have applied the technology (`datazuum.com/5-data-actions-2018/`).

These facets become quickly self-evident in conversations with our enterprise clients. In discussing data warehousing and data lakes, the conversation often involves answers such as, "Which one? We have many of each." It often happens that a department within an organization needs a repository for its data, but their requirements are not satisfied by previous data storage efforts. So instead of attempting to reform or update older data warehouses or lakes, the department creates a new data store. The result is a hodgepodge of data storage solutions that don't always play well together, resulting in lost opportunities for data analysis.

Obviously, new technologies can provide many tangible benefits, but those benefits cannot be realized unless the technologies are deployed and managed with care. Unlike designing a building as in traditional architecture, information architecture is not a set-it-and-forget-it prospect.

While an organization can control how data is ingested, your organization can't always control how the data it needs changes over time. Organizations tend to be fragile in that they can break when circumstances change. Only flexible, adaptive information architectures can adjust to new environmental conditions. Designing and deploying solutions against a moving target is difficult, but the challenge is not insurmountable.

The glib assertion that garbage in will equal garbage out is treated as being passé by many IT professionals. While in truth garbage data has plagued analytics and decision-making for decades, mismanaged data and inconsistent representations will remain a red flag for each AI project you undertake.

The level of data quality demanded by machine learning and deep learning can be significant. Like a coin with two sides, low data quality can have two separate and equally devastating impacts. On the one hand, low-quality data associated with historical data can distort the training of a predictive model. On the other, new data can distort the model and negatively impact decision-making.

As a sharable resource, data is exposed across your organization through layers of services that can behave like a virus when the level of data quality is poor—unilaterally affecting all those who touch the data. Therefore, an information architecture for artificial intelligence must be able to mitigate traditional issues associated with data quality, foster the movement of data, and, when necessary, provide isolation.

The purpose of this book is to provide you with an understanding of how the enterprise must approach the work of building an information architecture in order to make way for successful, sustainable, and scalable AI deployments. The book includes a structured framework and advice that is both practical and actionable toward the goal of implementing an information architecture that's equipped to capitalize on the benefits of AI technologies.

What You'll Learn

We'll begin in Chapter 1, "Climbing the AI Ladder" with a discussion of the *AI Ladder,* an illustrative device developed by IBM to demonstrate the steps, or *rungs,* an organization must climb to realize sustainable benefits with the use of AI. From there, Chapters 2, "Framing Part I: Considerations for Organizations Using AI" and Chapter 3, "Framing Part II: Considerations for Working with Data and AI" cover an array of considerations data scientists and IT leaders must be aware of as they traverse their way up the ladder.

In Chapter 4, "A Look Back on Analytics: More Than One Hammer" and Chapter 5, "A Look Forward on Analytics: Not Everything Can Be a Nail," we'll explore some recent history: data warehouses and how they've given way to data lakes. We'll discuss how data lakes must be designed in terms of topography and topology. This will flow into a deeper dive into data ingestion, governance, storage, processing, access, management, and monitoring.

In Chapter 6, "Addressing Operational Disciplines on the AI Ladder," we'll discuss how DevOps, DataOps, and MLOps can enable an organization to better use its data in real time. In Chapter 7, "Maximizing the Use of Your Data: Being Value Driven," we'll delve into the elements of data governance and integrated data management. We'll cover the data value chain and the need for data to be accessible and discoverable in order for the data scientist to determine the data's value.

Chapter 8, "Valuing Data with Statistical Analysis and Enabling Meaningful Access" introduces different approaches for data access, as different roles within the organization will need to interact with data in different ways. The chapter also furthers the discussion of data valuation, with an explanation of how statistics can assist in ranking the value of data.

In Chapter 9, "Constructing for the Long-Term," we'll discuss some of the things that can go wrong in an information architecture and the importance of data literacy across the organization to prevent such issues.

Finally, Chapter 10, "A Journey's End: An IA for AI" will bring everything together with a detailed overview of developing an information architecture for artificial intelligence (IA for AI). This chapter provides practical, actionable steps that will bring the preceding theoretical backdrop to bear on real-world information architecture development.

Climbing the AI Ladder

*"The first characteristic of interest is the fraction of the computational load,
which is associated with data management housekeeping."*

—Gene Amdahl

"Approach to Achieving Large Scale Computing Capabilities"

To remain competitive, enterprises in every industry need to use advanced analytics to draw insights from their data. The urgency of this need is an accelerating imperative. Even public-sector and nonprofit organizations, which traditionally are less motivated by competition, believe that the rewards derived from the use of artificial intelligence (AI) are too attractive to ignore. Diagnostic analytics, predictive analytics, prescriptive analytics, machine learning, deep learning, and AI complement the use of traditional descriptive analytics and business intelligence (BI) to identify opportunities or to increase effectiveness.

Traditionally an organization used analytics to explain the past. Today analytics are harnessed to help explain the immediate now (the present) and the future for the opportunities and threats that await or are impending. These insights can enable the organization to become more proficient, efficient, and resilient.

However, successfully integrating advanced analytics is not turnkey, nor is it a binary state, where a company either does or doesn't possess AI readiness. Rather, it's a journey. As part of its own recent transformation, IBM developed a visual metaphor to explain a journey toward readiness that can be adopted and applied by any company: the AI Ladder.

As a ladder, the journey to AI can be thought of as a series of rungs to climb. Any attempt to zoom up the ladder in one hop will lead to failure. Only when each rung is firmly in hand can your organization move on to the next rung. The climb is not hapless or random, and climbers can reach the top only by approaching each rung with purpose and a clear-eyed understanding of what each rung represents for their business.

You don't need a crystal ball to know that your organization needs data science, but you do need some means of insight to know your organization's efforts can be effective and are moving toward the goal of AI-centricity. This chapter touches on the major concepts behind each rung of the metaphorical ladder for AI, why data must be addressed as a peer discipline to AI, and why you'll need to be creative as well as a polymath—showcasing your proficiency to incorporate multiple specializations that you'll be able to read about within this book.

Readying Data for AI

The limitations can be technological, but much of the journey to AI is made up of organizational change. The adoption of AI may require the creation of a new workforce category: the *new-collar* worker. New-collar jobs can include roles in cybersecurity, cloud computing, digital design, and cognitive business. New-collar work for the cognitive business has been invoked to describe the radically different ways AI-empowered employees will approach their duties. This worker must progress methodically from observing the results of a previous action to justifying a new course of action to suggesting and ultimately prescribing a course of action.

When an organization targets a future state for itself, the future state simply becomes the current state once it's attained. The continual need to define another future state is a cycle that propels the organization forward. Ideally, the organization can, over time, reduce the time and expense required to move from one state to the next, and these costs will be viewed not as expenses but as derived value, and money will cease to inhibit the cycle's progression.

Worldwide, most organizations now agree that AI will help them stay competitive, but many organizations can often still struggle with less advanced forms of analytics. For organizations that experience failure or less than optimal outcomes with AI, the natural recourse seems to be to remove rigor and not increase it. From the perspective of the AI Ladder, rungs are hurried or simply skipped altogether. When an organization begins to recognize and acknowledge this paradigm, they must revisit the fundamentals of analytics in order to prepare themselves for their desired future state and the ability to benefit from AI. They don't necessarily need to start from scratch, but they need to evaluate their capabilities to determine from which rung they can begin. Many of the technological pieces they need may already be in place.

Organizations will struggle to realize value from AI without first making data simple, accessible, and available across the enterprise, but this democratization of data must be tempered by methods to ensure security and privacy because, within the organization, not all data can be considered equal.

Technology Focus Areas

Illustrated in Figure 1-1, the level of analytics sophistication accessible to the organization increases with each rung. This sophistication can lead to a thriving data management practice that benefits from machine learning and the momentum of AI.

Organizations that possess large amounts of data will, at some point, need to explore a multicloud deployment. They'll need to consider three technology-based areas as they move up the ladder.

- **Hybrid data management** for the core of their machine learning
- **Governance and integration** to provide security and seamless user access within a secured user profile
- **Data science and AI** to support self-service and full-service user environments for both advanced and traditional analytics

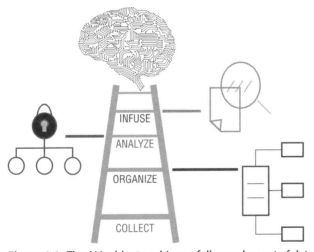

Figure 1-1: The AI Ladder to achieve a full complement of data and analytics

These foundational technologies must embrace modern cloud and microservice infrastructures to create pathways for the organization to move forward and upward with agility and speed. These technologies must be implemented at various rungs, enabling the movement of data and delivering predictive power from machine learning models in various types of deployment, from a single environment to a multicloud environment.

Taking the Ladder Rung by Rung

As shown in Figure 1-1, the rungs of the ladder are labeled Collect, Organize, Analyze, and Infuse. Each rung provides insight into elements that are required for an information architecture.

Collect, the first rung, represents a series of disciplines used to establish foundational data skills. Ideally, access to the data should be simplified and made available regardless of the form of the data and where it resides. Since the data used with advanced analytics and AI can be dynamic and fluid, not all data can be managed in a physical central location. With the ever-expanding number of data sources, virtualizing how data is collected is one of the critical activities that must be considered in an information architecture.

These are key themes included in the Collect rung:

- Collecting data with a common SQL engine, the use of APIs for NoSQL access, and support for data virtualization across a broad ecosystem of data that can be referred to as a *data estate*

- Deploying data warehouses, data lakes, and other analytical-based repositories with always-on resiliency and scalability

- Scaling with real-time data ingestion and advanced analytics simultaneously

- Storing or extracting all types of business data whether structured, semi-structured, or unstructured

- Optimizing collections with AI that may include graph databases, Python, machine learning SQL, and confidence-based queries

- Tapping into open source data stores that may include technologies such as MongoDB, Cloudera, PostgreSQL, Cloudant, or Parquet

The *Organize* rung infers that there is a need to create a trusted data foundation. The trusted data foundation must, at a minimum, catalog what is knowable to your organization. All forms of analytics are highly dependent upon digital assets. What assets are digitized forms the basis for what an organization can reasonably know: the corpus of the business is the basis for the organizational universe of discourse—the totality of what is knowable through digitized assets.

Having data that is business-ready for analytics is foundational to the data being business-ready for AI, but simply having access to data does not infer that the data is prepared for AI use cases. Bad data can paralyze AI and misguide any process that consumes output from an AI model. To organize, organizations must develop the disciplines to integrate, cleanse, curate, secure, catalog, and govern the full lifecycle of their data.

These are key themes included in the Organize rung:

- Cleansing, integrating, and cataloging all types of data, regardless of where the data originates

- Automating virtual data pipelines that can support and provide for self-service analytics

- Ensuring data governance and data lineage for the data, even across multiple clouds

- Deploying self-service data lakes with persona-based experiences that provide for personalization

- Gaining a 360-degree view by combing business-ready views from multicloud repositories of data

- Streamlining data privacy, data policy, and compliance controls

The *Analyze* rung incorporates essential business and planning analytics capabilities that are key for achieving sustained success with AI. The Analyze rung further encapsulates the capabilities needed to build, deploy, and manage AI models within an integrated organizational technology portfolio.

These are key themes included in the Analyze rung:

- Preparing data for use with AI models; building, running, and managing AI models within a unified experience

- Lowering the required skill levels to build an AI model with automated AI generation

- Applying predictive, prescriptive, and statistical analysis

- Allowing users to choose their own open source frameworks to develop AI models

- Continuously evolving models based upon accuracy analytics and quality controls

- Detecting bias and ensuring linear decision explanations and adhering to compliance

Infuse is a discipline involving the integration of AI into a meaningful business function. While many organizations are able to create useful AI models, they are rapidly forced to address operational challenges to achieve sustained and viable business value. The Infuse rung of the ladder highlights the disciplines that must be mastered to achieve trust and transparency in model-recommended decisions, explain decisions, detect untoward bias or ensure fairness, and provide a sufficient data trail for auditing. The Infuse rung seeks to operationalize AI use cases by addressing a time-to-value continuum.

These are key themes included in the Infuse rung:

- Improving the time to value with prebuilt AI applications for common use cases such as customer service and financial planning or bespoke AI applications for specialized use cases such as transportation logistics
- Optimizing knowledge work and business processes
- Employing AI-assisted business intelligence and data visualization
- Automating planning, budgeting, and forecasting analytics
- Customizing with industry-aligned AI-driven frameworks
- Innovating with new business models that are intelligently powered through the use of AI

Once each rung is mastered to the degree that new efforts are repeating prior patterns and that the efforts are not considered bespoke or deemed to require heroic efforts, the organization can earnestly act on its efforts toward a future state. The pinnacle of the ladder, the journey to AI, is to constantly modernize: to essentially reinvent oneself at will. The Modernize rung is simply an attained future state of being. But once reached, this state becomes the organizational current state. Upon reaching the pinnacle, dynamic organizations will begin the ladder's journey anew. This cycle is depicted in Figures 1-2 and 1-3.

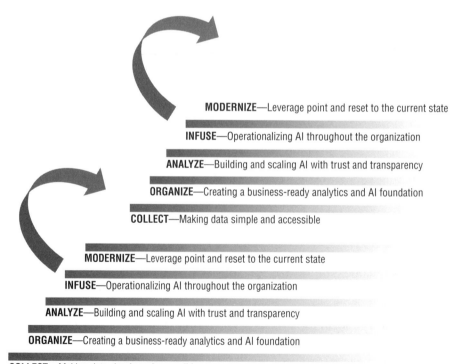

MODERNIZE—Leverage point and reset to the current state

INFUSE—Operationalizing AI throughout the organization

ANALYZE—Building and scaling AI with trust and transparency

ORGANIZE—Creating a business-ready analytics and AI foundation

COLLECT—Making data simple and accessible

MODERNIZE—Leverage point and reset to the current state

INFUSE—Operationalizing AI throughout the organization

ANALYZE—Building and scaling AI with trust and transparency

ORGANIZE—Creating a business-ready analytics and AI foundation

COLLECT—Making data simple and accessible

Figure 1-2: The ladder is part of a repetitive climb to continual improvement and adaptation.

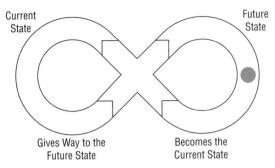

Figure 1-3: Current state ⇦ future state ⇦ current state

These are key themes included in the Modernize rung:

- Deploying a multicloud information architecture for AI
- Leveraging a uniform platform of choice across any private or public cloud
- Virtualizing data as a means of collecting data regardless of where the data is sourced
- Using DataOps and MLOps to establish trusted virtual data pipelines for self-service
- Using unified data and AI cloud services that are open and easily extensible
- Scaling dynamically and in real time to accommodate changing needs

Modernize refers to an ability to upgrade or update or, more specifically, to include net-new business capabilities or offerings resulting from transformational ideas or innovation that harness reimagined business models. The infrastructural underpinnings for organizations that are modernizing are likely to include elastic environments that embrace a multicloud topology. Given the dynamic nature of AI, modernizing an organization means building a flexible information architecture to constantly demonstrate relevance.

THE BIG PICTURE

In agile development, an *epic* is used to describe a user story that is considered far too big to be addressed in a single iteration or a single sprint. Therefore, an epic is used to provide the "big picture." The big picture provides an end-to-end perspective for what needs to be accomplished. The epic can then be decomposed into a series of workable stories that can be worked on. The epic serves to ensure the stories are threaded appropriately.

In the AI Ladder, the ladder represents the "big picture." The decomposition is represented by rungs. The ladder is used to ensure that the concepts for each rung—*collect, organize, analyze, infuse*—are threaded appropriately to ensure the best chance to succeed and deliver value.

Constantly Adapt to Retain Organizational Relevance

As the famous adage goes, "If you dislike change, you're going to dislike irrelevance even more" (www.network54.com/Forum/220604/thread/1073929871). In a world of rapid change, the endgame is to remain relevant. *Relevance* is an *ends*. Accordingly, transformation and disruption can be viewed as a *means*. Knowledge of the means provides the how (a course of action and the directives). Knowing the ends gives you a target (the desired result) for which to aim, as shown in Figure 1-4.

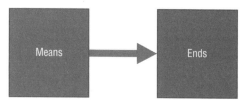

Figure 1-4: Ends and means model

The ends and means model can be iterated upon to adjust to continuous change and continuous course correction to drive toward sustained and improved relevance.

If an organization can combine relevance with uniqueness, then the path forward may offer greater opportunities, as the organization is unlikely to be viewed as another commodity player in a given space.

Formulating the ends is potentially more difficult than formulating the means. Words that are substitutes for *means* include *transformation* (including digital transformation) and *disruption*. An organization wanting to transform might simply do so by focusing on select technologies or capabilities that are newer; for example, cloud computing, agile development, big data, consumer-oriented platforms, blockchain, analytics, and even AI. Regardless of which technologies and capabilities are picked as a means, the question would remain: but, to what ends?

Relevance can be more difficult to articulate in terms of an *ends*, especially in the light of newer technologies and capabilities. The struggle with articulation might result from subject-matter experts and end users having minimal insight or experience with how a new solution can actually be positioned and leveraged.

Disruption can be viewed through its two adjectives: disruptive and disrupted. A disruptive organization is more likely to garner a leadership position in handling change, while a disrupted organization is likely to have a lagging position. For example, traditional publishing companies and journalists were found flat-footed in the wake of the digital publishing era. For more than a decade, profits and viability have dwindled in traditional publishing due to social media, blogs, and the proliferation of web-based content.

Another example of a business type in the midst of being disrupted is the hospital. In the United States, the population size has grown by approximately 100 million people in the past 35 years and by nearly 200 million people in the past 70 years. It would not be unreasonable to assume that the demand for hospital beds has steadily risen alongside population growth, especially with an aging population. However, the demand for hospital beds is approximately the same now as it was in the 1940s. In the United States, the need for hospital beds peaked in the early 1980s.

Not all that long ago, a hospital was not exactly the safest of places to go and get well. In one account from the 1800s, it was noted that "hospitals are the sinks of human life" (www.archive.org/stream/proceedingsconn08socigoog). Through the use of anesthesia and the adoption of sterilization techniques, along with the advent of X-rays in 1895, hospitals turned a corner from being a highly risky place to get treated. But now, in a throwback to the 18th and 19th centuries, hospitals are once again seen as a less-than-desirable place to receive therapeutic medical treatment, as cited in a CDC report on hospital-acquired infections (www.documentcloud.org/documents/701516-cdc-hai-infections-deaths.html).

Facilities currently challenging the traditional hospital include walk-in urgent care centers, imaging facilities, surgical centers, physician offices, and so on. Hospitals are being forced to consider mergers and acquisitions as well as downsizing. Hospitals are being disrupted and need to seek nontraditional ways to remain relevant. Could the use of advanced analytics be part of the approach?

Ultimately, if AI is going to augment human intelligence, AI will be part of the *means* to transform or disrupt. While AI can potentially hypothesize about what can be relevant, AI is likely going to be challenged to convey a de facto direction as what needs to be done to remain relevant. For AI and for humans, collaboration is an augmented opportunity to address a defining issue of our times: relevance.

Therefore, the sole purpose of an information architecture for AI can be postulated, as an aid in the transformation and disruption of an organization that is on a ladder to achieve sustained or regained relevance, whereby each point of leverage is based on data and the organization is willing and capable of harnessing the insights that can be derived from that data.

ECONOMICALLY VIABLE

Without data there's no AI. Period. AI works well because organizations now have the means to economically collect and hoard immense quantities of digital information. Augmenting our work with machines and AI is the norm.

For example, when was the last time you went a day without *Googling*? Chances are, you don't give machine learning a second thought when you're interacting with

AI-infused capabilities. We are augmenting our work with AI, and in large part, it feels totally natural.

Organizations still have a long way to go to fully realize how they can augment all of their processes with AI. For companies that are successful, the result should feel natural.

Data-Based Reasoning Is Part and Parcel in the Modern Business

Advanced analytics, including AI, can provide a basis for establishing reasoning by using inductive and deductive techniques. Being able to interpret user interactions as a series of signals can allow a system to offer content that is appropriate for the user's context in real time.

To maximize the usefulness of the content, the data should be of an appropriate level of quality, appropriately structured or tagged, and, as appropriate, correlated with information from disparate systems and processes. Ascertaining a user's context is also an analytical task and involves the system trying to understand the relationship between the user and the user's specific work task.

For an industrial-based business application, a user might have a need to uncover parts and tools that are required to complete maintenance on a hydraulic system. By using adaptive pattern-recognition software to help mine a reference manual about hydraulic systems and their repair, a system could derive a list of requisite tools and related parts. An advanced analytic search on hydraulic repair could present content that is dynamically generated and based on product relationships and correlated with any relevant company offerings.

Pulling content and understanding context is not arbitrary or random. Aligning and harmonizing data across an enterprise or ecosystem from various front-end, mid-end, and back-end systems takes planning, and one of the results of that planning is an information architecture.

Advances in computer processing power and the willingness for organizations to scale up their environments has significantly contributed to capabilities such as AI to be seen as both essential and viable. The ability to harness improved horsepower (e.g., faster computer chips) has made autonomous vehicles technologically feasible even with the required volume of real-time data. Speech recognition has become reliable and is able to differentiate between speakers, all without extensive speaker-dependent training sessions.

There is no hiding that AI can be a complex subject. However, much of the complexity associated with AI can be hidden from a user. While AI itself is not a black art, AI benefits when traditional IT activities such as data quality and data governance are retained and mastered. In fact, clean, well-organized, and managed data—whether the data is structured, semistructured, or unstructured—

is a basic necessity for being able to use data for input into machine learning algorithms.

There will be many situations when an AI system needs to process or analyze a corpus of data with far less structure than the type of organized data typically found in a financial or transactional system. Fortunately, learning algorithms can be used to extract meaning from ambiguous queries and seek to make sense of unstructured data inputs.

Learning and reasoning go hand in hand, and the number of learning techniques can become quite extensive. The following is a list of some learning techniques that may be leveraged when using machine learning and data science:

- Active learning
- Deductive inference
- Ensemble learning
- Inductive learning
- Multi-instance learning
- Multitask learning
- Online learning
- Reinforcement learning
- Self-supervised learning
- Semi-supervised learning
- Supervised learning
- Transduction
- Transfer learning
- Unsupervised learning

Some learning types are more complex than others. Supervised learning, for example, is comprised of many different types of algorithms, and transfer learning can be leveraged to accelerate solving other problems. All model learning for data science necessitates that your information architecture can cater to the needs of training models. Additionally, the information architecture must provide you with a means to reason through a series of hypotheses to determine an appropriate model or ensemble for use either standalone or infused into an application.

Models are frequently divided along the lines of supervised (passive learning) and unsupervised (active learning). The division can become less clear with the inclusion of hybrid learning techniques such as semisupervised, self-supervised, and multi-instance learning models. In addition to supervised learning and unsupervised learning, reinforcement learning models represent a third primary learning method that you can explore.

Supervised learning algorithms are referred to as such because the algorithms learn by making predictions that are based on your input training data against an expected target output that was included in your training dataset. Examples of supervised machine learning models include decision trees and vector machines.

Two specific techniques used with supervised learning include classification and regression.

- *Classification* is used for predicting a class label that is computed from attribute values.

- *Regression* is used to predict a numerical label, and the model is trained to predict a label for a new observation.

An unsupervised learning model operates on input data without any specified output or target variables. As such, unsupervised learning does not use a teacher to help correct the model. Two problems often encountered with unsupervised learning include clustering and density estimation. Clustering attempts to find groups in the data, and density estimation helps to summarize the distribution of data.

K-means is one type of clustering algorithm, where data is associated to a cluster based on a means. Kernel density estimation is a density estimation algorithm that uses small groups of closely related data to estimate a distribution.

In the book *Artificial Intelligence: A Modern Approach, 3rd edition* (Pearson Education India, 2015), Stuart Russell and Peter Norvig described an ability for an unsupervised model to learn patterns by using the input without any explicit feedback.

The most common unsupervised learning task is clustering: detecting potentially useful clusters of input examples. For example, a taxi agent might gradually develop a concept of "good traffic days" and "bad traffic days" without ever being given labeled examples of each by a teacher.

Reinforcement learning uses feedback as an aid in determining what to do next. In the example of the taxi ride, receiving or not receiving a tip along with the fare at the completion of a ride serves to imply goodness or badness.

The main statistical inference techniques for model learning are inductive learning, deductive inference, and transduction. Inductive learning is a common machine learning model that uses evidence to help determine an outcome. Deductive inference reasons top-down and requires that each premise is met before determining the conclusion. In contrast, induction is a bottom-up type of reasoning and uses data as evidence for an outcome. Transduction is used to refer to predicting specific examples given specific examples from a domain.

Other learning techniques include multitask learning, active learning, online learning, transfer learning, and ensemble learning. Multitask learning aims "to leverage useful information contained in multiple related tasks to help improve the generalization performance of all the tasks" (`arxiv.org/pdf/1707.08114.pdf`). With active learning, the learning process aims "to ease the data collection process by automatically deciding which instances an annotator should label to train an algorithm as quickly and effectively as possible" (`papers.nips.cc/paper/7010-learning-active-learning-from-data.pdf`). Online learning "is helpful when the data may be changing rapidly over time. It is also useful for applications that involve a large collection of data that is constantly growing, even if changes are gradual" (Stuart Russell and Peter Norvig, *Artificial Intelligence: A Modern Approach, 3rd edition,* Pearson Education India, 2015).

LEARNING

The variety of opportunities to apply machine learning is extensive. The sheer variety gives credence as to why so many different modes of learning are necessary:

- Advertisement serving
- Business analytics
- Call centers
- Computer vision
- Companionship
- Creating prose
- Cybersecurity
- Ecommerce
- Education
- Finance, algorithmic trading
- Finance, asset allocation
- First responder rescue operations
- Fraud detection
- Law
- Housekeeping
- Elderly care
- Manufacturing
- Mathematical theorems
- Medicine/surgery
- Military
- Music composition
- National security

- Natural language understanding
- Personalization
- Policing
- Political
- Recommendation engines
- Robotics, consumer
- Robotics, industry
- Robotics, military
- Robotics, outer space
- Route planning
- Scientific discovery
- Search
- Smart homes
- Speech recognition
- Translation
- Unmanned aerial vehicles (drones, cars, ambulance, trains, ships, submarines, planes, etc.)
- Virtual assistants

Evaluating how well a model learned can follow a five-point rubric.

- **Phenomenal:** It's not possible to do any better.
- **Crazy good:** Outcomes are better than what any individual could achieve.
- **Super-human:** Outcomes are better than what most people could achieve.
- **Par-human:** Outcomes are comparable to what most people could achieve.
- **Sub-human:** Outcomes are less than what most people could achieve.

Toward the AI-Centric Organization

As with the industrial age and then the information age, the age of AI is an advancement in tooling to help solve or address business problems. Driven by necessity, organizations are going to use AI to aid with automation and optimization. To support data-driven cultures, AI must also be used to predict and to diagnose. AI-centric organizations must revisit all aspects of their being, from strategy to structure and from technology to egos.

Before becoming AI-centric, organizations must first identify their problems, examine their priorities, and decide where to begin. While AI is best for detecting outcomes against a pattern, traditional business rules are not going to disappear. To be AI-centric is to understand what aspects of the business can best be addressed through patterns. Knowing how much tax to pay is never going to be a pattern; a tax calculation is always going to be rule-based.

There are always going to be situations where a decision or action requires a combination of pattern-based and rule-based outcomes. In much the same way, a person may leverage AI algorithms in conjunction with other analytical techniques.

Organizations that avoid or delay AI adoption will, in a worst-case scenario, become obsolete. The changing needs of an organization coupled with the use of AI are going to necessitate an evolution in jobs and skillsets needed. As previously stated, every single job is likely to be impacted in one way or another. Structural changes across industries will lead to new-collar workers spending more of their time on activities regarded as driving higher value.

Employees are likely to demand continuous skill development to remain competitive and relevant. As with any technological shift, AI may, for many years, be subject to scrutiny and debate. Concerns about widening economic divides, personal privacy, and ethical use are not always unfounded, but the potential for consistently providing a positive experience cannot be dismissed. Using a suitable information architecture for AI is likely to be regarded as a high-order imperative for consistently producing superior outcomes.

SCALE

On occasion, we are likely to have experienced a *gut feeling* about a situation. We have this sensation in the pit of our stomach that we know what we must do next or that something is right or that something is about to go awry. Inevitably, this feeling is not backed by data.

Gene Kranz was the flight director in NASA's Mission Control room during the Apollo 13 mission in 1970. As flight director, he made a number of *gut feel* decisions that allowed the lunar module to return safely to Earth after a significant malfunction. This is why we regard AI as augmenting the knowledge worker and not an outright replacement for the knowledge worker. Some decisions require a broader context for decision-making; even if that decision is a gut feel, the decision is still likely to manifest from years of practical experience.

For many businesses, the sheer scale of their operations already means that each decision can't be debated between man and machine to reach a final outcome. Scale, and not the need to find a replacement for repetitive tasks, is the primary driving factor toward needing to build the AI-centric organization.

Summary

Through climbing the ladder, organizations will develop practices for data science and be able to harness machine learning and deep learning as part of their enhanced analytical toolkit.

Data science is a *discipline*, in that the data scientist must be able to leverage and coordinate multiple skills to achieve an outcome, such as domain expertise, a deep understanding of data management, math skills, and programming. Machine learning and deep learning, on the other hand, are *techniques* that can be applied via the discipline. They are techniques insofar as they are optional tools within the data science toolkit.

AI puts machine learning and deep learning into practice, and the resulting models can help organizations reason about AI's hypotheses and apply AI's findings. To embed AI in an organization, a formal data and analytics foundation must be recognized as a prerequisite.

By climbing the ladder (from one rung to the next: collect, organize, analyze, and infuse), organizations are afforded with the ability to address questions that were either previously unknown (When will a repeat buyer buy again?) or previously unanswerable (What were the influencing factors as to why a given product was purchased?).

When users can ask new questions, users can benefit from new insights. Insights are therefore a direct means to empowerment. Empowered users are likely to let specific queries execute for multiple minutes, and, in some cases, even hours, when immediate near-zero-second response is not fully required. The allure of the ladder and to achieve AI through a programmatic stepwise progression is the ability to ask more profound and higher-value questions.

The reward for the climb is to firmly establish a formal organizational discipline in the use of AI that is serving to help the modern organization remain relevant and competitive.

In the next chapter, we will build on the AI Ladder by examining considerations that impact the organization as a whole.

Framing Part I: Considerations for Organizations Using AI

"We don't just pass along our DNA, we pass along our ideas."
—Lisa Seacat DeLuca
TEDBlog

The use of artificial intelligence (AI) is not exclusively about technology, though AI cannot exist without it. Organizational motivation to adopt digital transformation is, in large part, being driven by AI. Arguably, the rate of successful AI initiatives is far less than the number of AI initiatives that are started. The gap is not centered on the choice of which AI algorithm to use. This is why AI is not just about the tech.

AI does not force its own organizational agenda. AI augments how an organization works, driving how people think and participate in the organization. Through tying together organizational goals with AI tools, organizations can align strategies that guide business models in the right direction. An organization augmented as a coherent unit is likely to achieve its digital goals and experience a positive impact from using AI.

As organizations realize value from the use of AI, business processes will see further remediation to operate efficiently with data as a direct result of AI-generated predictions, solutions, and augmented human decision-making.

From pressures that emanate from within the organization as well as those from the outside, the need to develop a balanced tactical and strategic approach to AI is required for addressing options and trade-offs. AI is a revolutionary capability, and during its incorporation, organizational action must not be seen as remaining conventional.

As a data scientist, you'll determine what types of inputs, or features, will be of benefit to your models. Whether determining which features to include (feature engineering) or which features to exclude (feature selection), this chapter will help you determine which features you'll need for the models that you develop. You'll also learn about the importance of organizing data and the purpose of democratizing data.

Data-Driven Decision-Making

The most advanced algorithms cannot overcome a lack of data. Organizations that seek to prosper from AI by acting upon its revelations must have access to sufficient and relevant data. But even if an organization possesses the data it requires, the organization does not automatically become data-driven. A data-driven organization must be able to place trust in the data that goes into an AI model, as well as trust the concluding data from the AI model. The organization then needs to act on that data rather than on intuition, prior experience, or longstanding business policies.

Practitioners often communicate something like the following sentiment:

> [O]rganizations don't have the historical data required for the algorithms to extract patterns for robust predictions. For example, they'll bring us in to build a predictive maintenance solution for them, and then we'll find out that there are very few, if any, recorded failures. They expect AI to predict when there will be a failure, even though there are no examples to learn from.
>
> From "Reshaping Business with Artificial Intelligence: Closing the Gap Between Ambition and Action" by Sam Ransbotham, David Kiron, Philipp Gerbert, and Martin Reeves, September 06, 2017 (`sloanreview .mit.edu/projects/reshaping-business-with-artificial-intelligence`)

Even if an organization has a defined problem that could be solved by applying machine learning or deep learning algorithms, an absence of data can result in a negative experience if a model cannot be adequately trained. AI works through hidden neural layers without applying deterministic rules. Special attention needs to be paid as to how to trace the decision-making process in order to provide fairness and transparency with organizational and legal policies.

An issue arises as to how to know when it is appropriate to be *data-driven*. For many organizations, loose terms such as a *system of record* are qualitative signals that the data should be safe to use. In the absence of being able to apply a singular rule to grade data, other approaches must be considered. The primary interrogatives constitute a reasonable starting point to help gain insight for controlling all risk-based decisions associated with being a data-driven organization.

Using Interrogatives to Gain Insight

In Rudyard Kipling's 1902 book *Just So Stories,* the story of "The Elephant's Child" contains a poem that begins like this:

I keep six honest serving-men: (They taught me all I knew)

Their names are What and Where and When and How and Why and Who.

Kipling had codified the six primitive interrogatives of the English language. Collectively, these six words of inquiry—*what, where, when, how, why,* and *who*—can be regarded as a means to gain holistic insight into a given topic. It is why Kipling tells us, "They taught me all I knew."

The interrogatives became a foundational aspect of John Zachman's seminal 1987 and 1992 papers: "A Framework for Information Systems Architecture" and "Extending and Formalizing the Framework for Information Systems Architecture." Zachman correlated the interrogatives to a series of basic concepts that are of interest to an organization. While the actual sequence in which the interrogatives are presented is inconsequential and no one interrogative is more or less important than any of the others, Zachman typically used the following sequence: what, how, where, who, when, why.

- **What:** The data or information the organization produces
- **How:** A process or a function
- **Where:** A location or communication network
- **Who:** A role played by a person or computational agent
- **When:** A point in time, potentially associated with triggers that are fired or signals that are raised
- **Why:** A goal or subgoal revealing motivation

NOTE Zachman's article "A Framework for Information Systems Architecture" can be found at `ieeexplore.ieee.org/document/5387671`. "Extending and Formalizing the Framework for Information Systems Architecture" is available at `ieeexplore.ieee.org/document/5387433`.

By using Zachman's basic concepts of the six interrogatives, an organization can begin to understand or express how much the organization knows about something in order to infer a degree of trust and to help foster data-driven processes.

If a person or a machine had access to a piece of information or an outcome from an AI model, the person or machine could begin a line of inquiry to determine trust. For example, if the person or machine is given a score (representing the interrogative *what*), can they then ask, "*How* was this information produced? *Where* was this information produced? *Who* produced this information? *When* was this information produced? Is this information appropriate to meet my needs (*why*)?"

The Trust Matrix

To help visually grasp how the holistic nature of the six interrogatives can assist in trust and becoming data-driven, the interrogatives can be mapped to a trust matrix (shown in Figure 2-1) as the x-axis. The y-axis reflects the time horizons: past, present, and future.

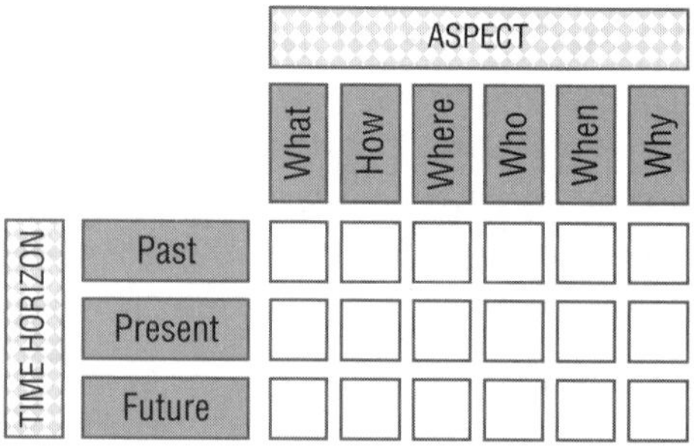

Figure 2-1: Trust matrix

The past represents something that has occurred. The past is a history and can inform as to what happened, what was built, what was bought, what was collected (in terms of money), and so on. The present is about the now and can inform us as to things that are underway or in motion. The present addresses what is happening, what is being built, who is buying, etc. The future is about things to be. We can prepare for the future by planning or forecasting. We can budget, and we can predict.

Revealing the past can yield hindsight, present insight, and future foresight. The spectrum across the time horizons provides the viewpoints for what happened, is happening, and could/will happen. While the divisions are straightforward, the concept of the present can actually span the past and the present. Consider, "this year." This year is part of the present, but the days gone are also part of the past, and the days to come are also part of the future. Normally, the context of inquiry can help to remove any untoward temporal complications.

At each x-y intersection lies what the organization can reasonably know. What is knowable has two dimensions, as shown in Figure 2-2. The two dimensions are breadth and depth. The breadth is a reflection of scope and represents a means to understand how much is known about a given topic. For example, some organizations may have a retention policy that requires information to be expunged after a given number of years—for example, seven years. In this example, the breadth of information an organization has access to is constrained to the most recent seven years.

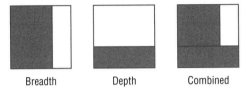

Figure 2-2: Breadth and depth slivers

Conversely, depth is a reflection of detail. The topic of ethnography is addressed here. For example, a person may purchase a product, and if that product is gifted to some other person, the organization may not have any indication as to the actual consumer of the product, representing a lack of depth.

Breadth and depth can be approximated in terms of percentages and mapped to an intersection. Figure 2-2 shows an example where a breadth sliver is shown to be approximately 75%, and a depth sliver is approximately 25%. The third box combines the breadth and depth slivers together.

In Figure 2-3, the quality of the information is graded against the breadth and depth. The diamond grid pattern indicates that the data quality is known to be poor. The diagonal stripes pattern indicates that the data quality is moderate, which means that the information in specific conditions may prove to be unreliable, while the square grid pattern is used to indicate that the information is of high quality and is reliable.

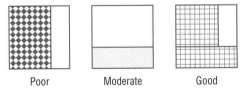

Figure 2-3: Grading

Therefore, even if the breadth and depth are not both 100%, the available data can be graded in the context of the information that is at hand.

Across the overall trust matrix, if the information for a particular need could be measured in terms of breadth and depth for each aspect across each time horizon and then graded, a person or a machine could evaluate an aspect of risk in terms of consuming information. Being able to accurately quantify a risk in terms of how much is known and at what level of detail, an organization can pursue being data-driven with confidence, knowing that all subsequent actions or decisions are being made on the merit of the data.

Furthermore, a data-driven organization using its data as critical evidence to help inform and influence on strategy will need a means to weigh options against any inherent risk. A data-driven organization must develop an evidence-based culture in which data can be evaluated against a means to establish trust and that the analytics and AI performed against the data is deemed to be highly relevant, informative, and useful in determining next steps.

The Importance of Metrics and Human Insight

For organizations that make gut-feel decisions and are apprehensive about pursuing data-driven means, the ability to measure is vital. The ends and means model shown in Chapter 1, "Climbing the AI Ladder," Figure 1-4 illustrates the necessity to balance what needs to be measured with something that can produce something that is measurable and is aligned to what ultimately needs to be measured.

The use of AI requires an organization to become data-driven, especially when a person is in a decision-making loop. Machine-to-machine communication fosters the ability of a machine to act independently to make decisions based purely on the information at hand. Orchestrating a person into a communication flow allows for decision augmentation and to act as a gatekeeper.

In the 1960s, the euphemism Mad Men was supposedly created by those working in the field of advertising, where—in the United States—the industry was heavily centered around Madison Avenue in New York City (the *men* of *Madi*son Avenue). Mad Men created messages for the masses. Whether messages were regionally appropriate or whether an advertisement resonated exceptionally well with the discrete needs of each singular individual was not the core focus. Eventually, the gut feel of the Mad Men approach gave way to the focus group–oriented view of the Media Men. In turn, the Media Men have given way to the Math Men. The Math Men are the men and women of data science whose provinces are the hordes of big data and thick data, algorithms, and machine learning that derive insight from data. As the new-collar worker expands into all aspects of corporate work from using model-based outcomes, each decision is going to be based on data. New-collar workers are data-driven and so are their decisions.

> **THE ZACHMAN FRAMEWORK**
>
> The six interrogatives—what, how, where, who, when, why—provide a methodical means toward inquiry. However, the use of the interrogatives in the Zachman Framework provide for a structural device in the framework. Because the Zachman

Framework is structural in nature and is not a methodology, the framework is actually an ontology for describing the enterprise.

The Zachman Framework is not a methodology because the framework is not prescriptive or anchored on a process. The framework is concerned about creating, operating, or changing essential components that are of interest to an enterprise. The components can be big or small and include the enterprise itself, a department, a cloud, an app, a container, a schema, and an AI model.

Democratizing Data and Data Science

Despite the explosion of interest in data collection and storage, many organizations will intentionally relegate data science knowledge to a discrete, small number of employees. While organizations must foster areas of specialization, the need to designate the data scientist label to a small cohort of employees seems to stem from a misguided belief that AI is somehow magic.

In the long-term, neither data science nor AI should be the sole purview of the data scientist. The democratization of data science involves opening up the fundamentals of data science to a broader set of employees, paving the way for the establishment of new roles, including the *citizen data scientist*.

For example, a citizen data scientist would "create or generate [AI] models that use advanced diagnostic analytics or predictive and prescriptive capabilities, and whose primary job function is outside the field of statistics and analytics" (www.gartner.com/en/newsroom/press-releases/ 2017-01-16-gartner-says-more-than-40-percent-of-data-science-tasks-will- be-automated-by-2020). Citizen data scientists would extend the type of analytics that can be associated with self-service paradigms that are offered by organizations.

A citizen data scientist is still able to make use of advanced analytics without having all of the skills that characterize the conventional data scientist. Skills associated with a conventional data scientist would include proficiency in a programming language, such as Python or R, and applied knowledge of advanced-level math and statistics. By contrast, a citizen data scientist may possess intrinsic and expert domain knowledge that the data scientist does not possess. When a data scientist does additionally possess domain knowledge, they are jokingly referred to as a *unicorn*.

Attempting to relegate the handling of data associated with AI to a small specialized team of people within a company can be fraught with challenges. Some data scientists may find it wearisome to communicate insight and nuance to other employees who lack specific data literacy skills, such as the ability to read and work with digitized data. Business stakeholders can become frustrated because data requests are not addressed quickly and may appear to fail at addressing their questions.

Many software tools that have been designed for use by the data scientist community end up residing solely within each data science team. But while logical, creating a silo of data software tools and restricting tool access to a small team (such as a team of data scientists) can create its own dilemma. All departments across an organization can generate analytical needs. Each need can span a spectrum of complexity: from ultra-simple to insanely tricky. But realistically, not every requirement is going to be anchored on the insanely tricky end of the analytical need spectrum. Many needs may be solvable or addressable by someone with basic analytical training. By instituting the citizen data scientist, organizations can better tailor the initiatives suited for the deep expertise of the data scientist.

Democratizing data science empowers as many people as possible to make data-driven decisions. Empowering begins with education and is sustained through continual education. If AI is to impact 100% of all future jobs, education on AI and data literacy (data literacy is addressed in Chapter 7, "Maximizing the Use of Your Data: Being Value Driven;" statistical literacy is covered in Chapter 6, "Addressing Operational Disciplines on the AI Ladder") should be viewed as a requisite offering that begins in grade school and must become part of the new-collar worker's continual learning within the workplace.

Building the organization's collective skills must encompass education in the use of collaborative software tools and socially oriented communication tools. Through being connected, employees can see who needs help and who can provide help, what problems need to be addressed, and how problems have been resolved. In democratizing data, organizations should notice that speed and value are moving in a positive direction, because sharing skills and knowledge can improve mutual understanding and business performance.

The impact of democratizing data and AI will circle back to refine existing job roles and responsibilities. Data scientists and citizen data scientists alike should be able to access and understand the curated datasets that are most relevant to support their own job functions. In building a workforce that is enabled to be data-driven through democratization, a new-collar workforce emerges. Organizations are faced with an unknown unknown in that this poses a new way to work but for which optimal organization structures have not been established. Change is upon the organization, but how that change manifests is not self-evident ahead of time. The new organizational structure of the enterprise is going to require frequent tuning.

Whether data science is applied by the data scientist or the citizen data scientist, sufficient oversight is necessary to ensure outcomes are not biased against the objectives of the organization. By empowering employees with essential skills, organizations can expand upon the opportunity to innovate and to find the next point of leverage. Sufficient oversight is also a concept that is distinct from sufficient insight. Sufficient insight would help to explain or articulate the what, how, where, who, when, and why of a singular outcome, whereas sufficient oversight would be the means to address causality across a series of outcomes.

Figure 2-4 shows the entwinement between the democratization of data and AI with data literacy and the ability to self-serve. The intersections should promote organizational collaboration, empowerment, and enablement of individuals and teams. The overall result is outcome-based in that the time-to-value proposition realized by an organization should be progressive and ultimately fair to all constituents.

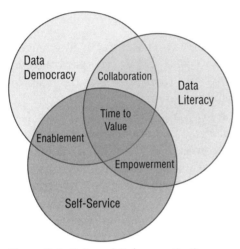

Figure 2-4: Data and AI democratization

DEMOCRATIZATION

Four critical elements for enabling data democratization are that the data for which a person or a machine is entitled to see should be:

- Easy to find
- Understandable
- Consumable
- Of sufficient quality

For the most part, being easy to find means that you'll need to unilaterally catalog (or inventory) all of the data that exists within the enterprise and all of the applicable data that exists outside of the enterprise. The other elements are potentially nonunilateral in that understandability, consumability, and data quality are contextual and may vary for different people or different machines. For example, the names *Kneel Fischman* and *Coal Striker* may be of insufficient quality for the payroll department but be of sufficient quality for the internal fraud department.

Aye, a Prerequisite: Organizing Data Must Be a Forethought

> **NOTE** The word *aye* is British English for "yes." The heading therefore reads as "Yes, a Prerequisite." As a pun and wordplay, the pronunciation "eye, a prerequisite" sounds the same as "IA prerequisite" where IA are the initials for information architecture, a focus topic of this book. Therefore, the heading also reads: "information architecture prerequisite."

All organizations, regardless of size and industry vertical, are actively engaged on a journey to Valhalla: a place of honor, glory, and sustained organizational happiness. This journey, with all of its twists and turns, involves the need to embrace analytics. The recent collective embrace of analytics stems from the observation that analytics has become the low-hanging fruit for addressing organizational change. The expression *low-hanging fruit* refers to tasks or actions that are most easily achieved. The analogy comes from the very literal task of picking fruit off a tree without the need to use a *ladder*. But organizations that believe they can retain their operational status quo run the risk of irrelevance or eventually obsolescence. For many organizations, analytics is now a vehicle for helping organizations figure out what can be done *now* and what can be done *next*.

Although AI and enabling technologies can carry a higher degree of panache, many of the foundational skills required to fully deliver on AI's promise are not well honed. These fundamentals of information architecture aim to address the problem of deriving value from data, which is inherently inert, not self-aware, and not self-organizing. Information architecture addresses these characteristics of data and aims to organize and contextualize data so that it can be mined for value.

> **NOTE** An enabling technology is an innovation that can be leveraged to drive radical change in the performance or the capabilities of an organization. The Internet and wireless communication are examples of enabling technologies.

Having an expectation that AI can consistently work its magic on any data source—regardless of the type of data and regardless of the level of data quality—without having a proper information architecture is a form of naivety that is all too widespread. Information architecture is the prerequisite to maximizing the benefit of advanced analytics, especially neural nets, machine learning, natural language processing, and other forms of AI.

Organizational leaders understand that change is constant, accelerating, and arriving from all sides. In the United States, the 1933 Glass-Steagall Act forbade commercial banks from owning securities firms.

NOTE   For more information, read Eric Weiner's book *What Goes Up: The Uncensored History of Modern Wall Street as Told by the Bankers, Brokers, CEOs, and Scoundrels Who Made It Happen* (New York, NY: Back Bay Books, 2005).

Seventy-five years later, the securities industry all but came to an end when the remaining large players, Morgan Stanley and Goldman Sachs, requested permission to become bank holding companies. Modern organizations must be willing to recognize that change can happen at any time and that when *something* changes, that *something* is also susceptible to being changed later. While the time horizon between changes can vary from seconds to years and decades, placing a corporate anchor on something that proves volatile can be disastrous.

NOTE   For more information about the changes at Morgan Stanley and Goldman Sachs, read Ben White's article in the *New York Times*, "Starting a New Era at Goldman and Morgan" (September 22, 2008).

Competitive companies tend not to remain stagnant, especially those that formally declare through a mission or vision statement the desire to improve shareholder value. By restructuring the organization, acquiring another organization, spinning off a line of business, or growing organically, organizations continually change and evolve. Companies that change in ways beyond an existing market niche can certainly reap assistance through the use of AI. Paradoxically, if an overarching strategy is to tightly align information technology with the business, that may be a surefire way to stifle or inhibit business growth and prevent the ability to rapidly change.

An information architecture that is loosely coupled to the business strategy, the underlying data, and the practice of AI can provide the requisite degree of agility to help respond to changing business needs while lessening the burden on an IT department to predict what needs to be changed to address a new business need. Assets built by IT need to be highly adaptive.

Preventing Design Pitfalls

One of the problems that arises in an information architecture is that the data can act as a binding agent and slow down IT's ability to rapidly respond to needed changes. For example, a common practice for instantiating data is to take a real-world concept and represent that concept in a literal and binding manner.

In our changing world, many real-world concepts are often just anchored to a point in time and may be susceptible to change or interpretation. Any concept that is stored is typically used, verbatim, in a program or an application and potentially on a user's screen.

Another example: a person's gender might be tagged/named as "gender" in a database, referred to as "gender" in program code, and then labeled "gender" on a screen. The data is now serving to tightly bind various components of an information architecture together. Moreover, the tight coupling is extended to the business.

Gender is a term that has changed in popular meaning and use. Formerly, gender was popularly considered an immutable designation as to a person being either male or female. Society has moved away from that binary. The binding aspects attributed to instantiating data can make it difficult for systems to adapt to a new use without a rippling effect that requires a system to go through a significant rewrite or modification.

To replace the historical use of gender, at least two concepts are needed: one to represent a biological interpretation and one to represent a mutable societal preference that can be updated to reflect any needs changes.

As indicated, a tightly coupled alignment between the business and IT may result in an inability to fully leverage data in a meaningful manner beyond the point in time that the alignment was established. Intrinsically, alignment is the result of a cognitive desire to satisfy a specific point-in-time requirement or need.

The futurist Alvin Toffler described how the speed of change forces decisions to be made at "a faster and faster pace" and reveals how waves of change are not just isolated instances but have intertwined correlations across "business, family life, technology, markets, politics, and personal life" (*The Third Wave*, New York: Bantam Books, 1981). If a system is too tightly coupled to a point in time, alterations that are made to a system can lag behind the necessary business decisions that need to be taken, resulting in poor decision-making or missed opportunities simply because the system cannot be revised at the speed of business.

Influences or mandates for change to an organization can be externally driven or internally driven. External influences such as competition, government regulation, the environment, the arrival of new technology, suppliers, vendors, and partners are a few different types of stimuli that can result in the need to define a new, potentially immediate point in time. Internal influencers such as new senior management or a shift in corporate values, the execution of a management prerogative, and the availability or unavailability of resources or skillsets may create new types of demand. An information technology solution backboned on alignment (e.g., tightly coupled) with the business is likely to result in a current solution being misused and potentially damaging to the quality of the corporate digital knowledge base. A test of an information architecture is its inherent ability to facilitate the winds of change.

ARCHITECTURE AND DESIGN

The difference between architecture and design is not immediately clear. Professor and author Philippe Kruchten has argued that all architecture is design. By using themes of difficulty and cost, an example can be used to help create a mental model for delineation.

A building has an external structure. Within the building, rooms are created, and furniture or other objects can be placed in each room. In this analogy, the external structure represents architecture, and the objects in a room represent design. The placement of the furniture, even if heavy, can be rearranged with minimal effort and cost. New elements can even be brought into the room over time, and other elements can be removed. The placement is designed.

The external walls may be immovable, especially if you just want to move the walls on the 50th story of a skyscraper. But, even if you could move the walls, the time, expense, and complexity can make the prospect inadvisable.

Elements within your designs that are anchor points and highly disruptive or expensive to change are architectural. Elements that can be reasonably changed over time are design elements. In an information architecture, the need to have an environment to support AI is architectural; the use of a machine learning library or the selection of features for use in a model is design.

Facilitating the Winds of Change: How Organized Data Facilitates Reaction Time

How much time an organization is given to respond to a change is a variant and is always predicated on being circumstantial. When the European Union introduced a law known as the General Data Protection Regulation (GDPR), all companies conducting business with individual citizens of the European Union and the European Economic Area were given a specific date by which they were required to comply with the changes the law introduced.

When the media company Netflix switched its core business model to subscription-based streaming from online DVD rentals, the company essentially gave notice to all brick-and-mortar DVD rental companies to switch their own existing business models or risk irrelevance. The response from the traditional DVD rental companies has proven to be overwhelmingly inadequate. So, while Netflix does have marketplace competition, the competition is not coming from the organizations that owned or operated the brick-and-mortar DVD rental facilities at the time Netflix switched its business model.

Sometimes transformations occur in a slow and progressive manner, while some companies can seemingly transform overnight. Some transformation needs can be sweeping (e.g., to comply with insider-trading rules). Adjustments might even blindside some employees in ways that they perceive as unwarranted.

Sweeping changes equivalent to eminent domain can be part and parcel of management prerogative. An internal IT department can be outsourced, a division can be sold, sales regions rearranged, and unsatisfactory deals made just to appease a self-imposed quota or sales mark. Some of these changes can be forced on an organization on a moment's notice or even appear to be made on a whim. Like eminent domain, sometimes change arrives at the organization swiftly and seemingly capriciously—but when it comes, reaction is not optional.

NOTE   Eminent domain is a government's right to expropriate private property. In 1646, Hugo Grotius (1583–1645) coined the term *eminent domain* as taking away by those in authority. In general, eminent domain is the procurement of an individual's property by a state for public purposes. An individual's right to own a home and the land beneath it is viewed as part of the liberty extended to all Americans by the Constitution of the United States. Varying degrees of land ownership is also a liberty afforded to individuals in many other nations around the world, too.

Within a corporate culture, eminent domain represents the ability for senior leaders to maneuver around previously accepted controls and protocols.

MUTABLE

In computing, a *mutable* object is an object whose state can be modified after it is created. An *immutable* object is an object whose state cannot be modified after it is created. Designing solutions to be mutable will make it easier to address new needs. When it comes to managing data, adding mutability concepts into a design will make adding a variable, deleting a variable, and modifying a variable's use or characteristics easier and more cost effective.

Quae Quaestio (Question Everything)

Different users might phrase comparable questions using different terminology, and even the same user from query to query might introduce nuances and various idiosyncrasies. Users are not always succinct or clear about their objectives or informational needs. Users may not necessarily know what to request.

Consequently, in business, there is a need to *question everything* to gain understanding. Although it might seem that to "question everything" stymies progress in an endless loop (Figure 2-5), ironically to "question everything" opens up all possibilities to exploration, and this is where the aforementioned trust matrix can help guide the development of a line of inquiry. This is also why human salespeople, as a technique, will often engage a prospect in conversation about their overall needs, rather than outright asking them what they are looking for.

Figure 2-5: Recognizing that the ability to skillfully ask questions is the root to insight

In Douglas Adams' *The Hitchhiker's Guide to the Galaxy*, when the answer to the ultimate question was met with a tad bit of disdain, the computer said, "I think the problem, to be quite honest with you, is that you've never actually known what the question is" (New York: Harmony Books, 1980). The computer then surmised that unless you fully come to grips with what you are asking, you will not always understand the answer. Being able to appropriately phrase a question (or query) is a topic that cannot be taken too lightly.

Inserting AI into a process is going to be more effective when users know what they want and can also clearly articulate that want. As there are variations as to the type of an AI system and many classes of algorithms that comprise an AI system, the basis to answer variations in the quality of question is to first seek quality and organization in the data.

However, data quality and data organization can seem out-of-place topics if an AI system is built to leverage many of its answers from unstructured data. For unstructured data that is textual—versus image, video, or audio—the data is typically in the form of text from pages, documents, comments, surveys, social media, and so on. But even nontextual data can yield text in the form of metadata, annotations, or tags via transcribing (in the case of audio) or annotating/tagging words or objects found in an image, as well as any other derivative information such as location, object sizes, time, etc. All types of unstructured data can still yield structured data from parameters associated with the source and the data's inherent context.

Social media data, for example, requires various additional data points to describe users, their posts, relationships, time of posts, location of posts, links, hashtags, and so on. This additional data is a form of metadata and is not characteristic of the typical meta-triad: business metadata, technical metadata, and operational metadata. While data associated with social media is regarded as unstructured data, there is still a need for an information architecture to manage the correlations between the core content: the unstructured data, along with the supporting content (the structured metadata). Taken in concert, the entire package of data can be used to shape patterns of interest.

Even in the case of unsupervised machine learning (a class of application that derives signals from data that has not previously been predefined by a person), the programmer must still describe the data with attributes/features and values.

QUESTIONING

When questioning, consider using the interrogatives as a guide—*what, how, where, who, when,* and *why*. The approach can be used iteratively. You can frame a series of questions based on the interrogatives for a complete understanding, and as you receive answers, you can reapply the interrogatives to further drill down on the original answer. This can be iteratively repeated until you have sufficient detail.

Summary

This chapter covered some of the organizational factors that help drive the need to establish an information architecture for AI. More broadly, an information architecture is also relevant for maximizing the benefit of all forms of analytics. The mind-set to think holistically was covered through the introduction of the six interrogatives of the English language—*what, how, where, who, when,* and *why*—over the time horizon of the past, present, and future.

Through democratizing data and data science, an organization can elevate the impact of AI to where it can more unilaterally benefit the organization and its culture. Democratizing data and data science must be placed squarely in the context of each person's role and responsibility and would therefore require sufficient oversight to attain organizational objectives.

While an information architecture can provide for efficiencies and flexibility, if the data is tied too closely to volatile business concepts, the effect can be too binding and stifle the rate of change that IT wants to deliver to the business.

Holistic thinking, democratization, AI, the use of an information architecture, etc., can all serve as a means for an organization to cut down on the time it needs to react. While organizations can plan for the changes they want to create, external factors and influences can hasten the time an organization has to respond. The better equipped an organization becomes with handling data and AI, the less reliance you'll need for responding with a *gut feel* to a situation.

In understanding that different organizational roles and responsibilities require different lenses by which to undertake a particular business problem, due diligence would require intended responses to be sufficiently questioned.

In the next chapter, we'll further explore aspects on framing concepts for preparing to work with data and AI.

Framing Part II: Considerations for Working with Data and AI

"I've learned that if you are not failing a lot, you're probably not being as creative as you could be—you aren't stretching your imagination."

—John Backus

In Chapter 1, "Climbing the AI Ladder," we mentioned that "not all data can be considered equal." Inequality is not just restricted to data. In many ways, the fact that the employees of the organizations we work for all have different jobs implies that we invariably will have different needs—we all don't have the same identical needs. Our unique needs define what data we use and how best we wish to consume that data. This chapter will lay the foundation as to why a modern environment for data analytics and artificial intelligence (AI) should not fixate on a single version of the truth paradigm.

AI can now be considered a necessary proxy for applying human knowledge, and the ripple effect of using AI will mean that the traditional ways that people work are going to be altered. The type of data that you'll need will change too. Beyond big data, specialized data that is far more precise in describing a real-world object (such as a person) or an event (such as a political rally or a business transaction) will be required, and so we will begin to examine how knowledge of ethnography can be blended with big data.

For AI to be of assistance, organizations must encapsulate knowledge in an *ontology*. An ontology is the result of organizing relationships or axioms for the concepts and features that make up the knowledge base. As such, an ontology may further aid in the removal of bias from outcomes and provide a means for outcomes to be viewed as fair and transparent.

Within the context of our jobs, data must be accessible, accurate, curated, and organized. Data shouldn't be difficult to consume. This sentiment also holds true for machine learning.

Personalizing the Data Experience for Every User

A single data store is not sufficient to provide all of the data needs for an organization. Unless latency can be eliminated for any type of interaction, a single data store is always going to be impractical, unfeasible, and far too complicated to ever be worth considering.

Information must flow through an information architecture in a precise, orderly, and orchestrated sequence (and ultimately, one that is repeatable and predictable). When you're planning for more than one data store, the ability to move data requires a high degree of discipline.

The paramount requirement to truly *personalize* a user experience (UX) is that information from any data domain be correctly organized. For certain domains like product or financial data, this also entails being appropriately structured.

Any process that involves data content must be integrated into an onboarding and data movement process. Associations must be established between data domains, context, and the user's behavior (these are the user's signals, digital footprints, and electronic body language) so that the user can be properly served with the information that is needed. Having some type of signal for a user's next action can help determine what information is then served. The resulting information may be in the form of lists, specifications, instructions (displayed, audible, or tactile), policies, reference materials, diagrams, images, and so on.

> **NOTE**   Electronic body language can be understood in terms of user interactions and navigations as to which screens are used, which buttons are clicked, the frequency in which messages are checked, the latencies involved in responding, and so on.

All too often organizations try to build a singular data store to represent a single version of the truth from the perspective of the enterprise. The assumption is that managing a single data store is preferable to managing multiple data stores, and only in a singular data store can organizational truth be adequately managed. The thinking behind this approach is that everybody associated with an organization wants to access information in the same way and with the same representations.

Here's an example: To maintain the truth and consistency, an organization might want all database references to New York City to be recorded as "New York City." However, the organization's legal department might want to use the legal name of the city, which is "The City of New York." The organization's travel department might want to use an airport code such as "JFK" or "LGA" in lieu of the destination, New York City. And, the sales department might want to use the post office's preferred name, which is simply "New York." Other departments might need to use one of the borough names such as "Manhattan," "Queens," "The Bronx," "Brooklyn," or "Staten Island." Conversely, the county names might need to be referenced such as "New York," "Bronx," "Queens," "Kings," and "Richmond."

A single version of the truth can sometimes be counterproductive to the various specialized needs of each line of business, department, and worker.

For many organizations, the notion of creating a custom, personalized, or hyper-personalized experience for each customer is a desirable business practice. Extreme personalization is to treat each client or customer in a cohort of one. But when looking inwardly, at the employees, personalization can be difficult for IT departments to grapple with. Instead of giving each worker specialized service, IT often opts to steer all workers to use a common, single service. But if hyper-personalization is appropriate for a customer, why not for an employee?

The problem arises because IT has historically viewed an organization as an enterprise. An enterprise is, by its nature, a singularity. IT has often offered the mantra that IT must align to the enterprise. . ."or else!" When viewing an enterprise or an organization as a whole, the opportunity to support specialized needs can be seen as frictional or counter to serving the perceived needs of the singularity. But this perceived oneness is a false illusion.

NOTE   For a viewpoint of the misalignment of IT with the enterprise, see `www.cio.com/article/3238844/align-your-it-and-business-strategy-or-else.html`.

To help you understand how specialization provides for efficiency and adaption, we can examine ourselves. As individuals, we are singular and a "one." However, below the surface, our bodies are made of a number of discrete systems: digestive system, nervous system, circulatory system, etc. Each system carries out a discrete purpose or a set of functions. These subsystems must know how to interoperate. For example, the gut–brain axis is the biochemical interoperability signaling that takes place between the gastrointestinal tract and the central nervous system. Our bodily enterprise, being comprised of specialized functions, allows us to be fast, flexible, and mended when we are broken. We are efficient and adaptive because our bodies are willing to make use of specialization. Analogously, by giving personalizing data for each user in a manner that is conducive to their function, the enterprise will be better equipped to perform. We'll discuss how this can be done in practical terms later.

> **WATER**
>
> What's in that bottle? Perhaps it's water. Water may be a sufficient answer. However, another person may need to know "H_2O." However, another person may want the information presented as "HOH" because that represents the physical structure of the molecule.
>
> Businesses are complex, and workers may have individual needs for how best they need to see the data they interact with. Progressive organizations can address the nuance between optimizing the enterprise and optimizing the worker. Historically, trends tended to solely optimize the enterprise.

Context Counts: Choosing the Right Way to Display Data

Enterprises perpetually pursue improvement, whether that's improving response rates from electronic correspondence, customer self-service, social media engagement, or the product experience.

In each of the following scenarios, the means to improve is derived from the ability to provide a relevant piece of information—in the right context, in a timely manner (which may literally be measured in nanoseconds), and in the most visually useful and appropriate form. The information provided may be in the form of a promotion, a special offer, a suggestion for a next-best action, a product or service for a cross-sell or an upsell, or an answer to aid a decision.

Providing relevant information in the right context is an aspect of UX design that must take into account accessibility, usability, and inclusion. Information can be provisioned digitally, visually, audibly, haptically, olfactorily, or kinesthetically.

As shown in Figure 3-1 and the close-up in Figure 3-2, visualization forms from the Mission Control Center for the International Space Station in Houston, Texas, highlight a preference for text-based representations of data.

In Figure 3-1, the command center is set up with a series of large monitor boards on the back wall. The placement of staff workstations is strategic across the command center, with each person's job role illuminated in blue lettering above their station. Each worker is given at least four different monitors with which to work and is assigned to a discrete set of responsibilities. The worker then monitors information relevant to those responsibilities.

The back panel on the left is showing general images of Earth from the Space Station—as such, nothing visually specific. The middle panel is showing the Space Station's projected orbital path around Earth. The rightmost panel is mirroring someone's workstation monitor.

Figure 3-2 is a closeup of the biomedical engineer's (BME) station. In the Mission Control Center, the BME serves as a direct link between the flight crew on the International Space Station and the Crew Health Care Systems' hardware and software and provides round-the-clock healthcare support for the crew.

Figure 3-1: Monitors at Mission Control Center for the International Space Station

Figure 3-2: A closer view

During the crewmembers' waking hours, a medical doctor who specializes in aerospace medicine is seated alongside the BME at the surgeon station. The BME's monitors contain windows of information, which is heavily tilted toward text rather than a visual graphic. In part, this is because explicit values are preferred when dealing with well-being, and text does a better job of representing explicit values.

Color can sometimes enhance explicit values as shown on the left monitor in Figure 3-2. Text highlighted in green would show acceptable values, and text highlighted in red would indicate values that are outside of acceptable norms.

Figure 3-3 shows the monitors in a modern hospital's emergency room. Here too, there is a heavy reliance on the use of text-based information, which often prevails over graphical views of the data. In the case of machine-to-machine interactions, text-based or binary data is also likely to prevail over graphic or visual representations.

Figure 3-3: Monitors in a hospital emergency room

To illustrate that there are not necessarily any hard and fast rules regarding when and where to use a visualization and when and where to use plain text, an electrocardiogram (EKG) provides an example of a visual that can communicatively work much faster than text.

An EKG is used by doctors to show electrical activity of the heart. Electrodes are placed on the body to detect small electrical changes that are the consequence of the cardiac muscle depolarizing followed by a repolarization during each heartbeat cycle. Changes in a normal EKG pattern—and *pattern* being the operative word—occur with numerous cardiac abnormalities, including cardiac rhythm disturbances such as atrial fibrillation.

The three main components of an EKG are shown in Figure 3-4. These components are the P wave, which represents the depolarization of the atria; the

QRS complex, which represents the depolarization of the ventricles; and the T wave, which represents the repolarization of the ventricles. During each heartbeat, a healthy heart has an orderly depolarization progression.

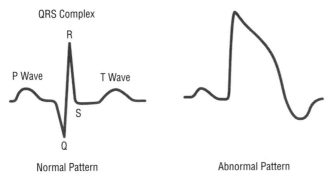

Figure 3-4: An electrocardiogram pattern showing normal and abnormal heartbeats

For the doctor, any pattern shown by the EKG gives way to having to know the exact values for the P wave, the T wave, and the QRS complex. A determination for normalcy is established through pattern detection and not the individual data values. Pattern detection often requires some degree of experience and understanding. However, should the exact values, with decimal precision, be required by the doctor, the text-based values could be leveraged. A normal value for a P wave is a value less than 80 milliseconds and is 160 milliseconds for the T wave. The QRS complex should be between 80 to 100 milliseconds.

A firefighter rushing into a burning building is not likely to make use of visual information even if the information can be relayed on a heads-up display built into the helmet. The firefighter is certainly not going to avert any attention to a handheld smart device or tablet. Studying user behaviors and understanding user motivations in low-stress or high-stress environments provides the necessary context for designing inclusionary experiences and knowing how best to present information that is immediately understandable and actionable. Ultimately, the means to present information to a person or a machine is essentially a signal to respond in some manner.

Data visualization is always going to rely on mixing a meaningful and intelligent blend of both text and graphics. The ratio will depend on the context.

CONTEXT

To establish context, you can consider the following:

■ Time

■ Location

■ Specific inclusions or exclusions

- Business objectives and activities
- Accountability and responsibilities
- Adherence to standards or mandates
- Legal, regulatory, and contractual needs
- Causation

Ethnography: Improving Understanding Through Specialized Data

The ability for an organization to ask any question against any data is no longer a luxury but a necessity. How sufficient or profound the sense of the answer may depend on the underlying information architecture.

Topics such as thick data or its more formal name, *ethnography*, can be complementary to big data in producing higher levels of insight from deeper levels of information. Big data can generate lots of data points, but through the use of ethnographic techniques, organizations can improve the sense they make of that data.

The phrase that someone's knowledge is "a mile wide and an inch deep" juxtaposes thick data with big data. Big data can have millions of data points for use in AI but represent only a broad sense of knowledge. Thick data can bring a granular level of detail to advanced analytics. In ethnography, the traits associated with the data tend to be more holistic and more fine-grained (detailed) when compared to the data collected through coarser-grained (or big data) techniques. For example, with big data, one might capture weather data across the country based on one-square kilometer grids. The weather data might include ambient temperature, wind speed, wind direction, and humidity captured in five-minute increments. With ethnography, other elements would be added such as the terrain, the use of the land (industrial, farming, city, urban), tidal times if near a body of water, population movements, vehicular movements, etc., which can all serve to further influence the general weather characteristics.

In descriptive statistics, an *interquartile range* is the measure of statistical dispersion. By looking at where data falls across an interquartile range, an organization can garner sufficient information to determine whether a data point lies within the norm or is an outlier. The ability to leverage discriminant functions over the data can lead to the use of multiple AI models. These models can be specifically trained to address the characteristics or the special nuances of a designated cohort or classification. Being able to apply the right model to the right situation promotes sustainable viability and relevancy. Especially when addressing outliers, adding thick data/ethnography techniques might help improve pattern detection with AI models.

DRILLING DOWN

When we look at another person, we see a oneness: one person. However, if we were to figuratively peel away the layers, we would encounter numerous other physical systems under the covers (the skin): a respiratory system, nervous system, digestive system, muscular system, the skeleton, etc. In turn, each system can be decomposed. This is just the physical part of the oneness. There is a mental component too.

A system often distills down the oneness to name, address, date of birth, and last product bought. The collective data about a person often gets combined to form a 360-degree view of the oneness. Upon closer examination, we can quickly uncover that far more attributes or facts are missing from a 360° view than are actually included in the view. Often, far more can be known if we are willing to collect the data.

Data Governance and Data Quality

A potential misconception surrounding data lakes that are built from big data sources is that because the ingestion side of the environment is regarded as schema-less (meaning, that the data is written without the necessity to have a predefined structure), no structure is actually required.

As applicable across all forms of analytics, including machine learning and pattern identification, having properly prepared data increases the utility of the data in terms of the results that can be presented for insight or decision-making. Properly preparing data often involves addressing some form of structure.

The Value of Decomposing Data

There might be instances when a machine learning method proves to be more useful when it is used on a decomposed or split attribute as part of feature engineering. In AI, feature engineering is an essential process in using the domain knowledge associated with data to create data points that can make machine learning algorithms more effective.

Consider a timestamp. A timestamp can be represented by its constituent parts, date and time, both of which can also be further decomposed. The date can be split into a year, a month, and a day, while the time can be further split into hours, minutes, and seconds. There could be a business need, for instance, where only the hour is relevant to a machine learning model. Additionally, other features can be derived or engineered from a date such as the day of the week or the proximity to a solstice.

Providing Structure Through Data Governance

Data governance is an essential element in organizing data, providing mechanisms to perform the necessary oversight to ensure that the data is appropriately used to assist in making certain types of decisions. Metrics are used to monitor the effectiveness of those decisions, and data quality helps ensure that those decisions are based on the best possible answers.

Figure 3-5 illustrates how data governance can be applied, proactively or reactively, by an organization. *Proactive* data governance seeks to prevent issues from arising, while *reactive* data governance addresses issues that have already risen.

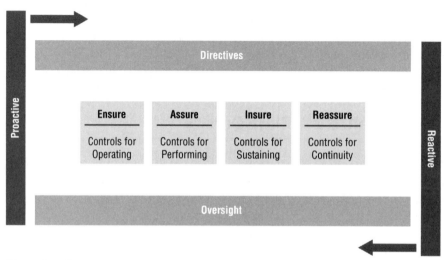

Figure 3-5: Data governance

Directives are used to provide guidance for others to follow when producing or consuming data, while *oversight* provides the means to observe people and the associated outcomes related to the data that they are producing and consuming.

Ensure, assure, insure, and reassure create an orchestrated flow in the production of data and comprise the practice of data governance.

- **Ensure:** Various governance controls associated with the creation of standards and guidelines for data and AI
- **Assure:** Governance controls associated with the creation of data values
- **Insure:** Governance controls required to sustain governance for AI in an operational mode
- **Reassure:** Governance controls to provide the continuity and transparency to demonstrate that the use of AI is functioning as intended and fairly

Through data governance, activities such as data quality and data curation are established as part of an organizational set of disciplines and practices.

Curating Data for Training

Data quality should be considered part of the preparation when curating training data. Curation is a process that involves the ability to subset data based on some type of subject-matter bias, and, often, the more highly curated the better. Curating depends on being able to identify the most appropriate data sources, business use cases, and objectives. Curated data can be culled from the following sources:

- Content and data relationships from call center recordings
- Answers to questions from chat logs
- Correlating maintenance data with streaming sensor data
- Use cases and user problems from search logs
- Customer purchase history to look for similarities in buyers and predict responses to offers
- Surfacing buyer segments from email response metrics
- Attributes and attribute values from product catalogs and data sheets
- Procedures, tool lists, and product associations from public references
- Product associations can be mined from transcribed audio tracks from YouTube video content
- Correlating offers and dynamic content to website behavior patterns
- Extracting knowledge and user-intent signals from sentiment analysis, user-generated content, and social graph data

Additional Considerations for Creating Value

AI and cognitive computing require data to be managed in much the same way as data that is used for business intelligence (BI) and other analytical systems, by applying practices from a data governance initiative. Executive sponsorship, charters, roles and responsibilities, decision-making protocols, escalation processes, defined agendas, and linkages to specific business objectives and processes apply *equally* to all forms of data and analytics.

But, as discussed earlier, data is inert. Data is not self-aware and is not self-organizing. Data, by itself, cannot recognize value. Data requires applications and other processes to ascertain and derive value. Moreover, data must be used if the data is to provide any value at all. Data that sits unused on a spinning disk or is stagnant on a flash drive is just an expense.

The better structured/tagged, the better organized, the better curated, and the better governed the data, the more utility the data will afford to the organization.

Using advanced analytics and AI is to affect a process outcome through accessing the enterprise's data. AI and cognitive computing programs must be aligned to enterprise metrics. Data and data quality are necessary to aiding process effectiveness and achieving the enterprise's business imperatives. Advancing advanced analytics requires capturing and curating data through a pragmatic information architecture.

STANDARDIZATION

Remediation for data quality often falls into one of two categories: standardization or cleansing.

Most data quality initiatives are limited to standardization, as it is easier to address, creating a conformed representation of the value. Cleansing often involves correcting a value where an incorrect value was used. Invariably, the correct value is not always easy to remediate.

Ontologies: A Means for Encapsulating Knowledge

Applying techniques from information engineering to information architecture provides the opportunity to plan and incorporate the right type of information organization and schema design.

For AI, knowledge is often leveraged by means of an ontology. An ontology can consist of a number of elements including taxonomies, controlled vocabularies, thesaurus structures, and all of the relationships between terms and concepts.

An ontology represents a domain of knowledge, and the organization's ability to access and retrieve answers in specific contexts is ultimately made possible through information architecture. Therefore, an information architecture plays a strong role in shaping analytical outcomes. Ontologies can be specialized, such as in the ability to support an autonomous driving car, or more generalized, for broader uses in artificial general intelligence (AGI).

Ontologies capture commonsense knowledge and relationships for objects, processes, materials, actions, events, and so on. An ontology forms a foundation for computer reasoning, even if the answer to a question is not explicitly contained within the organization's body of knowledge or corpus.

As nonexplicit answers can be inferred from the facts, terms, and relationships expressed within an ontology, this makes the use of an ontology a vehicle to provide additional business value. In a practical sense, the ability to infer—as an analytical capability—can make a system more user-friendly and forgiving, such as when a user makes a request using phrase variations or when encountering foreign use cases.

An ontology can express the following:

- **Entity types:** An entity type could be a person, an organization, a bank account, a meeting, a terrorist attack.

- **Relationships:** These are types between entity types (for example, a person can own a bank account, a person can be a member of an organization, or a person can be the parent of another person).

- **Properties of entity types:** A person typically has a first name; an organization has an establishment date.

- **Hierarchies between entity types:** Every cat is a mammal; a tomato is a fruit.

- **Logical entities definitions:** An orphan is a person where both parents are deceased.

- **Logical relationships definitions**: If Adam is a parent to Brenda, and Brenda is a parent to Charlie, then Adam is a grandparent to Charlie; in jest, if Michael is a parent to Nigel, Olive is a parent to Penelope, and Michael marries Penelope, Nigel is his own grandfather.

- **Assertions:** If Deborah is the parent to Edward, then Edward cannot be the parent to Deborah.

Ontology-based information extraction is a form of uncovering facts from the use of an ontology to drive outcomes. By harnessing the knowledge and the rules embedded within an ontology, many complex extraction problems can be solved. Figure 3-6 shows how a basic ontology model can be used to understand contextual facts.

A jaguar can also be a lot of different things, such as a type of car, a ping-pong team, an animal, and so on, as shown in Figure 3-7. A guitar model known as a Jaguar could be inferred from the use of other facts and terms uncovered in natural language processing such as: "The signature jaguar used by Johnny Marr features a taller tremolo arm as well as a four-position slider pickup selector. The modifications were implemented to reflect several of the changes found on other vintage models. . . ."

The inference to a guitar can conclude that the description is not that of a wild animal or an automobile, etc., but is in fact that of a guitar by the use of the words "tremolo arm," "pickup selector," and the awareness that Johnny Marr is known as a guitarist.

Through encapsulating knowledge using techniques as ontologies to assist with AI, organizations can begin to reason on various hypotheses.

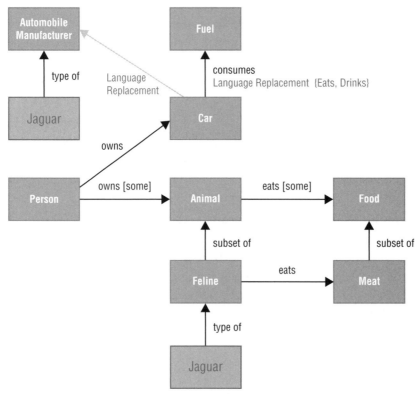

Figure 3-6: An ontological model

Figure 3-7: Inference

SEMANTICALLY DISAMBIGUATE

Imagine creating a spreadsheet, where it can be easy to create abbreviated column names. Perhaps it's easier to type in "org nm" instead of "organization name"; but what if someone thought that it meant "organism name"? How do you ensure when a spreadsheet has a column named "org nm" that it means the same thing as another person's spreadsheet that uses "company name"?

These concepts matter significantly when you're trying to make use of multiple datasets to piece together a more complete picture of the world. It may not seem like a big deal on a handful of datasets, but when a problem takes hundreds of datasets to get a complete picture and the datasets change drastically over time, it demands a more robust solution than solely a human in the loop.

When managing many datasets, you need to understand the following:

- Company names in the data
- Their addresses
- Information that tells me the mailing address is different from the headquarters address

By labeling information and their explicit relations to other pieces of information, we can take a step forward into semantically answering these questions. Ontologies help with semantically disambiguating references to entities that would otherwise appear the same.

Fairness, Trust, and Transparency in AI Outcomes

Machine learning algorithms that parse data, extract patterns, learn, and make predictions and decisions based on gleaned insights are readily applied for use in common applications for search engines, facial recognition, and digital assistants. But despite good intentions, unfairness (often called out as *bias*) can creep into machine learning and AI.

The more data that is fed into a machine learning algorithm, the smarter it gets, assuming that the data has an appropriate level of quality and that the data is not inherently skewed. If the data is biased in some manner—either through the level of data quality or the choices made to avoid incorporating specific types of data—negative outcomes result.

In 2016, AI was used as a means to judge a beauty contest. More than 6,000 women from more than 100 countries submitted their photographs. AI was promoted as being able to relieve mankind from the social biases that human judges are believed to exert. The deep-learning algorithm selected 44 winners from all of the entrants. Only one of the winners had dark-colored skin. Although there were not any explicit algorithms to favor lighter-skinned women, the limited variety of training data (people of color were vastly underrepresented) was sufficient to establish that level of bias by AI.

> **NOTE** For more information about the bias of the AI used in this beauty contest, see `www.theguardian.com/technology/2016/sep/08/artificial-intelligence-beauty-contest-doesnt-like-black-people`.

Erasing bias from insight is key to creating impartial machine learning algorithms. AI requires a body of knowledge: the corpus of the business and the basis for the organizational universe of discourse. The body of knowledge ultimately contains all of the clues that AI uses for processing and subsequently for interpretation and inferencing. To properly train a predictive model, historical data must meet broad and high-quality standards. While many organizations have created data quality programs with varying degrees of success, organizations will be forced into stepping up their game and also addressing the breadth and representation of their data if they are to maximize their investments in AI.

Fairness, a linguistic antonym to bias, can be a form of corrective bias in its own right. Fairness can help ensure that specific data is included or excluded from analysis. Fairness can ensure that a study, for example, on prostate health or ovarian cysts, will be limited to the appropriate cohort groups, so as not to distort any observations or insights.

Other examples that warrant biased data to achieve fairness in outcomes include AI initiatives that support child welfare and safety, whereby the study of data is limited to juveniles. A gaming vendor that provides cloud gaming capabilities should also understand when a juvenile is playing to avoid inappropriate interactive offers. A financial services company wanting to upsell clients should train models on clients that already use existing services and products. An airline wanting to adequately manage the availability of space in overhead bins as passengers board an aircraft may want to train its models exclusively on the types of baggage brought into the main cabin versus all of the passenger luggage that is loaded onto the plane.

Achieving fairness may also require capturing a deeper level of knowledge in specific areas. For example, Figures 3-8 and 3-9 show the blood test results from a hospitalized patient. The routine blood work results failed to detect any anomaly in the patient's body. Further discrete tests were subsequently required to go deeper into finding or understanding a probable cause for suffering. Bias can therefore result from an insufficient knowledge base from which to draw conclusions, observations, or patterns.

Because certain AI algorithms can learn from the data received, the algorithms can be heavily influenced. An extreme example of the influence data can have upon AI is Microsoft's 2016 chatbot known as Tay. Tay lasted only 16 hours before its plug was pulled. During its short time on Earth, Tay turned homophobic and used Nazi references.

Laboratory Results:	Result Value	Result Value Ranges
Liver Function Panel (▬▬▬▬▬ AM)		
Cancellation Reason		[-]
Urinalysis, Dipstick with Microscopic Exam on Positives (▬▬▬▬▬ AM)		
Color Urine	Yellow	[Yellow-]
Appearance Urine	Clear	[Clear-]
Urine Glucose (Urinalysis)	Negative	[Negative-]
Bilirubin Urine	Negative	[Negative-]
Specific Gravity Ur	<1.005	[1.003–1.030]
Ketones Urine	Negative	[Negative-]
Blood Urine	Trace	[Negative- mg/dL]
pH, Urine	6.5	[4.5–8.0]
Protein Urine	Negative	[Negative-]
Urobilinogen Urine	Normal	[Normal-]
Nitrite Urine	Negative	[Negative-]
Leukocyte Esterase U	Negative	[Negative-]
.Estimated Glomerular Filtration Rate (▬▬▬▬▬ AM)		
eGFR African-American (MDRD)	>60	[>=60- mL/min/1.73 m2]
eGFR Non African-American (MDRD)	>60	[>=60- mL/min/1.73 m2]
HCG (Total Beta) (▬▬▬▬▬ AM)		
HCG (Total Beta)	<1.20	[0.00–4.80 mIU/mL]
Auto Differential (▬▬▬▬▬ AM)		
Nucleated RBC Auto	0.1	[0.0–1.0 /100 WBC's]
Neutrophil percent auto	52.2	[45.0–70.0 %]
Lymphocyte Automated	32.8	[22.0–40.0 %]
Monocyte percent auto	10.7	[0.0–12.0 %]
Eosinophil percent auto	3.8	[0.0–8.0 %]
Basophile percent auto	0.5	[0.0-2.0 %]
Neutrophil Absolute Number	2.90	[1.80–7.70 x10(9)/L]
Lymph Absolute # (Westchester)	1.8	[1.0–5.0 x10(9)/L]
Monocyte Absolute Number	0.60	[0.00–1.32 x10(9)/L]
Eosinophil Abs #	0.20	[0.00–0.88 x10(9)/L]
Basophil Absolute Number	0.10	[0.00–0.22 x10(9)/L]

Figure 3-8: Blood test results showing normalcy, part A

NOTE More information about Tay's bias problem can be found at fortune.com/longform/ai-bias-problem.

Organizations must find ways to fine-tune AI so that any defects can be addressed almost immediately after they are identified. AI without the aid of transparency creates a "black box," implying a need to operate in a mode of blind trust. In contrast, AI with transparency can be a white box, critical to understanding causation. We'll explore trust a bit deeper in a few pages.

<u>**Basic Metabolic Panel**</u> (▬▬▬▬▬▬ AM)

Sodium Serum	139	[137–145 mmol/L]
Potassium Serum	3.9	[3.6–5.0 mmol/L]
Chloride Serum	103	[98–107 mmol/L]
CO2	24.0	[22.0–30.0 mmol/L]
Urea Nitrogen (BUN)	10.0	[7.0–20.0 mg/dL]
Creatinine Serum	0.7	[0.6–1.1 mg/dL]
Glucose Random	89	[70–100 mg/dL]
Anion Gap	12.0	[5.0–17.0]
Calcium, Serum	9.0	[8.4–10.2 mg/dL]
BUN/Creatinine Ratio	14.3	[6.0–22.0]

<u>**Complete Blood Count with Differential**</u> (▬▬▬▬▬▬▬ AM)

WBC Count	5.5	[4.0–11.0 x10(9)/L]
Red Blood Cell Count	4.53	[4.20–5.40 x10(12)/L]
Hemoglobin	13.1	[12.0–16.0 g/dL]
Hematocrit	39.4	[38.0–47.0 %]
Mean Corpuscular Vol	87.0	[80.0–95.0 fL]
Mean Corp Hgb (Mch)	29.0	[26.0–33.0 pg]
Mean Corp Hgb Conc	33.4	[31.0–36.0 g/dL]
RDW-CV	14.2	[11.5–14.5 %]
Platelet Count	291	[150–430 x10(9)/L]
Mean Platelet Volume	9.80	[8.00–12.00 fL]

<u>**Urinalysis Microscopic UF-100**</u> (▬▬▬▬▬▬ AM)

White Blood Cells Ur	1	[0–5 /HPF]
Red Blood Cells Ur	1	[0–0 /HPF]
Bacteria	None	[None-]
Squamous Epith Cells	None	[None-]

Figure 3-9: Blood test results showing normalcy, part B

ETHICS

Things that are ethical are not always legal, and things that are legal are not always ethical. For example, speeding while driving someone to an emergency room for life-saving medical treatment may be ethical; however, it's still illegal to drive faster than the speed limit. On the other hand, it's legal to allow a tap to drip water for months on end; however, ethically, you shouldn't waste water.

Fairness and bias can be juxtaposed against ethical and legal viewpoints. Are we being fair and ethical? Are we being fair and legal? Secondarily, we can pose the questions, are we being fair to our customer (and their value system) and are we being fair to ourselves/organization (and our own value system)?

Accessible, Accurate, Curated, and Organized

When using machine learning or AI, behaviors such as signals, digital footprints, and electronic body language from a user's current and past interactions can be evaluated and interpreted. By successfully evaluating the user's behaviors, the options with the highest probability of impact can be delivered.

Such behaviors can include a multitude of various data points. The data points may include prior purchases, real-time click-stream data, support center interactions, consumed content, preferences, buying characteristics, demographics, firmographics (which are to businesses and organizations what demographics are to people), social media information, and any other behavioral traits that can be captured by marketing automation and integration technologies.

Results from search queries can be tuned—such that they may even be dissimilar from one interaction to the next—to accommodate nuances between different users based on factors that span precision and generalization. For example, a search engine, in many ways, is nothing more than a recommendation engine.

The signal is the search phrase, and the recommendations form the result set. The more that is known about the user, the more the recommendation (or personalization) can be tailored to that user. This is an example of how ethnography can be leveraged and applied.

If the recommendation from a search is related to a business domain such as product or finance—and regardless of how tailored the result set—there is a fundamental precondition that the data associated with the domain be accessible, accurate, curated, and organized.

The precondition is part of the necessity to establish and maintain an information architecture. Figure 3-10 shows that between the access methods to data (APIs, SQL, or NoSQL) and the users themselves lies the information (the data). At a minimum, the data needs to be:

- **Accessible:** The data is located in a place and within a medium that makes the data available to a user community for on-demand use.

- **Accurate:** Here, accuracy is multidimensional and includes a reflection of the exactness in digital form from something in the real world. If the data is supposed to be a person's name, the accuracy of the data should reflect the actual name along with the full and complete spelling. Accuracy also reflects the data's timeliness for consumption.

- **Curated:** For an intended use, the data provided is of meaning and utility. An aspect of curation is to be able to establish an appropriate subset of data. The subset is created from the total amount of information that is accessible to the enterprise. The curated data (the subset) should be useful to a user so that irrelevant data is not accidently consumed and inadvertently used in a decision or action. Curation also infers that the data is properly annotated and described.

- **Organized:** Each data point does not occur in isolation. Organization ensures that all relationships across the data are navigable and stored in a technology that makes certain types of navigation easier to perform.

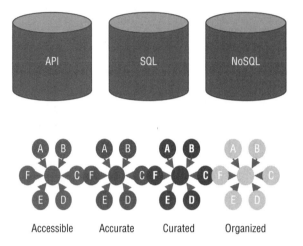

Accessible   Accurate   Curated   Organized

Behaviors

Figure 3-10: Recognizing preconditions

When data is made accessible, accurate, curated, and organized to a business user, the user is better enabled to carry out their job functions with greater effect.

CURATED

A curated dataset is something that, content-wise, can constantly change. Curated data may differ from one day to the next based on the needs of an individual or team. Curated data should always be relevant to the contextual needs associated with roles and responsibilities.

Summary

This chapter covered some of the driving factors that are required for an information architecture to be effective for use with AI. Considerations must be taken into account for the data that goes into a model as well as the data that comes out. These considerations result in both human and machine implications where each human has unique needs as well as each machine having unique needs too.

As all users are not created equal, they don't consistently have the same needs and the same demands. In fact, most people have a specialized function within an organization and may prefer to interact with data using different paradigms: text-based, graphical, with haptic technology, etc. In all cases, the most efficient means to harness information will be contextual to the consumer. Assuming that all user needs are equivalent can be a mistake. To support a cadre of needs, specialized data stores for users and AI should be considered. In fact, hyper-personalized experiences should not exclusively be reserved for customers.

The use of ontologies can help with making AI effective, but building an ontology also benefits from an appropriate information architecture. A well-formed information architecture built on the specialized needs of an organization is likely to provide for completeness of information to users even when questions are asked in a multitude of ways.

Data quality and metadata are imperatives to be realized through an information architecture and to allow for AI to realize its potential to be a transformative tool. Data is inert and is not self-organizing. Data cannot realize any inherent value. These things must come from the information architecture.

In the next chapter, we'll review and critique the environments that have been traditionally built to handle analytics.

A Look Back on Analytics: More Than One Hammer

"It does little good to forecast the future of . . . if the forecast springs from the premise that everything else will remain unchanged."

—Alvin Toffler

The Third Wave

This chapter explores some of the pitfalls associated with traditional analytical environments and how modern data lakes attempt to remediate many of the gaps found in a data warehouse, especially in terms of handling unstructured data and providing support for artificial intelligence (AI). The lessons learned from the failures of previous analytics solutions reveal that further progress is necessary. Organizations need to develop a robust and modern information architecture. Newer solutions must address the needs of multiple personas along with data quality and data governance so that multiple forms of analytics, including AI, can be readily incorporated to yield a sustainable data and analytical environment.

Been Here Before: Reviewing the Enterprise Data Warehouse

Historically, organizations requiring analytics have turned to an *enterprise data warehouse* (EDW) for answers. The traditional EDW was used to store important business data and was designed to capture the essence of the business from other enterprise-based systems such as customer relationship management, inventory, and sales. These systems allowed analysts and business users to gain insight and to make important business decisions from the *business's* data.

For many years, techno-religious wars played out to see which employee had the most mettle to sway a direction, the winner to triumphantly select the enterprise's EDW deployment style. But as the technology landscape changed, driven in part by much higher data volumes from streaming data, social data feeds, and the magnitude of growth in connected devices, so rose the enterprise's expectations from data and analytics. IT departments began to realize that traditional EDW technologies, by themselves, were ill-suited to meet the newer and more complicated needs of the business.

The relational database, the tool of choice for most data warehouses, is still a viable technology for analytics. Even in the era of cloud computing, resilient cloud-native varieties do exist. However, relational technologies are being usurped by distributed ledgers (such as blockchains), graph databases, key-value databases, object databases, triplestores, document stores, wide-column stores, and so on—all seeking to offer alternative ways to store and retrieve corporate data.

> **NOTE**   One example of a resilient, cloud-native relational database is CockroachDB by Cockroach Labs.

The traditional EDW has ironically suffered heavily from its intended use. The relational model of data, the underpinning philosophy of the relational database, was first described by Ted Codd in the late 1960s. In the relational model, relations manifest as tables in a relational database. In turn, a table contains rows and columns. The table, rows, and columns all obey certain rules to retain the notion of being relational. The fact that the database was based on a formal model paved the way for data integrity (but not necessarily for data quality).

Codd set about establishing a number of rules to ensure the overall integrity of data within a relational database, and many are appropriate to many other database types as well.

> **NOTE**   Codd's rules were published in a two-part article by *Computerworld* magazine in 1985: "Is Your DBMS Really Relational?" and "Does Your DBMS Run by the Rules?"

These rules included the following:

Rule 0: The *foundation rule*. For any system that is advertised as, or claims to be, a relational database management system, that system must be able to manage databases entirely through its relational capabilities.

Rule 1: The *information rule*. All information in a relational database is represented explicitly at the logical level and in exactly one way—by values in tables.

Rule 2: The *guaranteed access rule.* Each and every datum (atomic value) in a relational database is guaranteed to be logically accessible by resorting to a combination of table name, primary key value, and column name.

Rule 3: The *systematic treatment of null values rule.* Null values (distinct from the empty character string or a string of blank characters and distinct from zero or any other number) are supported in fully relational database management systems (RDBMSs) for representing missing information and inapplicable information in a systematic way, independent of data type.

Rule 4: The *dynamic online catalog based on the relational model rule.* The database description is represented at the logical level in the same way as ordinary data so that authorized users can apply the same relational language to its interrogation as they apply to the regular data.

Rule 5: The *comprehensive data sublanguage rule.* A relational system may support several languages and various modes of terminal use (for example, the fill-in-the-blanks mode). However, there must be at least one language whose statements are expressible, per some well-defined syntax, as character strings and that is comprehensive in supporting all of the following items:

- Data definition
- View definition
- Data manipulation (interactive and by program)
- Integrity constraints
- Authorization
- Transaction boundaries (begin, commit, and rollback)

Rule 6: The *view-updating rule.* All views that are theoretically updatable are also updatable by the system.

Rule 7: *Possible for high-level insert, update, and delete.* The capability of handling a base relation or a derived relation as a single operand applies not only to the retrieval of data but also to the insertion, update, and deletion of data.

Rule 8: The *physical data independence rule.* Application programs and terminal activities remain logically unimpaired whenever any changes are made in either storage representations or access methods.

Rule 9: The *logical data independence rule.* Application programs and terminal activities remain logically unimpaired when information-preserving changes of any kind that theoretically permit unimpairment are made to the base tables.

Rule 10: The *integrity independence rule*. Integrity constraints specific to a particular relational database must be definable in the relational data sublanguage and storable in the catalog, not in the application programs.

Rule 11: The *distribution independence rule*. The data manipulation sublanguage of an RDBMS must enable application programs and terminal activities to remain logically unimpaired whether and whenever data are physically centralized or distributed.

Rule 12: The *nonsubversion rule*. If a relational system has a low-level (single-record-at-a-time) language, that low level cannot be used to subvert or bypass the integrity rules and constraints expressed in the higher-level relational (multiple-records-at-a-time) language.

While not all databases, relational and nonrelational, adhere to these rules, fundamentally the rules apply in spirit to an information architecture and to what an information architecture seeks to accomplish.

In a relational database, a table is intended to store information about a particular type of *thing*, such as a customer, a product, or an order, and so on. Each row in the table is also intended to store information about the *thing*, such as an individual customer, an individual product, and an individual order. Each column of each row is intended to hold atomic pieces of data that describe the *thing* that the row now represents. And herein lies the crux of the EDW problem.

The problem was not, as may be initially thought, what to include in a primary key or even whether the data was properly **normalized**.

> **NOTE** The principles of normalization are intended to provide rigor in establishing the overall schema of the database.

The problem was the *atomic piece of data*. Atomicity, as shown in Figure 4-1, caused, and still causes, table designers to limit their thinking for deploying business-oriented solutions.

The term *atomic* is used to connote the idea that a business concept must be expressed in its lowest common form of meaningful decomposition. Understanding the composition of data and what constitutes an atomic value can significantly aid in how you approach engineering features for an AI model.

> **NOTE** The lowest common form of decomposition is a bit (the decomposition of a byte), but that would not hold meaning to a businessperson.

To some businesspeople, the term *mailing address* can be considered atomic (refer to Figure 4-1). However, a mailing address, in the United States, could be decomposed as street number, street name, city, state, and ZIP code. But then, the street name could also be further decomposed into a pre-direction, the street name, a post-direction, and a suite or apartment number.

Rule 2: Guaranteed Access Rule
Each and every datum (atomic value) is guaranteed to be logically accessible by resorting to a combination of table name, primary key value, and column name.

Mailing Address

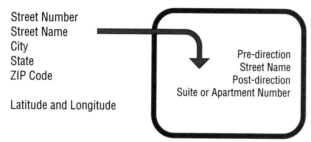

Street Number
Street Name
City
State
ZIP Code

Latitude and Longitude

Pre-direction
Street Name
Post-direction
Suite or Apartment Number

Figure 4-1: Reviewing atomic data

In fact, the U.S. Postal Service further defines alternative atomic rules that include general addresses versus rural route addresses versus post office box addresses. The Postal Service also delineates rules of format between business addresses and residential addresses.

But while there are all of these different approaches to representing a mailing address, two other atomic values could act as a surrogate: a latitude and a longitude.

Even the notion of a mailing address, from an atomic aspect, is therefore distinct from other uses of an address such as a billing address or for a mobile location. One must also consider that not all addresses represent a geographically fixed location.

In another example, a person's name can be decomposed into first name, middle name, and last name with honorifics such as Mr., Mrs., and Dr. also separated along with any separation for name suffixes, such as academic achievements (e.g., Ph.D.), honorary titles (e.g., K.B.E), professional title (e.g., CPA), or generational title (e.g., Sr., Jr., and III)—leading to column design that may begin as follows:

Order_Name_Prefix

Order_Name_First

Order_Name_Middle

Order_Name_Last

Order_Name_Suffix

Depending on cultural needs, the previous approach can also be too restrictive. In some cultures, a last name can contain many names representing paternal or maternal lineage. But across different cultures, the sequence in how portions of a name are represented may vary too. All of these factors played heavily into where people drew the line as to how the guaranteed access rule should be interpreted and applied.

In many cases, too many designers choose to hard-code atomic attributes to the prevailing business vernacular rather than to pursue more forgiving (and adaptive) abstractions. The adopted practices created a technique that served to literally hard-code the business to a point in time and prevented an easier route to making changes to a database schema. The binding nature of data was also addressed in Chapter 2, "Framing Part I: Considerations for Organizations Using AI."

Following on from the "gender" example that was used in Chapter 2, if an organization wanted to add a *biology* or a *sex code* to a table that already had an existing *gender code*, this could be simply accomplished by using a structured query language (SQL) statement named ALTER. The ALTER statement would allow someone to specify the table name and to provide the new column name with an appropriately designated data type, such as string or numeric.

However, what proved to be difficult was the time required to effect the change when a table contained billions of stored rows and when potentially hundreds of application programs and procedures were dependent and tied to the original schema.

Atomicity was relentlessly infused as a best practice. Few practitioners took note that concepts such as the built-in data type TIMESTAMP were themselves not atomic. The TIMESTAMP data type could be decomposed by the query language and even participate in temporal (time-series) equations—but a column with this data type was not technically atomic in its representation. While subtle, this meant that people referred to designs as having certain characteristics that they, in fact, did not have.

> **NOTE**   A TIMESTAMP is a composite column containing both a date and a time. Both the date and the time portions are also composite in their own right. The date consists of the month, the day, and the year. The time contains the hour, the minutes, the seconds, and optionally the number of subseconds. The American National Standards Institute (ANSI) standard for SQL specifies the number of subseconds and *n*. The *n* allows each database vendor to choose what fraction to support. Common fractions are 0, 3, 6, and 8. While the precision can vary by database implementation, they all conform to the ANSI SQL standard. Therefore, the standard does not promote likeness or consistency.

Later, character large objects (CLOBs) and binary large objects (BLOBs) were introduced as data types that were highly suited for nonatomic attributes and concepts. These data types were essentially NoSQL friendly. Relational technology was essentially doomed by best practices that ended up paving the way for future nimbler and more adaptive techniques and technologies.

Some successful implementations broke away from the atomic column-defined design model when using a relational database. For example, Initiate Systems, bought by IBM in 2010, used alternative design techniques in its relational database Master Data Management offering that were driven by external metadata. The metadata was managed externally to the table and allowed the column structure to be inferred and interpreted through the metadata. Ultimately, though, the inherent schema-on-write best practice of relational databases was perceived as being far too slow and restrictive to address constant business changes.

NOTE   A schema-on-write means that a schema for the data must preexist prior to writing or persisting any data into a database.

With schema-on-write approaches, enterprises must design the data model and articulate the analytical needs before loading any data into the traditional EDW. In other words, each enterprise must know ahead of time how it plans to use the data. For many organizations, this approach can be highly constraining.

Beginning with the use of eXtensible Markup Language (XML), smaller data stores benefited from using a far less rigid and formalized method for describing a structure. By using flat files, programmers could work around formal database administrator (DBA) groups, and, at the time, DBAs were happy to give up control of flat-file designs as they were often just viewed as *tinker toys* compared to a *real* database.

Soon after the insurgence of XML, database technologies that could support a schema-less-write began to appear in the marketplace. A schema-less-write could be used to extract data from a source and then place that data into a data store without first transforming the data in a way that would have been necessary with a traditional EDW.

NOTE   A schema-less-write is the same thing as a schema-on-read. The difference between a schema-less-write and a schema-on write is that the schema-less-write only requires that a schema be used for reading the data.

The newer approaches to managing data began to highlight some of the drawbacks associated with the traditional methods used in the creation of an analytical environment.

A RELATIONSHIP IS NOT JUST A LINE BETWEEN OBJECTS

A customer is a type of relationship and not an independent concept. The same applies to an employee. An employee is also a type of relationship. In general terms, a customer is a person (or organization) that may engage with another party in a transaction.

If a person has not yet engaged with the other party in a transaction, the person can be regarded as a prospective customer. Additionally, if a person has not transacted with the other party for an extended period of time, the person may be considered to be a former customer. Therefore, the person and the party exist independently of time, while the aspects of the relationship are time-dependent.

An employee is a person who performs paid work for another party. In terms of the relationship, a person may be a prospective hire, an active employee, or a former employee. Often, relationships are designed and implemented as standalone concepts that can complicate our understanding of what the data is telling us. When an individual participates in multiple relationships such as a customer, an employee, a vendor, etc., our ability to derive insight from analytics or machine learning can become obscured if an inappropriate organizational technique is used.

Drawbacks of the Traditional Data Warehouse

The simplified EDW architecture shown in Figure 4-2 helps to illustrate some of the drawbacks associated with the traditional EDW. There are three major areas for data stores: the staging area, the normalized data stores, and the marts.

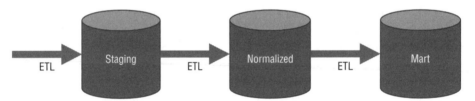

Figure 4-2: Simplified information architecture for an EDW

The *staging area* was used as a transition area between the source data and the data being formally incorporated into the data warehouse environment for end-user access. The *normalized area* is a broad array of cross-subject area domain models for the enterprise to support general analytical needs, while the *mart area* is comprised of discrete models to address certain types of specific analytical needs.

Each data store area required its own distinct data model for which multiple data models could actually be created: a *conceptual data model*, a *logical data model*, and a *physical data model*. In all, some organizations attempted to build nine different models to support the hypothetical architecture that is shown in Figure 4-2.

The approach to designing the staging data may have been based on a denormalized design inherited from multiple source systems and accompanied by separate conceptual, logical, and physical models. The normalized data may have used a normalized design and also be accompanied by separate conceptual, logical, and physical models. The mart data may have used a star schema or snowflake design and also is supported by a cadre of underlying models.

Approaches to normalization, denormalization, and even star schemas boil down to affinities between concepts and whether to organize the concepts together or separately and with what degree of applied rigor. In each case, the physical data model would be the source for the writing or generating data definition language (DDL) so that the necessary tables can be installed.

In addition to the three data store areas, three separate data integration processes are required: one to move data into the staging area, another to move data into the normalized area, and a third to move data into the marts. These processes are often referred to as or extract, transform, and load (ETL). There are variants such as ELT: extract, load, and then transform.

Each operational source, data file, or relational table requires its own ETL line. Figure 4-2 illustrates why a schema-on-write approach for the traditional EDW can consume a tremendous amount of time and cost in extensive data modeling and data preparation.

NOTE   Each of the modeled areas needs to be aligned and support the data flows. Each data flow is dependent on the models in each area. A change in place can have a ripple effect of change along the entire chain.

Under the guise of data governance, many organizations invested in a paradigm known as *analysis paralysis*. Resulting standardization or governance committees were formed, and they met to deliberate over standards and terminology—sometimes for years and without actually completing all of the tasks at hand.

NOTE   The phrase *analysis paralysis* is used to denote a process when overanalyzing and overthinking a situation can cause forward motion or decision-making to become all but impossible so that no solution or course of action can be taken or decided upon.

For example, the outcome of lengthy deliberation for defining what a customer actually means to an organization may result in a definition such as "a party that has purchased, been shipped, or used products." While this might be amenable to an IT department, most business-facing employees found little value or meaning with such lackluster and terse definitions.

NOTE   The quote in the preceding paragraph comes from Len Silverston's *The Data Model Resource Book, Volume 1: A Library of Universal Data Models for All Enterprises* (Wiley, 2001).

A committee process normally involves creating many up-front definitions. Before formally beginning, committees must often deliberate upon the problems they want to solve. Then, the committee must decide what types of business questions are likely to be frequently asked. The committee process is perceived to help ensure that the correct supporting data can be identified. From that, a committee will commission the design of a database schema capable of supporting the questions brought to light by the committee.

Because of the time and energy to onboard new data sources, after a schema has been finalized, a committee can spend an inordinate amount of time deciding what information should be included and what information should be excluded from a data warehouse. Such a time-intensive process helped to render the traditional EDW fairly static in composition and content.

If a committee became gridlocked, meaningful work and progress could stall. In some organizations, gridlocks have been known to drag on for many months. A gridlock can be short-circuited when a committee member, sometimes dubbed as the 800-pound gorilla in the room, decides to simply *edict* an answer.

NOTE The aspect of an 800-pound gorilla in a committee means that a strong personality can take over and force a direction that is in their favor and not necessarily in the favor of the committee. A strong personality can be overbearing and cause some people to refrain from offering a challenge or a dissenting opinion.

However, such answers can often be biased and can be detrimental to both the short-term and long-term success of an EDW. The lack of success is evident by the consistency of EDW project failures, as reported by numerous advisory services.

NOTE For example, M. Gordon Hunter's *Strategic Information Systems: Concepts, Methodologies, Tools, and Applications* (Information Science Reference, 2009).

The question must be asked as to why an organization would use a committee as a means to create an EDW. The answer is twofold.

First, the *enterprise* aspect of a traditional EDW denotes that it represents the entire enterprise and that the enterprise nature of the warehouse would prevent it from becoming another siloed function or siloed data store. Second, as a best practice, the hierarchical organization chart used by all major organizations is based on lines of business (which are themselves silos that are created by following a best practice on organizational models) where only one enterprise-wide decision-maker actually exists, *the company president*.

As repeatedly asking the organization's president to decide on what should or should not go into a data warehouse is probably not a viable option, committees were therefore established as a way to facilitate a cross line-of-business activity. In a matrixed organization where employees may report into multiple managers, *interlocking*, or the coordination with others, becomes a surrogate means to provision a committee or governance authority.

Using a traditional EDW approach, business analysts and data scientists cannot consistently seek answers to ad hoc questions from the data. A business analyst or data scientist would have to form a hypothesis ahead of creating the requisite data structures and analytics so as to test out their hypothesis. A restrictive aspect of the EDW was that analytic users had to follow a predefined path of access to the data so as to avoid performance or response time issues. System administrators often canceled wayward (or ad hoc) requests because they were seen as consuming too many computer resources.

The only feasible analytic results that were consistently produced by a traditional EDW were those that the EDW had been explicitly designed to return. Certainly, this is not an issue if the original hypothesis was absolutely correct and the underlying business (and the business-side business model) is stagnant from one year to the next. The closed-loop techniques adopted by EDW designers can be restrictive for a business that consistently requires new ways to view data and new data to support a changing business landscape.

The successor environment to the data warehouse was the *data lake,* and it sought to eliminate many of the issues just described as both structured and unstructured data could be readily ingested—without any data modeling or standardization. Structured data from conventional databases can be placed into the rows of the data lake table in a largely automated process. Technologies associated with the data lake were also better prepared to handle big data.

Because the schema for storing data does not need to be defined up front, expensive and time-consuming modeling is not needed (or can be deferred). Once data is in the data lake, analysts can annotate or choose which tag and tag groups to assign. The tags are typically pulled from the source's table-based information. Data can receive multiple tags, and tags can be changed or added over time.

THE LOGIC BEHIND A BEST PRACTICE

For a best practice to even be considered a best practice, the practice must work, as prescribed, in more than one situation. For a best practice to achieve consistent and reliable outcomes multiple times, across various industries, there is a strong likelihood that the practice only represents the *best* average practice. A logical conclusion would dictate that there is no such thing as a best practice.

A team is likely to seek out and adopt a best practice so as to avoid reinventing the wheel. But, if nobody ever reinvented the wheel, it would still be made out of stone. A downside to reusing a best practice is that it can sustain a legacy mentality and inhibit innovation. When using any best practice, the practice should be considered as your starting point and not your goal.

Even if you use a particular technique to yield success—methodology, process, rule, concept, theory, and so on—that will not automatically make the technique a universal truth for all other situations.

Paradigm Shift

Driven both by the enormous data volumes associated with big data and by the perceived lower cost of ownership, schema-less-write technologies such as Hadoop found open doors in many organizations.

In 2010, Pentaho's James Dixon wrote about the limitations of the EDW and the benefits of Hadoop. He more or less stated that in the EDW, the standard way to handle reporting and analysis is to identify the most interesting attributes and to aggregate these attributes into a data mart. There are several problems with this approach. First, only a subset of the attributes can be examined, so only predetermined questions can be answered. Second, the data is aggregated so that visibility into the lowest levels are lost.

> **NOTE** Dixon's article is available at `www.pentaho.com/blog/2010/10/15/` `pentaho-hadoop-and-data-lakes`.

Based on the requirement needs of the modern organization and to address the problems of the traditional EDW, Dixon created a concept called the *data lake* to describe an optimal solution, which he expressed through this analogy:

> *If you think of a data mart as a store of bottled water—cleansed and packaged and structured for easy consumption—the data lake is a large body of water in a more natural state. The contents of the data lake stream in from a source to fill the lake, and various users of the lake can come to examine, dive in, or take samples.*

While the term has caught on and has continued to gain in popularity as a concept, data lake projects have not all been smooth sailing. Many data lakes have been turned into data swamps—an all but useless collection of data where any hope of performing analytics has become all but lost. When a data lake becomes a data swamp, starting a new data lake project is simpler than attempting to drain (otherwise known as *reorganizing*) the swamp.

ANY VOLUME IN ZERO SECONDS

If you could design an analytic and AI solution to respond in something approaching zero seconds for any sized model, for any volume of data, and regardless of any other processing complexity, what would that design look like? The organization of data, network connectivity, processing time, data volumes, data cleanliness, processing cores, and solid-state drives all serve to help mitigate physics. Designing things for the physical world often means de-optimizing our preferred designs.

The preferred design would constitute an optimized design. A paradigm shift should allow us to get closer to our optimized designs for operating at any level of complexity with any volume of data in near-zero time.

Modern Analytical Environments: The Data Lake

Many modern analytical environments primarily seek to address big data. One of the approaches to managing big data is the data lake, a central location in which to store the enterprise's data, regardless of its source and format.

The data lake technology of choice has been to sit on top of the Hadoop Distributed File System (HDFS) or cloud object storage. The data can be structured or unstructured and can be used by a variety of storage and processing tools to extract result sets.

For example, cloud object storage aids with managing the needs associated with aggressive storage capacity growth demands by enabling capacity-on-demand and other benefits. Similarly, the scalability, simplicity, and accessibility for managing storage on public, private, and on-premise clouds are compelling.

Cloud object storage normally has the following traits:

- Provides a cost-efficient storage capability that can supersede some of the complexities and restrictions associated with older file systems that support network attached storage (NAS) and storage array networks (SANs).

- Provides any time and any device storage access via HTTP protocols and can be delivered via a storage-as-a-service (SaaS) application.

- Provides for elastic and on-demand services. Cloud object storage systems do not use directory hierarchy and can provide for location transparency without imposed limits on the number of files that can be maintained, mandate a threshold as to how large a file can grow, or place a restriction on the amount of space that can be allocated.

- Helps to eliminate hot spots and provides for near-linear performance as nodes are added. A cloud object storage cluster is symmetrical, which allows for the workload to be automatically load balanced across the nodes in the cluster.

- Helps to avoid the need for cloud backup and recovery as the entire cloud object storage cluster is an online, scalable file repository.

When the big data era began, it was defined by volume, variety, velocity, and veracity. Data lakes became a welcoming beacon for managing these types of data traits because the underlying storage mechanisms were far more flexible than those that had been used to support an EDW.

- **Volume:** Large

  Making petabytes and exabytes a viable storage number

- **Variety:** Unbounded

  Making it possible to store structured, semistructured, and richly varied unstructured data that included text, documents, audio, video, and images

- **Velocity:** Tolerable

    Broad acceptance of eventually consistent data copies across the distributed storage made HDFS and cloud object storage an underpinning for capturing data associated with devices and sensors associated with the Internet of Things (IoT)

- **Veracity:** Naivety

    Believing the enterprise was capable of deriving insights from inconsistent content

If data lakes could put out a flashing neon sign, it would likely read "All data is welcome" as a mark of its intended flexibility and capability. Data lakes have arisen as a dominant alternative to the traditional EDW, especially as organizations seek to expand their mobile, IoT, and multicloud data footprints.

The following are some of the benefits you would experience in building a data lake:

- Deriving business value from any type of data

- Persisting any type of data format

- Hoarding data without having to understand its immediate utility

- Refining data as understanding, need, and insight improves

- Fewer restrictions on how data can be queried

- Not restricted to proprietary tools to gain insight into what the data means

- Data can be democratized (allow for nonspecialists to be able to gather and analyze data without requiring outside help) and helping data silos to be eradicated.

- Democratized access can provide a single, unified view of data across the organization.

- Supports complete analytical needs from traditional business intelligence to AI

As indicated earlier in Figure 4-2, several distinct styles of table design emerged to support the EDW. As previously discussed, one style was based on a normalized model of data. The target level of normalization that was sought by many practitioners was third normal form, often abbreviated as 3NF. Third normal form defined design guidelines for associating data to a table's primary key. As data is inert, the data itself could not tell whether it was in or out of 3NF, and practitioners who cited their designs as conforming with 3NF were, at times, making invalid claims.

Other popular data modeling techniques for the EDW include the previously mentioned star schema and snowflake. The star schema and the snowflake were typically known as a *data mart*. The normalized model and the data mart can co-exist in an information architecture for data warehousing. But the differences between an EDW and a data lake can be significant.

While machine learning and AI models invariably use denormalized data, understanding the process and mechanics associated with normalization can pay huge dividends when examining results from the execution of a model—especially in terms of identifying false positives in pattern detection.

By Contrast

While both the EDW and the data lake cater to an organization's analytical needs, how those needs are met have more than a semantic difference. As the *E* in EDW stands for enterprise, the approach organizations took to schema design in the traditional EDW was (and is) often based on establishing a unifying canonical model. Canonical data models are normally developed to present data entities and relationships in a simple and singular form—which may often result in a series of designs that represent a lowest-common denominator.

As few applications could conform to the structure of a canonical model, a production EDW often provided a warehousing environment had limited use. The EDW also paved the way for the establishment of the departmental data warehouse (DDW), where the implemented data model was never intended to have enterprise-wide appeal and thus had a stronger affinity to the source schemas or the schemas of the supported transactional applications. Both the EDW and the DDW always made use of a predefined schema.

NOTE   A departmental data warehouse is focused on supporting the needs of a single business department or line of business. The DDW could be used in conjunction with an EDW.

The operational data store (ODS) was also the result of the limitations to a canonical approach to data modeling but also required schemas to be predefined. The ODS was often built to support intraday analytical needs for front-office applications. Today, the ODS can be replaced with hybrid transactional/analytical processing (HTAP) database technologies.

NOTE   An operational data store is designed to support operational reporting needs and not generalized forms of analytics, such as comprehensive business intelligence and machine learning.

In many organizational implementations, the EDW was designed only to collect data that is controlled for quality and conforms with the enterprise data model. As a result, the traditional EDW was only able to address a limited number of questions, specifically, the preconceived questions that the environment was *theoretically* capable of answering.

Once implemented, the traditional EDW also proved difficult to manage. At one point, the research and advisory firm Gartner cautioned that more than 50 percent of data warehouse projects would have limited acceptance. Later, another advisory service, Dresner, found that only 41 percent of survey respondents considered their data warehouse projects to be successful, and Forrester reported that 64 percent of analytics users had trouble relating the data that was available to the business questions they were trying to answer. More recently, Forbes has commented that the trend is not dissipating: "For too many companies, the data warehouse remains an unfulfilled promise."

NOTE The reference to Gartner's remarks is at `www.cioinsight.com/c/a/Technology/Data-Management-Getting-Clean/1`

The Dresner study is available at `portal.yellowfinbi.com/Document.i4?DocumentId=159663`.

The Forrester report is at `go.thoughtspot.com/forrester-white-paper-0315.html`.

The Forbes article is at `www.forbes.com/sites/danwoods/2017/02/07/snowflakes-vision-for-the-rebirth-of-the-data-warehouse/#11e66ed15d4d`.

Indigenous Data

While the data warehouse often focused a tremendous amount of effort on recasting data into new data models, the data lake inherently onboards data in its original form. Little or no preprocessing is performed for adapting the structure to an enterprise schema—this does not imply that data is not subsequently cleansed or standardized. The structure of the data collected for the data lake is not always known when it is fed into the data lake. The structure is often found only through discovery, when the data is read.

Flexibility is one of the biggest advantages of the data lake. By allowing data to remain in its native format, the data can often be made available for analysis in a much quicker time frame and in greater quantities. But, acting on the flexibility in this manner can be a double-edged sword, resulting in the following problems:

- Too much dirty data as few controls are put into place to reject redundant copies of data, to reject data from unauthorized sources, or to refine the numerous and various anomalies that are often found in source systems

- Trouble with actually collecting data resulting from a lack of data governance to ensure repeatable and consistent feed schedules are put in place
- Trouble with users accessing data due to few controls being placed on publishing a schema design or when a change occurs on a schema
- Not realizing value beyond the collection of data for the sake of collecting data without business objectives in place or identified
- Limited business value beyond keyword search because the data may not easily lend itself to analytics or AI
- Difficulty in properly securing the data lake because the security profiles of different stakeholders, custodians, and users were not sufficiently captured prior to onboarding the data

Cleansing and reconciling data from its contributing sources is central to understanding the differences between an EDW and a data lake. The primary purpose of the traditional EDW is to provide for reliable, consistent, and accessible data to business users in support of decision-making, especially for lawful actions, performance tracking, and problem determination. The data lake's primary purpose was to expand on the type of data that could be collected and made available to the organization. In addition, the data lake was meant to also provide higher degrees of flexibility, to reduce the amount of time spent in system design and on development lifecycles.

The EDW's detailed data originates from operational (largely transactional) systems. The data is often subdivided (especially in the data mart) and summarized (aggregated) by the time the data is accessed by a user. The discussion of data zones in Chapter 5, "A Look Forward on Analytics: Not Everything Can Be a Nail," further elaborates on some of the data characteristics within the data lake and illustrates some of the differences to the EDW.

Attributes of Difference

In contrast to the EDW, a data lake is often defined by several key attributes. The first of these key attributes is the ability to collect anything and everything. Please note that there is a difference between an ability to collect anything and everything and then acting on that ability. Prudence should be used as to what data to place into a data lake. Citing, again, the discussion on data zones in Chapter 5, specific areas can be carved out within a data lake to better manage data that is of an exploratory nature.

The data lake persists both the inbound raw data and any data that has been subsequently processed. Second, a data lake is also characterized by a dive-in-anywhere approach. As access paths are not predefined, users are free to refine, explore, and enrich data based on their terms, implying that a data lake can be cobbled together without much forethought or planning. While the data lake serves to mitigate some of the shortcomings associated with the EDW, an absence of an information architecture does not help with the success rate of a data lake.

Another key attribute is flexible access. Flexible access accommodates multiple data access patterns across a shared infrastructure that may stretch over a hybrid cloud or a multicloud approach and includes batch processing, interactive processing, online processing, cognitive search, in-memory data access, and so on.

The final key attribute of the data lake is that many of the elements are available through open source technologies and not solely on the availability of proprietary software.

RAW DATA

A date is a simple enough thing. Month, day, year. Done! But, representing a date can be far from simple. Consider the following:

dd-mmm-yy	e.g., 31-Jan-25
dd-mmm-yyyy	e.g., 31-Jan-2025
mm/dd/yy	e.g., 01/31/25
mm/dd/yyyy	e.g., 01/31/2025
dd.mm.yy	e.g., 31.01.25
dd.mm.yyyy	e.g., 31.01.2025
yyddd	e.g., 25031
yyyyddd	e.g., 2025031
yy/mm/dd	e.g., 25/01/31
yyyy/mm/dd	e.g., 2025/01/31
qQyy	e.g., 1Q25
qQyyyy	e.g., 1Q2025
mmm yy	e.g., Jan 25
mmm yyyy	e.g., Jan 2025
ww WK yy	e.g., 05 WK 25
ww WK yyyy	e.g., 05 WK 2025
name of day	e.g., Friday
name of month	e.g., January
etc.	

If all data types and data sources are held only in their raw form, inconsistencies are more likely to creep in across the enterprise, as different individuals and teams begin to wrangle the data and apply their own discrete needs and interpretations. Data virtualization should be considered as an alternative form of raw data.

Elements of the Data Lake

Data lakes were born out of the big data movement with the notion that a single shared data repository was a necessity. Because of the affinity between big data and the data lake, the technology of choice for many organizations was Hadoop. A repository built to conform to the Hadoop framework would, as previously mentioned, likely sit on top of HDFS or cloud object storage. In a hybrid or multicloud environment, there may be a need for more than one data lake, although a single data lake can span multiple topographies and will be covered in more detail in Chapter 5 on data topologies. In spanning more than one cloud deployment, a data lake can be partitioned to optimize analytic and AI functions for the supported users and the applications.

Hadoop data lakes often aimed to preserve data in its original form and to capture changes to data and contextual semantics throughout the data's lifecycle. This approach can be especially useful for compliance and internal auditing activities that need to have insight into the changing characteristics of the data and the analytical demands.

In contrast to the traditional EDW, there can be numerous challenges to piecing together a longitudinal perspective of the data after the data has undergone transformations, aggregations, and updates, resulting from a loss of provenance at the column or row level.

Orchestration and job scheduling capabilities are also important elements of the data lake. Within the Hadoop framework, these capabilities are often provided through the use of YARN, which is an acronym for Yet Another Resource Negotiator. YARN is a generic and flexible framework to administer the computing resources in the Hadoop cluster.

YARN provides resource management by using a central platform to deliver tools for consistent operations, security, and data governance. The tools are used across Hadoop clusters and ensure that the analytic workflows have access to the data and the required computing resources. Figure 4-3 shows the architecture for YARN.

The architecture shows specialized application clients submitting processing jobs to YARN's resource manager, which works with ApplicationMasters and NodeManagers to schedule, run, and monitor the jobs.

YARN containers are typically set up in nodes and scheduled to execute jobs only if there are system resources available for them. Hadoop supports creating opportunistic containers that can be queued up at NodeManagers to wait for resources to become available. An opportunistic container concept aims to optimize the use of cluster resources and, ultimately, increase overall processing throughput.

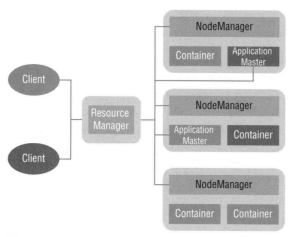

Figure 4-3: YARN architecture

Easy user access is one of the premises associated with a data lake due to the fact that organizations can preserve the data in its original form. This is opposite of the canonical data model approach that was previously described for EDWs. Data lakes seek to provide a set of applications or workflows for consuming, processing, and acting upon the data. Whether the data is structured, semistructured, or unstructured, the data is typically loaded and stored in its raw form.

By leveraging the raw data, the data lake offers data owners the chance to readily consolidate customer, supplier, and operations data, thereby eliminating many of the roadblocks that inhibit sharing data. However, in practice, the raw data is as much an inhibitor to the various data owners. The inherent nature of the raw data can prevent any easy consolidation and may serve to limit the number of data sharing opportunities, especially when using a self-service model.

The paradox between providing a means to consolidate data easily and the raw data preventing easy consolidation is that the raw data brought into the data lake can suffer from many traditional data quality issues seen in many systems. The promise of easy data consolidation requires that the raw ingested data of the data lake contain a level of data quality that is deemed reasonably accurate and consistent. Invariably, many organizations have business data that contains a series of significant data quality issues. If these issues are transferred into the data lake, they persist and are not always easily overcome.

The challenges that the EDW tried to proactively overcome are often addressed reactively within the data lake environment. Reactively addressing data quality issues means that AI models can be erroneously trained on big data, and other analytic processes can lead to misleading insights.

BIG DATA QUALITY

Often, data quality in the data lake can be viewed as being binary: clean or dirty. When dealing with big data, elements of financial cost, elapsed time, and impacts to system performance can influence an organization's decisions as to whether to evaluate and clean the data or to just leave it in a dirty condition.

A third option can be considered: *good enough*. We've already discussed how not all data is created equal and how when it comes to remediating data to improve its quality, not all data needs to be cleansed. You can pick which data to cleanse and which data to ignore (from a cleansing standpoint). Triaging what to cleanse can leave the data in a *good enough* state, even if it's not perfect.

The New Normal: Big Data Is Now Normal Data

Since the dawning of the computer era for mass commercial business purposes—which began in the mid-1960s with the introduction of the IBM 360—provisioning reports for analytical and insight purposes has been critical.

The genesis for the data warehouse began in the late-1980s and was quickly adopted as the de facto environment type for producing (seemingly) complex analytics and reports. But in the era of big data, where traditional complex analytics have taken a back seat to higher-levels of complex analytics—prescriptive analytics, machine learning, cognitive analytics, and AI, along with much higher volumes of data and broader varieties of data—the traditional EDW environment is overwhelmed and sometimes ill-suited.

Initially, big data was data that was deemed either too large or too complex for traditional data-processing methods to handle. As previously indicated, big data was often characterized by volume, variety, velocity, and veracity. Over time, these characteristics became accepted as the new normal.

In the face of this new normal, organizations were faced with the need to continuously change and adapt traditional EDW data models as well as manipulate the rigid field-to-field data integration mappings, all of which proved highly cumbersome. The move toward data lakes was a direct result of recognizing the necessity for a different analytical paradigm for end users and one that was already better equipped to handle big data.

Another weakness in the EDW model was the organization's sole reliance on IT departments to perform any manipulation or enrichment to the data. The dependency arose from the inflexible designs, system complexities, and misguided perception that human error could be eradicated from the environment. On the surface, data lakes were an easy answer for solving these types of challenges because they were not tied to any rigidity associated with a single data model.

Liberation from the Rigidity of a Single Data Model

Because data can be unstructured as well as structured, a data lake can be used to persist anything from blog posts to product reviews to order taking and order fulfillment. Because the data lake is not driven by a canonical data model, the data does not have to be stored in a uniform manner.

For example, one data source may render gender as "male" and "female," another data source might use an encoding technique such as "m" and "f," and a third system may choose to distinguish between biology and societal gender preferences and persist the information as two separate concepts. A system that uses both biology and gender may choose to represent the biology at birth and the gender to represent the individual's portrayal in society; this also includes the ability for a system to recognize gender neutrality.

Onboarding three or more different data source techniques such as streaming, bulk-batch, micro-batch, message queues, etc., in a traditional EDW can be considered problematic; in a data lake, however, you can put all sorts of data into a single repository without worrying about schemas that define the integration points between different datasets.

This approach affords the ability that not every user must conform to using data that is not helpful in making their job easier and more efficient. In the discussion on data zones in Chapter 7, "Maximizing the Use of Your Data: Being Value Driven," we'll cover how the zones can be developed to provide curated data. Data that has been curated makes it easier to consume data in a meaningful and useful manner.

Streaming Data

Once a capability of a select few organizations like stock markets, space agencies, and Formula 1 racers, tapping into streaming data has transcended from being a rare use case.

Streamed data can be brought into the data lake to cover a variety of near-real time or trending data needs from video and audio feeds, social media content, log data, news feeds, surveillance, machine operations (such as an engine from an in-flight airplane), and business transactions.

As the quote in Chapter 2 from Alvin Toffler stated, organizations are having to make decisions at "a faster and faster pace." Streaming data affords decisions to be made faster as analytics can be performed on many streams while the data is transient and still inflight. Being able to assess data while the data is still inflight reduces the need to wait for data to be written to a database. Technologies suitable for the task at hand can reduce latencies associated with decision-making.

Suitable Tools for the Task

While a traditional EDW can meet the needs of some business users for general types of business intelligence activity like aggregation and ranking, the use of tools like Spark, MapReduce, Pig, and Hive in the preparation of data for analysis for an EDW can take far more time than performing the actual analytics.

In a data lake, the data can often be processed more efficiently through these tools without requiring excessive preparation work. As data lakes do not enforce a rigid metadata schema, integrating data can involve fewer steps. Schema-on-read allows users to build custom schemas into their queries upon query execution for easier accessibility.

Easier Accessibility

By using infrastructures designed for big data, ever-larger data volumes can be managed for all forms of analytics, including cognitive analytics and AI. Unlike the potential monolithic view of a single enterprise-wide data model, the data lake accommodates delaying any data modeling activities. Data modeling can be delayed until the end user actually intends to use the data.

The delay may be seen as creating opportunities for enhanced operational insights through the lens of just-in-time data discovery practices. This type of advantage is perceived to grow with increasing data volumes and data varieties along with an increase in the richness of the metadata.

Reducing Costs

Because of economies associated with open source distributions and the use of the infrastructure-as-a-service (IaaS) and platform-as-a-service (PaaS) computing models, data lakes built on Hadoop clusters can be less expensive than comparable on-premise solutions using a commercial relational database.

However, an unmanaged data lake can become more expensive than it needs to be because of the relatively easy tendency to hoard data. Waiting for data to be discovered in a data lake carries a certain number of organizational risks as well as potential rewards. For example, all of the data in the data lake can be subject to search during an e-discovery process for litigation purposes. Not knowing if any of the data that was persisted conflicts with regulatory or compliance requirements is not normally viewed as a sufficient legal defense.

Scalability

Big data is typically defined as an intersection between volume, variety, and velocity. Traditional EDWs are notorious for not being able to scale beyond a certain volume due to restrictions within the architecture. Data processing in an EDW can take so long that organizations are prevented from exploiting all of their data to its fullest extent. Using Hadoop, petabyte-scale and beyond data lakes are more cost-efficient and relatively simple to build and maintain at the level of scale that is organizationally desired.

Veracity and value were two other *v* words that became associated with the big data movement. In a number of ways, veracity and value only highlighted the gap between the promise of the data lake and the realization that some other approach would ultimately be needed.

Data Management and Data Governance for AI

If an organization uses data and advanced analytics, especially AI, for mission-critical purposes, then data management and data governance cannot be lax or ad hoc.

While the traditional EDW was initially embraced because of the formal processes and strict controls, the processes themselves became overwhelmed by the growth in data volume as well as the speed required to handle the ingestion rates along with the broad variety of data types. A knee-jerk reaction for using the data lake is another type of extreme: a convenient place to dump gobs and gobs of data.

Early adopters of the data lake were likely to exhibit the tendency to load data without any attempt to manage the data using a formalized process. Although this type of situation may still exist as organizations go through the trials and errors of using a data lake, the dumping ground for data is rarely considered an optimal business choice.

In situations where the data has not been standardized, where data errors are unacceptable, and when the accuracy of the data is regarded as more than just a high priority, a data dump will work against any organizational efforts to derive value from the data lake.

The data lake can still be a data lake even if it borrows certain formalities from a traditional EDW. A data lake is intended to be flexible, scalable, and cost-effective, but it can also adopt some of the disciplines from a traditional EDW, especially practices associated with data management and data governance.

Incorporating data management and data governance disciplines into the data lake environment requires organizations to avoid the temptation to freely load data at will. While machine learning techniques can sometimes help discover structures in large volumes of disorganized and uncleansed data, this is not something that can ordinarily be left to the unsupervised learning techniques of AI.

Even the most sophisticated inference engine would require a place to start in the vast amounts of data that comprise a data lake. Based on the potential volume, an inference engine would, in all likelihood, need to ignore some of the data. Organizations can run the risk that parts of the data lake may result in data that becomes stagnant and isolated—also known as *dark data*. In addition, the data lake may contain data with so little context or structure that even the most specialized automated tools, or data scientists, can find the terrain tough to rationalize.

The level of data quality in the data can deteriorate over time, and the deterioration can potentially escalate as the volume of data accumulates in the data lake. When similar semantic questions are asked in a slightly different way and yield different answers, users may begin to distrust the data lake or require that the data lake be metaphorically "drained" and begun all over again.

Tools that were used with the traditional EDW can often be applied or adapted for use in the data lake. Invariably, a big data equivalent tool or a specialized data connector can be found. As the marketplace for big data matures, so too will the capabilities that are offered. Evolving capabilities would include the means to allow data—whether written via a schema-on-write approach or through a schema-less-write (schema-on-read)—to be readily cataloged across a hybrid or multicloud environment. Other necessary capabilities would also include improved support for the management of workflows and to assist in the improvement of data quality regardless of where the data is located. Such capabilities would further foster the ability to infuse AI into more applications.

FACTORS

Some of the datasets that are used for training AI models can be so large that they aren't preserved. Therefore, a conundrum exists in how reproducible the results from a model can be should it ever require to be retrained. Several factors that can be considered when governing data and AI include hypothesis data, training data, validation data, test data, and results.

- **Hypothesis data:** How is the hypothesis data developed? How is the hypothesis data validated? Is the resulting hypothesis data kept and managed? If not, is the hypothesis dataset reproducible?

- **Training data:** How is the training data selected? How is the training data validated? Is the training data kept and managed? If not, is the training dataset reproducible?

- **Validation data:** How is the validation data selected? How is the validation data actually validated? Is the validation data kept and managed? If not, is the validation dataset reproducible?

- **Test data:** How is the test data selected? How is the test data validated? Is the test data kept and managed? If not, is the test dataset reproducible?

- **Results:** Are the results validated? Are the results kept and managed? If not, are the results reproducible?

Schema-on-Read vs. Schema-on-Write

This is an oversimplified but useful characterization: the EDW centered on schema-on-write, and the data lake has centered upon schema-on-read.

Some of the advantages associated with a schema-on-write approach include the following:

- The location of the data is known.
- The structure is optimized for predefined purposes.
- The SQL queries are reasonably simple.
- Response times are often very fast.
- Checking the data's quality is an important requisite function.
- Business rules are used to help ensure integrity.
- Answers are largely seen as being precise and trustworthy.

These are some of the disadvantages associated with a schema-on-write approach:

- Data is modified and structured to serve a specific purpose and predefined need.
- There can be certain limitations placed on how long a query can run.
- There can be certain limitations on writing complex queries without the aid of a stored procedure or a program.
- ETL processes and validation rules can take a long time to build.
- Certain ETL processes—due in part to the nature of batch processing—can take a long time to execute.
- ETL processes can take a long time to be adapted to address new needs.

The following are some of the advantages that can be associated with a schema-on-read approach:

- Query capabilities can be flexible.
- Different types of data that are generated by different types of sources can all be stored in the same location.
- The previous two points allow for querying multiple data stores and types at the same time.
- This approach more readily supports agile development approaches.
- This approach more easily accommodates unstructured data.

These are some of the disadvantages associated with a schema-on-read approach:

- The data may not be subjected to data cleaning or data rationalization/ validation processes.

- Some necessary data may be missing, duplicated, or invalid.
- The SQL queries can become complex—taking time to write and time to execute.

Schema-on-write has been an accepted approach since the inception of hierarchical databases such as IBM's IMS database and IBM's relational database Db2 and its forerunner, System R. Before any data is written in the database, the structure of that data is strictly defined, and that metadata is stored and tracked. The schema, comprising the columns, rows, tables, and relationships, is defined for the specific purpose that the database is intended to address. Data is filled into its predefined positions within the schema. In the majority of cases, the data is cleansed, transformed, and made to fit in the structure before the information is persisted.

Schema-on-read is a concept where the programmer is not burdened with knowing what is going to happen to the data before persistence takes place. Data of many types, sizes, shapes, and structures can be thrown into the data storage system or data lake. Only at the time that the data is to be accessed is the schema structure required.

In essence, the two approaches represent opposite ends of a shared spectrum. In earnest, a data-centered environment that supports analytics and AI is likely to benefit from an appropriate blend of the two approaches that is anchored toward providing value to the organization based on organizational business objectives. Rather than establishing a mind-set as to which is better, a mind-set as to which is prudent might yield better odds that a data-centered environment can result in business success.

Data lake successes have not been unilateral. Benefits of the data lake have often been voiced by IT and not because of realized outcomes experienced by a business. While EDWs often started life under a "build it and they will come" mentally, data lakes have often been set up without specific goals in mind other than to build a single corporate version of the truth and to finally democratize the corporate data asset. The downside of many data lakes has been that their setup has been neither strategically aligned to the business nor sufficient in tactical innovation.

Often data lakes succeed where the approach is not enterprise-wide and where specific analytic use cases are specifically being addressed. The use cases tend to be oriented to smaller business groups within a department or line of business.

Realistically, both the EDW and the data lake are infrastructures. As an infrastructure, neither one is a substitute for being an isolated and disenfranchised strategy. In Chapter 5, design considerations for a data lake implementation are explored within the context of information architecture. Backboning a data lake, especially one that is intended to promote advanced analytics and AI with an information architecture, can reinvigorate the data management program to look more closely at all of the aspects that contribute toward a successful analytical platform.

AN UNDERLYING METAMODEL

Whether schema-on-read or schema-on-write, herein lies a simple underlying metamodel that can be used to start understanding any schema. The metamodel is *thing-relationship-thing*. In the metamodel, a thing is a term for something that is of interest, such as an enterprise, a line-of-business, a customer, a name, a transaction, an amount, a community of interest, this book, etc.

A relationship is a connection between things and is used to establish a correlation. A relationship is normally bidirectional where both ends of the relationship, each of the things, have explicit or an implied awareness of the other. But a relationship can also be unidirectional. You and the U.S. President can be used to illustrate a unidirectional relationship: *you know who the president is, but the president doesn't know who you are*!

A relationship is likely to be one of two types. It'll be either a *hasa* relationship or an *isa* relationship. A *hasa* relationship reads as "the thing *has a* correlation to another thing." An *isa* relationship would read as "the thing *is a* specific type of thing."

Linguistically, a *hasa* relationship consists of a holonym and a meronym. A holonym is something that consists of other things that have unique terms. For example, a customer is a holonym to a name, an address, and a national identifier. In turn, a name is a holonym with a first name, a middle name, and a last name. A meronym is the inverse where a postal code is part of an address.

An *isa* relationship is often used for taxonomies and consists of a hypernym and a hyponym. For example, a tiger is a type of mammal, where a mammal is the hypernym, and a tiger is the hyponym.

A verb phrase can often be used to express the nature of a relationship that exists between things. For example, if we have two things (terms), a business concept and a business term, then we have this:

- A business concept *is represented by a* business term.
- A business term is defined by a business concept.

Whether the schema is associated with a relational model or a JSON document, the relationship is often implicit and assumed (ill-defined).

Summary

While half of the EDWs that were attempted have reportedly failed to succeed, the number of data lake and big data projects that have been attempted have outpaced the EDW in terms of failure. As expressed in the introduction, Gartner analysts have, in the past, projected that the failure rate of data lakes may be as high as 60 percent. However, that number was subsequently regarded as being too much on the conservative side, with the actual failure rate being much closer to 85 percent.

> **NOTE**   Gartner's discussion of data lake failure rates is at `blogs.gartner.com/`
> `nick-heudecker/big-data-challenges-move-from-tech-to-the-`
> `organization`.
>
> A discussion of the assessments leading to the higher failure rate is at `www.infoworld`
> `.com/article/3393467/4-reasons-big-data-projects-failand-4-ways-to-`
> `succeed.html`.

Interestingly, the higher rate of failure for data lakes and big data initiatives has not been attributed to technology but rather to the technologists who have applied the technology.

> **NOTE**   For a fuller discussion of the causes of and cures for the high rate of data
> failures, see `datazuum.com/5-data-actions-2018`.

For much the same reasons that the EDW failed, the underlying approaches taken by practitioners in the era of data lakes and big data have failed to fully understand the nature of the enterprise or the business of the organization, that change is stochastic and can be gargantuan, that data quality really does matter, and that the techniques applied to schema design and an information architecture can have consequences in how readily the environment can be adapted.

While new technologies can provide many new and tangible advantages, technologies are not always impervious to how they are deployed and can have difficulty being impervious to the data they have to ingest.

Only the organization can control how data is entered and how and what data is entered changes over time. In some ways, an organization can be thought of as a fragile entity. Rarely does it stay the same for any length of time. Creating design solutions against a moving target has proven to be difficult, but the challenge is not insurmountable. Some of the potential methods to combat organizational volatility when providing advanced analytics and AI capabilities to the organization are themes discussed in the next chapter.

A Look Forward on Analytics: Not Everything Can Be a Nail

"Order doesn't come by itself."
—Benoit Mandelbrot
The Fractalist: Memoir of a Scientific Maverick

This chapter reviews the use of a data topology for organizing and arranging data that can transcend a dedicated analytical environment, such as a data lake, and encompass all of the data needs of an organization and the broader enterprise ecosystem. A data topology covers three primary areas: creating a zone map, defining the data flows, and establishing the data topography. Overall, the data topology is a critical aspect when developing an information architecture for artificial intelligence (AI) because the inherent use of AI is now transcendent to the vitality of your organization.

A Need for Organization

Data can enter the data lake from anywhere. This includes online transaction processing (OLTP) systems, operational data stores, data warehouses, logs or other machine data, or cloud services, etc. Data that is brought into a data lake from one or more of these source systems is likely to encompass different types of data-based technologies and data formats. Variations may also transcend the spoken word (for audio files) and written language (for electronic documents) and include variations in page set encoding for storing data, such as Unicode and Extended Binary Coded Decimal Interchange Code (EBCDIC).

Regardless of format, data needs to be brought into the data lake by some means. However, the data lake is not best served by acting as a single cauldron for the enterprise's analytical needs. Like most complex solutions that require flexibility and the ability to adapt to changes, data should be partitioned or separated in some way. Data partitioning can accommodate varying degrees of specialization required to operate the organization. These partitions are known as *zones*.

Zones instantiate intent, priorities, and purposes for consuming information. A properly zoned data lake allows access to data in various states of being, transformation, and consistency. Zones are intended to provide agility and flexibility, serve as a means to enable additional data security, and foster the ability to democratize curated data assets. The concept of a zone is not that different from the way that the traditional enterprise data warehouse (EDW) was architected in that both are forms of partitioning. As shown in Figure 4-2 (Chapter 4, "A Look Back on Analytics: More Than One Hammer"), the simplified data architecture for a traditional EDW included areas for staging data, managing normalized data, and organizing data in a data mart. Each of these areas is certainly zone-like.

> **NOTE**   While placing a tangible value on data can be difficult, data can be associated with a value chain. As business processes move through various workflows and additional data is accumulated by an organization, the accumulation of data can reflect value. Potentially, the more information that is available to the organization, the better enabled the organization becomes in generating additional insights and understanding through the use of the accumulated data. Additionally, as data can be correlated or integrated with other digital assets along the value chain, the correlations may also lead to deriving increased value. You'll learn more about this in Chapter 7, "Maximizing the Use of Your Data: Being Value Driven."

Having one lone database to accommodate all of the enterprise's data would be unduly complicated to manage and update. It would create an inordinate challenge for security, and users would likely suffer from extreme performance and latency issues. But if having just one database is not the ultimate answer to managing enterprise data, then how many databases are actually required? Four, 40, 400, 4,000, four-trillion-gazillion? Could there be a number that would represent a best practice?

The answer lies not in the number of databases but in the clustering of data for a given purpose or a given community of interest. This clustering manifests in the data lake as a series of zones. We're first going to discuss a series of different zone types and then delve further into the nature of data topologies. Then, we will explain how the zones are mapped and how data flows from one zone to another and illustrate how the various components of a multicloud deployment fit together in terms of these zones.

> **NOTE** A community of interest in analytics would be a group of individuals who share a commonality in the data that is consumed, the data types of insights required, or the types of questions asked. There is an inherent overlap or association across one or more facets of consuming data and performing analytics.

While the number of zones and the purpose of each zone may differ from organization to organization for their analytical implementations, there are six essential data zones that can be considered as a starter set for contemplation in a data topology, as shown in Figure 5-1. The use of the phrase *starter set* is intended to be distinct and separate from that of a reference architecture. The starter set is not a reference architecture, in part, because it is not specifically framing an endpoint. The starter set includes the following zones:

- Staging
- Raw
- Discovery and Exploration
- Aligned
- Harmonized
- Curated

> **NOTE** A reference architecture provides recommended structures and integra-tions of IT products and services. A reference architecture is often created to illustrate appropriate pre-established practices or to lead the way for exploring new capabilities in a manner that suggests an optimal delivery method. Reference architectures can help managers, software developers, analysts, and architects collaborate and commu-nicate effectively about an implementation. A reference architecture can be used as a rallying point to address concerns, advantages, and questions, allowing teams to avoid errors and delays.

While each data zone has been established for a given purpose, a zone designer may choose to combine some of the starter set zones into a single zone or to determine that some of the starter zones are unnecessary for a particular use case or need. A designer may also include zone variants of their own choosing.

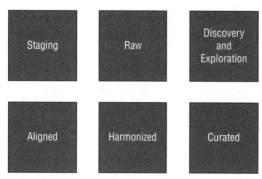

Figure 5-1: Starter set zones

The Staging Zone

The data's first touchpoint in the data lake is likely to be the *staging zone*. The data in this zone is held temporarily and subsequently removed after the data has been moved to a different zone or after an allotted period of time has transpired.

An allotted period of time, for example, might be a rolling schedule where data from the staging data zone is physically removed (or deleted) after 24 hours. Each organization can set the timeframe for the allotted period of time, and the organization can set a different allotment time for different data types or classes.

The staging zone can act as a gatekeeper, authorizing data to proceed into another zone or holding data if it is deemed unauthorized or inappropriate. Being able to prevent the movement of data into other zones is one way in which the integrity of the overall analytical environment can be improved—a vital capability for AI. The staging data zone's ability to pass judgment on the worthiness of the data is the first part of *data provenance.*

Data provenance is the recording of ownership. Often the word *provenance* is used in conjunction with artwork or an antique. The provenance is a type of evidence that helps guide the actual authenticity and quality of the work. The provenance is also used as a means to counter fraud.

With data provenance, the work is not that of art but of information. Data is frequently moved from one location to another, say from an operational system to a data warehouse or from an operational system to a series of data zones within the data topology. Data provenance is used to help authenticate the data and can prove that the data has not been adversely affected—that is, data that has been either intentionally or unintentionally modified.

With data provenance, the staging zone can be used to verify the authenticity of the data's origins and provide subsequent markings so that a chain of provenance can be established as the data moves from its original source through a series of multiple data zones. Basic data quality checks can be performed. In addition to authenticating the feed, data quality checks can be applied to determine whether the data is sufficiently complete, such that the data is not deemed to be incomplete or corrupted and that the data is not a duplication of the same data that has been previously sent.

If the data's structure (or nonstructure) is both known and understood, certain information might be redacted or obfuscated for the purposes of security, sensitivity, or privacy. A person's name, a national identifier, a telephone number, a driver's license number, a passport number, a credit card number, and a residential address are all candidate features that might require additional treatment to satisfy privacy needs.

In general, when ingesting data from a data source, persisting each payload can be a good idea, regardless of how much of the data is in the payload and how much of that data will ultimately be used or redacted. Subsetting the data too soon can require processes within the data lake to reach back out to the originating source system to request or pull back additional data. Once the data quality checks have been performed, the data can be loaded into the raw zone.

The Raw Zone

As the name implies, the data lake's raw zone persists data in its transmitted form. The data is considered raw, as the information has not been subject to any remediation, reconfiguration, or enhancement. In most instances, raw data may mean that the data is not suitable for general analytics or reporting use.

Data in the raw zone is analogous to the raw image format that is used by many digital cameras. A digital camera's raw image file contains minimally processed data from the onboard image sensor. Raw files are raw in the sense that they have not yet been processed and therefore are not in a ready state to be printed or edited. A converter is used to make color adjustments and other alterations before creating an image in a standard format such as JPG (or JPEG: Joint Photographic Experts Group). If you mess up the JPG by overlaying the wrong emoji or cropping what should not have been cropped, being able to fall back on the raw file to start over can be an advantage.

Data from the raw zone can provide value, as is, to an advanced user, such as a skilled data scientist, to apply machine learning or AI for purposes of exploration and the determination of a hypothesis. Potentially, far more data exists in the raw zone than exists in any other zone. In part, this implies that data from the raw zone is likely to contain attributes and columns (or even whole datasets) from sources that are not formally pushed into the other zones.

For example, if the original data contains auditing information from an operational system, such as the name of the program that inserted or updated a row, that information may not always be passed on to a subsequent zone. Other examples of information that is passed from one zone to another can include stateful processing codes, surrogate keys, etc.

The lineage of data for data movement should be established as a disciplined practice. *Data lineage* is the exercise of formally tracking the movement of information across data zones, from where the data enters the first data zone and as the data passes through to other zones. Data lineage provides general movement information all the way through to the data's consumption. Establishing data lineage and augmenting the lineage with data definitions and other management techniques can allow users to search and better understand the data in the data topology.

Data lineage and data provenance are complementary means of tracking data. Data provenance refers to explicitly annotated inputs, entities, systems, and processes that influence data of interest, providing a historical record of the data, its origins, and exactly how it has been pipelined. Data lineage provides visibility to trace errors back to a root cause in an analytics process.

The raw zone allows new sources of data to be ingested quickly and the lineage of the data into other zones to be tracked. For example, the raw zone can be a preferred zone for data scientists to obtain data that has not been previously augmented.

The Discovery and Exploration Zone

The *discovery and exploration zone* is used for data scientists to analyze and experiment with the data in a "sandbox" environment. For example, a data scientist working with data that seeks to uncover fraudulent or inappropriate activity might be able to uncover links that would otherwise be masked if the data was refined to any degree.

While data scientists are generally granted access privileges to some of the other data zones, such as the raw zone, the harmonized zone, and the curated data zone, if the data scientist requires additional information to augment the data that is at hand through the discovery and exploration data zone, the data scientist is likely to pull additional data from the aligned data zone, as data in the aligned zone is remediated in the context of the systems from where the data originated.

Depending on the tools being used, the discovery and exploration data zone is expected to be exercised through the use of self-service tools rather than the data scientist having to follow a formal request to IT for data wrangling services, etc. Data scientists should be allowed to import their own data into the discovery and exploration data zone, possibly bypassing all other prestaging zones, if the data is being used for one-off purposes.

A good practice is to proactively engage any data scientist in data governance and operations processes that allow them to understand the attributes and limitations of certain datasets. Helping the data scientist understand the nature of the data through metadata catalog capabilities can assist with handling datasets that may not be 100 percent accurate or complete. In addition, a metadata catalog may help the data scientist with removing any data that is no longer required or useful.

If the data scientist wants to use data that is potentially of a higher level of data quality, the data scientist may choose to use the harmonized data zone. The harmonized data zone might contain contents that have been remediated in the context of democratization for general data sharing. Alternatively, the data scientist may use the aligned zone that, as mentioned, is remediated in the context of the system from which the data originated.

The Aligned Zone

The *aligned zone* contains structures that provide the first stage of transformation for data from the raw data zone. An aligned data zone contains data from typed table structures. For data that has been ingested from structured sources, the benefit is gained from the data being available in a typed column and not as a generic string.

For data from nonstructured sources, certain processing probably needs to be performed to extract structured-type data. For example, if a video file is being brought into the aligned data zone, a process to transcribe the audio track may be initiated to populate a transcribed column in a table that provides information about the video file. Data from the transcription may also be pushed to a graph database to aid with correlation, context, and associative themes. In addition, information regarding the various scenes may also be loaded into typed tables within the aligned data zone.

A properly designed ingestion process would populate the aligned data zone automatically after the data has flowed through the staging data zone and the raw data zone. Without processes to quickly add new sources to the raw data zone and then immediately process them for the aligned data zone, much of the benefit of the aligned data zone can be lost.

Aligned data is data from a source that has been made consistent with the intended values of that source. Therefore, if any transformations need to be performed for the purposes of data quality, standardization, or consistency, the source definitions are used as the basis for a guide, as shown in Figures 5-2 through 5-8.

Figures 5-2 through 5-8 are connected, but each source is reflective of data that, in this case, is being managed by distinct worldwide offices. In the aligned zone, each separate file would be remediated or corrected based on the utilization guides set by each geographic office location.

Each file uses a distinct annotation to specify whether each individual record is to be regarded as being active or inactive. The office would use active records for current business needs, and inactive records would not be used any further. The inactive data is preserved as part of the historical records of the office.

In Figure 5-2, the column labeled Active has domain values of Y and N. Y means the record is active, and N means the record is inactive. If a value contains a value that is not an uppercase *Y* or *N*, the value would be modified to one of the valid domain values. Therefore, a lowercase *y* or the word *yes* would be modified to an uppercase *Y*. This is making the data consistent with the source.

Region	Country Code	COMMENTS	Active
IMPF	US		Y
IP2	BE	New DUNS as of 24.DE.25 283116366	Y
IP2	BE		Y
IMPF	US		Y
IP2	AT		Y

Figure 5-2: Consistent to Active

In Figure 5-3, the column labeled Inactive also has domain values of Y and N. However, the meanings are opposite to that of the domain values in Figure 5-2. For example, within the Inactive column, Y means *yes* the record is inactive, and N means *no* the record is still active.

LBE ID	LBE Description	Country	Inactive
91	General Motors Corporation	US	N
91	General Motors Corporation	US	N
37	Genasys L.C.	US	N
91	General Motors Corporation	US	N
44	GM of Canada Ltd.	CA	N
44	GM of Canada Ltd.	CA	N
4	Delphi Canada Incorporated	CA	Y
44	GM of Canada Ltd.	CA	N

Figure 5-3: Consistent to Inactive

Although the domain values of the ones used in Figure 5-2 are the same as those in Figure 5-3, the meanings and interpretations are not modified in the aligned zone; they are simply made consistent (with the source). Therefore, the values will be evaluated and changed to an uppercase Y or N if some other value is present.

In Figure 5-4, the column labeled CISCO_INACTIVE_IND also has domain values of Y and N. Here, the meanings are the same as those in Figure 5-3, but the column name is distinct. Again, within the aligned zone, the values would be made consistent to uppercase Y or uppercase N, and the column name would also be left as it is known in the source system.

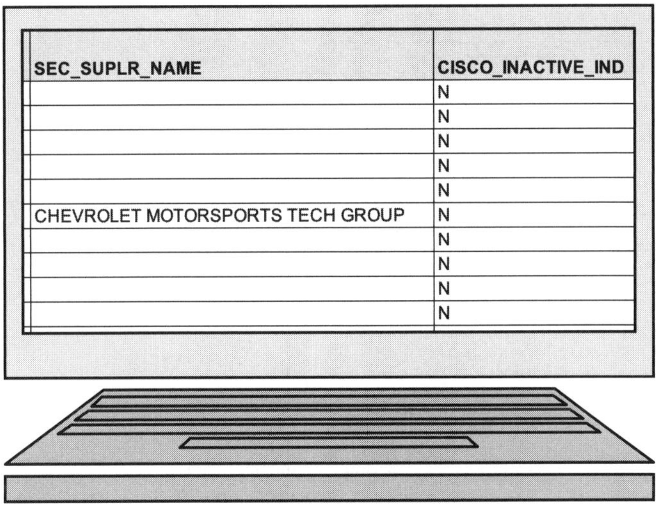

SEC_SUPLR_NAME	CISCO_INACTIVE_IND
	N
	N
	N
	N
	N
CHEVROLET MOTORSPORTS TECH GROUP	N
	N
	N
	N
	N

Figure 5-4: Consistent to CISCO_INACTIVE_IND

In Figure 5-5, the column labeled STATUS has different valid domain values. In the file from this source origination, the domain value A means active, and the domain value I means inactive. Again, the semantics are equivalent to the previous examples in Figures 5-2, 5-3, and 5-4. Any remediation would make the values consistent to uppercase A and uppercase I.

In Figure 5-6, columns are not used to denote active and inactive. Here, separate worksheets are used: the worksheet for active data is labeled STEERING, and the worksheet with the inactive data is labeled STEERING OLD. Therefore, the active and inactive records are provided with a consistent representation because they come into the data zone as two separate files. The type of file would be used to imply the active or inactive state of the record without an explicit domain value.

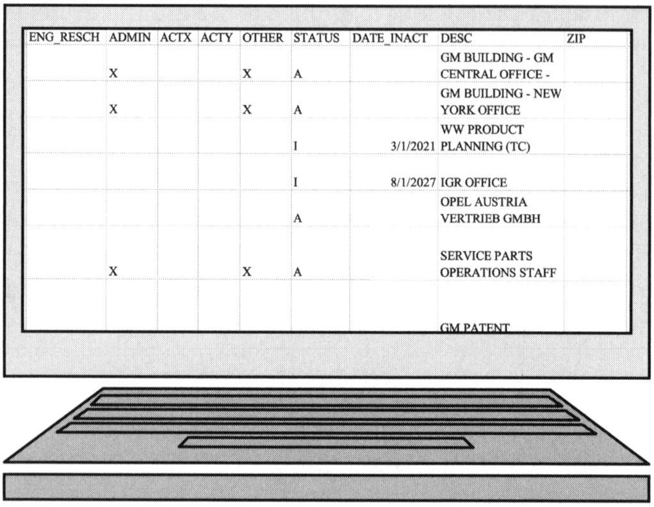

ENG_RESCH	ADMIN	ACTX	ACTY	OTHER	STATUS	DATE_INACT	DESC	ZIP
	X			X	A		GM BUILDING - GM CENTRAL OFFICE -	
	X			X	A		GM BUILDING - NEW YORK OFFICE	
					I	3/1/2021	WW PRODUCT PLANNING (TC)	
					I	8/1/2027	IGR OFFICE	
					A		OPEL AUSTRIA VERTRIEB GMBH	
	X			X	A		SERVICE PARTS OPERATIONS STAFF	
							GM PATENT	

Figure 5-5: Consistent to Status

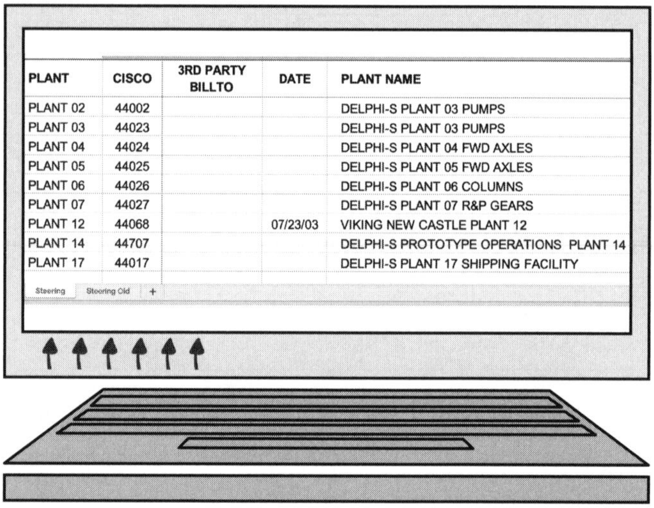

PLANT	CISCO	3RD PARTY BILLTO	DATE	PLANT NAME
PLANT 02	44002			DELPHI-S PLANT 03 PUMPS
PLANT 03	44023			DELPHI-S PLANT 03 PUMPS
PLANT 04	44024			DELPHI-S PLANT 04 FWD AXLES
PLANT 05	44025			DELPHI-S PLANT 05 FWD AXLES
PLANT 06	44026			DELPHI-S PLANT 06 COLUMNS
PLANT 07	44027			DELPHI-S PLANT 07 R&P GEARS
PLANT 12	44068		07/23/03	VIKING NEW CASTLE PLANT 12
PLANT 14	44707			DELPHI-S PROTOTYPE OPERATIONS PLANT 14
PLANT 17	44017			DELPHI-S PLANT 17 SHIPPING FACILITY

Steering | Steering Old | +

Figure 5-6: Consistent to Worksheets

In Figure 5-7, the column labeled Name has a special marking to imply the semantic interpretation of an active or inactive record. The users in this geographical office have chosen to prefix names with a leading asterisk if the record is to be treated as an inactive record. Therefore, the absence of an asterisk implies activeness.

As asterisks do not have distinct uppercase and lowercase representations, any asterisks would already be consistent to the source system marking. However, if other special characters are uncovered as the first character of the Name, rules would need to be established if a conversion is appropriate. If so, the conversion would be to use an asterisk to enforce consistency.

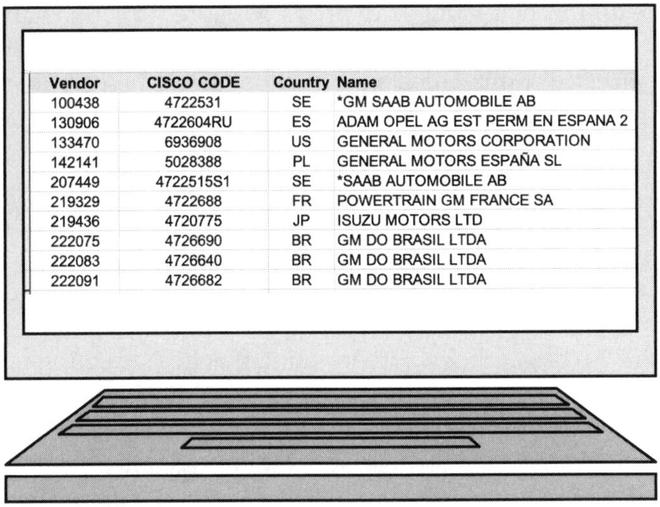

Vendor	CISCO CODE	Country	Name
100438	4722531	SE	*GM SAAB AUTOMOBILE AB
130906	4722604RU	ES	ADAM OPEL AG EST PERM EN ESPANA 2
133470	6936908	US	GENERAL MOTORS CORPORATION
142141	5028388	PL	GENERAL MOTORS ESPAÑA SL
207449	4722515S1	SE	*SAAB AUTOMOBILE AB
219329	4722688	FR	POWERTRAIN GM FRANCE SA
219436	4720775	JP	ISUZU MOTORS LTD
222075	4726690	BR	GM DO BRASIL LTDA
222083	4726640	BR	GM DO BRASIL LTDA
222091	4726682	BR	GM DO BRASIL LTDA

Figure 5-7: Consistent to Implied Meaning

In Figure 5-8, the column labeled Facility Receiving Plant Description uses yet another technique to represent active and inactive records. This particular geographic office has chosen to denote an inactive record by using a strike-through across the receiving plant's description. As with Figure 5-7, a technique of absence is used to identify or imply records that are active.

The strikethrough technique can be challenging to address. Without prior knowledge of this method being used, the strikethrough could be omitted when it is sent to the data zone. Here, the strikethrough is held as formatting metadata within the original file, which is likely to get excluded when the file is extracted and transmitted.

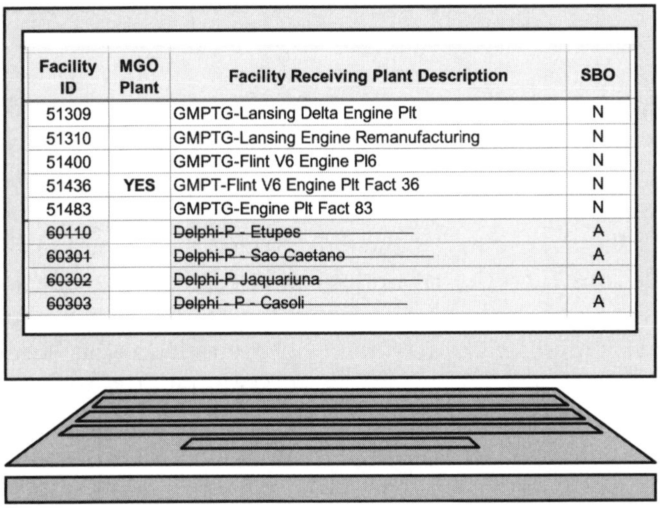

Facility ID	MGO Plant	Facility Receiving Plant Description	SBO
51309		GMPTG-Lansing Delta Engine Plt	N
51310		GMPTG-Lansing Engine Remanufacturing	N
51400		GMPTG-Flint V6 Engine Pl6	N
51436	YES	GMPT-Flint V6 Engine Plt Fact 36	N
51483		GMPTG-Engine Plt Fact 83	N
60110		Delphi-P - Etupes	A
60301		Delphi-P - Sao Caetano	A
60302		Delphi-P Jaquariuna	A
60303		Delphi - P - Casoli	A

Figure 5-8: Consistent to Metadata

Attempting to manage an implicit value is likely to be more difficult than trying to manage an explicit value. When a value is explicit, there is at least an intent to clearly and directly communicate a business fact. When a value is implicit, there is a situation that goes beyond uncertainty. An implicit value provides no way of knowing what is known or what can be known. In addition, when selecting a name for a column, a positive word or phrase is often easier to understand than a negative word or phrase, for example, active (positive) versus inactive (negative).

Within AI, feature engineering can be so important when trying to compensate for implicit information. Feature engineering can help the data scientist make explicit what would otherwise be implicit, further aiding machine learning or deep learning algorithms with overall feature selection.

For example, as mentioned in the video file example earlier in this section, aligned data can be augmented through metadata, annotation, and other tagging or extraction mechanisms such as transcribed audio. The aligned data zone is the first destination where practical analytics can be performed.

Whereas the aligned zone focuses on making data consistent to the source, the harmonized zone focuses on making data consistent to a target.

The Harmonized Zone

The *harmonized zone* contains data that is often organized in a data model that combines like-data from a variety of sources and mimics the traditional data warehouse use of a canonical model. The harmonized data zone may be used as a feed to an existing data warehouse or even subsume the functions and purpose of a legacy data warehouse.

Data in the harmonized data zone is likely to be augmented with derived data or aggregations or correlated with data from another source. Derived data is data that can be interpolated or extrapolated from other data points, inferred, or otherwise calculated.

Checks for referential integrity, data quality, or missing data can be performed in the harmonized data zone. Feeds to downstream systems can be created here as well.

Whereas the aligned data zone transforms data to conform with the data source as shown through Figures 5-2 to 5-8, the harmonized data zone transforms data so that correlations and other affinities can be readily ascertained through consuming analytical processes. In the case of the examples shown in Figures 5-2 to 5-8, a common representation would be chosen such as the word ACTIVE with domain values Y to mean yes, and INACTIVE with the domain value N to mean that the record is no longer used.

Figure 5-2 used a column named Active with domain values Y and N, and the column and the domain values would remain the same through the harmonized process.

Figure 5-3 used a column named Inactive with domain values Y and N. The column would get renamed, and the domain value Y would become N, and the domain value N would become Y.

Figure 5-4 used a column named CISCO_INACTIVE_IND with domain values Y and N. Similarly, the column would be renamed, and the domain value Y would be modified to N, and likewise, the domain value N would be modified to Y.

Figure 5-5 used a column named STATUS with the domain values A and I. The column would be renamed, and the domain value A would become Y, and the domain value I would become N.

Figure 5-6 used an implied inference through separate worksheets. A column named Active would be added to the STEERING worksheet (or file in a data lake), and each record would be given a domain value of Y. The worksheet named STEERING OLD would also receive a column named ACTIVE, and all records would be assigned a domain value of N. As both worksheets in the harmonized zone will have explicit columns, the information can be correlated.

Figure 5-7 used an implied reference through the absence of a prefix and an explicit reference by prefixing with an asterisk. Here too, a column named ACTIVE would be added, and when the column named Name did not begin with an asterisk, a Y would be assigned to the ACTIVE column, and when an asterisk appeared in the first byte, two things would occur. First, a domain value of N would be assigned to the ACTIVE column, and the asterisk would be stripped as a prefix and removed.

Figure 5-8 used an implied reference through the absence of formatting metadata and an explicit reference by using a strikethrough as formatting metadata. The techniques for addressing the strikethrough would follow the previous technique to add a column and remove the metadata for the strikethrough.

The ending result in the harmonize zone is that now all of the data is complementary, explicit, and with a consistent meaning. Using a two-step process between the aligned zone and the harmonized zone helps to simplify the overall translation process for data quality, as well as provide the data scientist a choice of which zone to use for populating the discovery and exploration zone.

While a final implementation may choose to consolidate the aligned and harmonized zones into a single zone with just one series of transformations, designers should be aware that some transformations are not reversible. For example, in the Danish language, the English word for "yes" has two separate words, *je* and *jo*. Jo is used when answering in the affirmative to a question that was posed in the negative. Translating both *je* and *jo* to yes would lose the subtlety of the original value.

Once the data has been harmonized, the data is now much easier to address for pushing the information out to the various communities of interests as curated data files.

The Curated Zone

Whereas the aligned zone and the harmonized zones contain ingested data from various sources (via the raw zone), the *curated zone* may be restricted to data that has been predetermined or ascertained by other means to be of specific value and usefulness.

Curation is the ability to produce a crafted subset. By analogy, curation can be thought of as a playlist, where songs are hand-picked based on a theme, a preference, a mood, a purpose, or a desire, etc. The playlist is not every song; it is just certain songs. Like a playlist, the data in a curated data zone is not immutable. The curated data zone can be refined over time with new types of data, and old or unwanted data can be removed.

The data topology's curated data zone provides an easy access point for business users to access the data they need without having to filter out unnecessary noise.

While the harmonized data zone can be thought of as being analogous to the normalized area of the traditional data warehouse, the curated data zone can be analogous to data marts. The data in the curated data zone is organized so that business users can easily and readily fetch the data they need.

As many organizational topographies are complex, consisting of on-premise computing as well as cloud computing, the curated zone may not be singular, as multiple curated zones may be necessary to address the needs of different lines of business or the needs created by supporting different regions or geographies.

As previously mentioned, the six zones were presented as a starter set and not a reference architecture. In part, this is because the zones by themselves cannot always adequately address some of the analytical and AI complications that you are apt to face. The establishment of a data topology takes the data zone concept a step further toward a reference architecture and smarter data science.

DATA RICH, INFORMATION POOR

DRIP is an acronym for *data rich, information poor* and is symptomatic of an organization that has not been able to keep its information sufficiently organized. Adding more data sources or arming users with more analytic tools will not remediate long-term needs for driving insights and leveraging AI. The disorganization of information is a symptom and not a root cause. The root cause is likely to be embedded in the behaviors of the organization: its underlying culture.

Data Topologies

A data topology is an approach for classifying and managing real-world data scenarios. These scenarios cover any aspect of a business: operational, accounting, regulatory and compliance, reporting, advanced analytics, AI, and more.

A data topology complements the analytical environment and is foundational for success with analytics.

A data topology is expressed by building a zone map that is holistic and meaningful to an enterprise that needs to continually address competing priorities and shifts in technologies. A data topology can provide a path forward to help manage any type of analytic for any use or for any type of enterprise.

The concepts of an enterprise and that of an organization aren't necessarily synonymous—a delineation can be drawn in terms of orientation. An organization can look inwardly upon itself even when taking into account customers and clients, whereas an enterprise can often take an outward-looking approach, recognizing the broader ecosystem in which the organization participates.

When viewing the enterprise as an ecosystem, understanding the place and purpose of data is viewed in a different light, demarcating between data created and consumed by the organization and data created and consumed by the enterprise.

Within an organization, all data is often assumed to be governable through some type of data governance program, whereas within the auspices of the enterprise (the ecosystem), not all data can automatically be assumed to be governable by an organizationally oriented and established data governance program.

Figure 5-9 represents an oversimplified diagram that organizations often draw for their analytical environments. Data governance is shown as a horizontal bar to illustrate that the entire architecture is to be actively governed. But this is not an entirely accurate representation. While an organization can choose to include or exclude data from its analytical platform, the organization may not always be able to actually assert governance over third-party data.

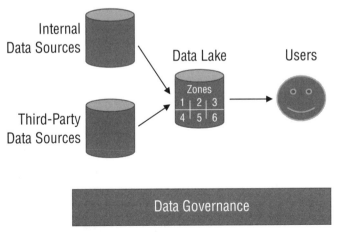

Figure 5-9: Misrepresenting the nature of data governance

For example, if third-party data includes aggregation from a company providing social media feeds, a governance initiative cannot cry "foul" on the levels of data quality from a particular tweet or post if they have misspelled the organization's name. You have to be able to handle the situation without going back to the author and saying, "Stop that!" This is an example of the concept of proactive versus reactive data governance that was shown in Chapter 3, "Framing Part II: Considerations for Working with Data and AI" Figure 3-5. Here data governance must be applied reactively to handle data anomalies.

A properly designed data topology should be sustainable over time and resilient to future needs, new technologies, and adaptive to the continuous changes associated with data characteristics, including volume, variety, velocity, veracity, and perception of the data's value.

As shown in Figure 5-10, the core elements of a data topology include the following:

- Zone map
- Data flow
- Data topography

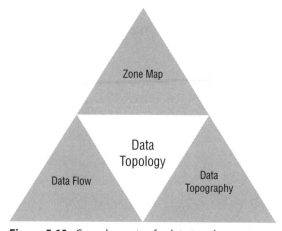

Figure 5-10: Core elements of a data topology

The zone map details the zones of the environment. The zone map can include all aspects of an organization's data estate so that when AI is infused into an application, all relevant data can be taken into account for the information architecture and not limited to what exists in one particular capability area or for one particular line of business.

The zones are organized around a taxonomy from root to nonleaf to leaf levels. The *root* level in the taxonomy encompasses all of the data available for processing. The *nonleaf* levels represent a logical cluster of the data that can be made available for use, and the *leaf* levels help simplify security, access, and database options that are deployed.

The data flow consists of three types of informational flow. These are preflight, inflight, and post-flight. Each flight point is an opportunity to perform analytics and AI that can trigger an appropriate signal or provide varying degrees of insight. *Preflight* involves analytics or processing that is performed before a flow formally begins. *Inflight* involves analytical processes that are invoked during the flow and while the data is still transient. *Post-flight* involves performing analytics after the flow ends.

> **NOTE**   The degrees of insight across the flight path are foresight, insight, and hindsight. Preflight is forward-looking and is aligned to foresight. Inflight looks at the now and is aligned with insight, and post-flight is backward-looking and is aligned with hindsight.

The data topography follows a cloud, fog, mist computing model of distribution (discussed in more detail in the "Data Topography" section later in this chapter). Elements within the data topography must include hardware, software, storage, and networking connectivity. Within the cloud-fog-mist hierarchical distributed computing model, the cloud offers the most elastic and option-rich environment, while the mist offers the least elastic and least option-rich environment. The fog lies between cloud and mist.

Zone Map

The *zone map* identifies and names each zone. All of the data zones are inherently abstract and conceptual in nature as a data zone is not a deployed object in and of itself. However, the data zones themselves are representative of something that is used for grouping or clustering. Ultimately, a group or cluster is associated with the instantiation or deployment of data. Whether that data is transient or persistent, the instantiation is always part of a leaf node data zone.

Figure 5-11 shows the primitive zones that are used in a zone map and are shown using two separate diagrammatic styles: taxonomical and box-in-box. Only a leaf zone is associated with the actual instantiation of data. Nonprimitive zones include a virtual zone that may cluster multiple zones together and reflect groups for data virtualization or data federation.

For a given context, the root zone represents a universe of discourse representing the entire body of data that forms what can be known. When building models for AI, understanding the bounds of the corpus is important for determining all of the features that are necessary when building a useful model.

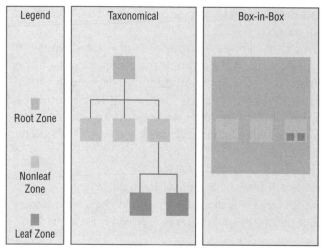

Figure 5-11: Primitive zone types

Data Pipelines

The *data flow* helps to illustrate the points of integration or interoperability for the data pipelines across the various zones. When circular data flows occur across the zones, this is a flag for investigation. A circular data flow may potentially compromise the data integrity if the data zones are not well managed (designed and governed). Here is where the concepts of data provenance and data lineage can help toward ensuring integrity across all data assets as information flows.

> **NOTE** An example of a circular data flow has data from *ZoneA* flow into *ZoneB*, which in turn has data that flows into *ZoneC*. A circle appears when *ZoneC* subsequently flows data into *ZoneA*.

The primitive data flows preflight, inflight, and post-flight give way to signals being raised at an appropriate point in time. Preflight analytical processing occurs at a source, and the source may use either in-memory or persistent database technologies. Preflight processing can also serve to filter data for inflight transmission such as choosing to send a median reading between time periods in lieu of each individual reading that may be present within the source.

Inflight analytics occurs while the data is transient between begin and end-points and, especially for real-time AI needs, offers distinct advantages to act in a timely manner. Post-flight analytics occurs at the target and may also make use of any type of available technology. For each type of flight, analytics can be performed, signals can be triggered and sent, and subsequent processing can take place.

Data Topography

The *data topography* is reflective of a cloud-fog-mist distributed computing model, where data can be highly dispersed across an organization and certainly across an enterprise. A common aspect across any cloud, fog, and mist node is that each will have compute power (that includes both hardware and software), storage capabilities, and network connectivity.

Mixed deployment data topographies include the following:

- Cloud, e.g., public cloud provider
- Fog, e.g., an on-premise private cloud
- Mist, e.g., a smart device

The data topography allows for the creation of complex solutions that are adaptive, flexible, and not reliant on centralized computing deployments. The cloud-fog-mist distributed architecture can place analytical and AI processing at a location that minimizes latency and the movement of data—bringing the analytics to the data.

The cloud-fog-mist paradigm follows a meteorological analogy. In real life, a cloud can be expansive and heavy from condensed water hanging high in the sky, far away from the ground. A fog, on the other hand, is less expansive and is far lighter than a cloud. The mist is very localized and is a thin layer of floating water droplets located around ground level.

Cloud computing follows this metrological analogy, where the cloud has great computing power and is located far away from general business activities. Fog computing takes place beneath the cloud, in a layer where the infrastructure can be more tightly controlled. On the other hand, mist computing takes place on the ground, where lightweight computing power such as a smart device operates on the very edge of the network and may even be able to operate temporarily in a disconnected mode, providing for a degree of resiliency. The mist may also include sensors and actuators built into smart devices.

One critical aspect of design for the data topography, data flows, and zone maps is the notion of *resiliency*. Resilient architectures are composed of critical components that provide a meaningful level of functionality in a disconnected mode within the cloud, within the fog, and within the mist.

As each layer or node within the data topology also has storage capabilities, distinct data management opportunities come to light. Within the paradigm of cloud, fog, and mist, different data capabilities can be realized and rationalized through a comparable meteorological analogy. If the cloud hosts a data lake, the fog could host a *data pond*, and the mist could host a *data puddle*, as shown in Figure 5-12. Each data location would maintain data that is relevant to the layer within the topography and be curated to support the needs of the associated users.

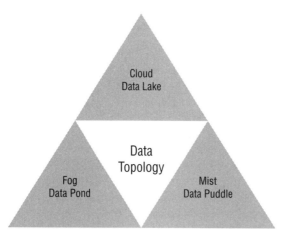

Figure 5-12: Data lakes, data ponds, and data puddles

The data puddle is characterized by the predominant use of in-memory and flash storage media. The data tends to be raw sensor data, and the analytics and AI tend to be primitive in nature, such as preemptively turning off a machine because of a predictive concern about a malfunction. The mist is restricted by the availability of data to make certain complex assertions.

The data pond is characterized by the ability to handle raw sensor data, structured data, and limited unstructured data. The analytic capabilities are broader when compared to the data puddle. Improved storage capability accommodates reasonable amounts of historical data.

In contrast, the data lake is characterized by an ability to handle any data type and provide meaningful and contextual data to a mixed and broad set of end-user needs and other interfaced machines. The analytic capabilities extend to all forms of business intelligence and AI and include descriptive, predictive, diagnostic, prescriptive, sensemaking, and cognitive forms of analytics.

With a flexible data topography and approach to managing data, disciplines must be established to help expand, add, move, or remove data zones.

MISGUIDED TENETS

Eliminating multiple copies of data and reducing the movement of data are often architectural tenets that are little more than knee-jerk reactions to a sustained problem. A data topology can certainly be achieved with a few data stores (or even a single data store), but the topology itself is an approach for managing data with confidence and not fear.

A data topology can help an organization manage one or more replica copies of data across the cloud, fog, and mist compute nodes as a positive aspect of managing data to help drive opportunities and outcomes. Even in the absence of replica copies, a data topology can be used to assist with controlling a complex distribution of data. A data topology adequately addresses the realization that organizations need to operate their IT workloads with decentralized compute nodes and that each workload addresses a specialized functional capability.

Expanding, Adding, Moving, and Removing Zones

Different organizations have different needs and priorities, and organizations find that needs change over time. The data topology provides a basis for establishing an information architecture as the data topology can identify a complex data distribution that is aligned to the business and can also address the necessary data flows as well as security, etc.

The zone map is a clustering of data stores, and the data topology is, in part, a clustering of data zones. The purpose of the clustering is to make the management and governance of data in support of analytics and AI much easier to accomplish. As mentioned at the beginning of the chapter, the purpose of clustering (or partitioning) is to promote agility and flexibility through specialization.

If an organization, for example, does not need the rigor of a staging data zone, then the zone should be removed from implementation plans. If your organization has an inordinate amount of video, then creating a zone just for the preservation of the video can be pragmatic. Decisions as to what zones are or aren't appropriate should be based on what your data users need.

The zone map portion of the data topology also serves to create a conceptual overview of the types of organization that are needed to cater to all of the various analytical needs of the organization, from the data scientist to business users to the extended ecosystem that may share in the generated insights.

The zone map is built on a taxonomy whereby the zones can be augmented without breaking the overall zone map. Setting an appropriate scope for the root-level universe of discourse is important, as it provides context for the zones that are contained within. But if necessary, the definition for the root level can be modified and expanded to build on a successful deployment.

The leaf levels are always instantiations of databases or files. An architect could establish a situation where two or more leaf-level zones contain identical data but decide that each zone of like data uses different underlying technologies. For example, one zone may organize the data within a graph database such as GraphDB and another zone to organize the data in a document store such as MongoDB. While a zone could contain multiple technologies, restricting a zone to a single technology provides for easier data management.

However, should two leaf nodes with separate technologies have a tight affinity, a nonleaf zone can be used to diagrammatically cluster the two zones. Clustering is an important role of the nonleaf zones and serves the purpose of helping to communicate intent and purpose.

Data zones should always be regarded as temporal in that new zones can be added, old zones removed, existing zones expanded in scope, or a zone moved to a separate part of the zone map. The temporal aspect is a foundational attribute in enabling the zone.

LEAF ZONES

At the leaf level, the management of a zone can be simplified if it can be limited to a single technology for a single location. Additionally, security access for the zone can be simplified if the zone is designed for a security policy or model that supports binary access control: either you have access or you don't. Technology, location, and security are three singular aspects that can guide how to define a leaf within the zone map.

Enabling the Zones

Underlying any zone is a cadre of functions that are needed to make the overall data topology a viable implementation environment. Such required functions include managing and monitoring the environment, governing the metadata, managing the data quality, provisioning users with a data catalog, and ensuring the security of the topographical data environment.

In addition, the leaf zones should be defined in a simplified way such that a leaf zone is limited to a single technology and a single topographical layer. The leaf zone should also support a simplified means to implement security models to ensure data privacy and protection.

The initial aspect of enabling the zone is being able to bring data into the zone.

Ingestion

Establishing a managed *ingestion* process allows for control over the data. This control helps to establish the governance, lineage, and provenance required to provide insight as to where the data comes from, when the data arrives, and where the data is stored in the data topology.

A key benefit of using a managed ingestion capability is that an organization can troubleshoot and diagnose potential ingestion issues before they manifest themselves as a problem. Data ingestion tools should allow for data movement to be defined in advance, tracked, and additionally logged; the processes that are enabled should be repeatable and scalable as well as transcend the ability to navigate over (or across) a hybrid or multicloud topographical environment.

Including unstructured data in a zone map is a way to realize many of the benefits that a data topology can provide. Videos, images, audio files, blog posts, log data, and contracts all provide opportunities for deriving additional business value from the data collected. Some of the limitations associated with the schema-on-write process of the traditional data warehouse meant that very few unstructured files were incorporated into the environment, and fewer still were fully analyzed.

While a managed ingestion mechanism is a basic prerequisite, to storing data from any system that is responsible in the manufacturing (creation) of data, by making unstructured data accessible for analytics, some transformations may be required to establish a standard for audio frequency persistence, image encoding, and the creation of thumbnails, etc.

Another behavioral side effect of the traditional data warehouse was the tendency to defer any attempt to add new data items (fields) or new data sources. Even when there was an inherent belief that the data could provide valuable business insights, the time and costs associated with adding new data to a data warehouse often overwhelmed the organization.

With a data lake, there is no inherent risk from ingesting data from a new source. Any format of data can be ingested quickly into the data lake and stored in the Hadoop Distributed File System (HDFS) or cloud object storage until the data is ready to be consumed for analysis. This type of paradigm removes some of the worry associated with data of questionable use. Because the costs and risks of adding data in the data lake are lowered, there is a pervasive hope of usefulness, rather than uselessness.

The mentality associated with the usefulness of data versus the uselessness of data can be seen in other behavioral areas of organizations adopting an agile approach, in that there can be a perception that the work itself is generating value rather than the outcome of the work.

In many agile organizations, deliberations on whether a new initiative should be pursued begin with "yes," and then dialogue follows to poke holes in the initiative. A more risk-averse approach would begin with a "no" and then dialoguing to justify an initiative's worth (moving to a "yes"). The agile approach says, "Let's go ahead and bring in the data and see if it has any utility." The more traditional risk-averse approach says, "Let's hold off for now and see how many times people ask for this type of data." Understanding how tolerant or intolerant to risk your organization feels it needs to be can help in how you propose and scope work.

With managed ingestion, the data should be appropriately cataloged and inventoried, which is accomplished by capturing metadata. Such a capability is not always found in a traditional analytical environment. Using managed ingestion, the environment should provide a means to protect sensitive information. As data is ingested and moves into the raw zone, data can be tagged according to how accessible the data should be to different users.

For example, a retailer might want customer names and contact data to be available to business analysts in sales and customer service, but to restrict more sensitive personally identifiable information (PII) data to business analysts in the finance department. That way, when users execute an analytic request, their access rights can restrict their visibility, based on stipulations arising from data security and governance.

Technology tools for ingestion into the data lake may include the following:

- **BigIntegrate:** BigIntegrate is an IBM product that provides a massively scalable, shared-nothing, in-memory data integration engine that can natively run in a Hadoop cluster thereby bringing robust enterprise capabilities to an analytical environment.

- **Streams:** Streams is IBM's advanced stream processing platform that can correlate massive volumes of continuous data streams. Streams provides an integrated development environment for applications, a runtime system that can execute applications on a single or distributed set of hosts, and analytic toolkits to speed development for ingesting data.

- **Flume:** Flume is a distributed service for streaming logs into Hadoop. Flume can collect, aggregate, and move large amounts of streamed data into HDFS. YARN (Yet Another Resource Negotiator) can be used to coordinate the ingesting of data from Flume and other services that deliver data.

- **Kafka:** Kafka is a scalable, durable, and fault-tolerant publish-subscribe messaging system. Kafka is often used in place of message brokers like Java Message Service (JMS) and Advanced Message Queuing Protocol (AMQP) because of Kafka's throughput, reliability, and replication.

- **Storm:** Storm is a system for processing streaming data in real time. Storm adds reliable real-time data processing capabilities. Storm can be used with YARN for scenarios that require real-time analytics, machine learning, and continuous monitoring of operations.

- **Sqoop:** Sqoop is a tool designed for transferring bulk data between Hadoop and structured data stores such as relational databases. Sqoop can import data from external structured data stores into HDFS or related systems like Hive and HBase.

- **NiFi:** NiFi is an integrated data logistics platform. NiFi was based on NiagaraFiles (the basis for the name NiFi) that automated the movement of data between disparate systems. NiFi can provide real-time control that makes the movement of data between any source and any destination easier to manage.

- **Airflow:** Airflow is a tool for orchestrating complex computational workflows and data processing pipelines. An Airflow workflow is designed as a directed acyclic graph (DAG), which means that a workflow should be designed to execute as independent tasks.

- **NFS Gateway:** The NFS Gateway allows HDFS to be mounted as part of the local filesystem enabling the following:

  - Browsing of an HDFS filesystem through the local filesystem on client-compatible operating systems

- File downloads from an HDFS file system onto a local filesystem
- File uploads from a local filesystem directly to an HDFS filesystem
- Streaming data directly to HDFS through the mount point

The technology tools move data by supporting various types of data transport protocols, which can vary from one tool to the next. In addition to gathering, integrating, and processing data, data ingestion tools can often assist with analytics and storage by allowing the data to be modified or formatted either within the tool or by allowing other remediation processes to be invoked from the tool.

Choices as to which tool is preferable can, in part, be based on ingestion needs, as shown here:

- A continuous real-time feed or a near-real-time feed based on committed units of work
- Guaranteed delivery to the target or not
- Delivered asynchronously or synchronously
- Microbatching or batch feeds are sufficient between the source and the target

In all likelihood, a data topology must be able to support multiple ingestion techniques. To that end, ingestion mechanisms must also be considered part of a data governance initiative.

Data Governance

As mentioned earlier in the chapter, an important part of the data flow associated with the data topology (and the data lake within the data topology) is to initially place data into a transitional area: the staging zone. Only from the staging zone does the data move into the raw zone and later into one or more of the other data zones.

Using the staging zone affords the opportunity to discard data, whether from internal or external data sources, before it can potentially taint the core data lake. While discarding data is one aspect of unified data governance, a managed ingestion process helps to enforce all applicable governance rules against the data used for general-purpose analytics and AI.

The ability to discard data is an ability to maintain the integrity of the overall data topology. Discarded data could be pushed to its own separate data zone for evaluation by any designated data stewards. A zone that manages discarded data for review acts as a pseudo demilitarized zone (DMZ), as the data is not formally included (or excluded) from the analytically leveraged data zones.

Unified data governance rules can include any or all of the following:

- **Encryption:** If data needs to be protected by encryption, the data should be encrypted before it enters into a data zone.

- **Data provenance and data lineage:** How data travels across the zone map (the data flow) should be planned and maintained as data lineage and data provenance. In addition, retaining insight into the dynamics associated with the creation of the data at its source is also an important aspect of managing the overall health and trustworthiness of the data. For example, organizations may want to create rules to prevent a data source from entering a given data zone if its data provenance is not verifiable.

- **Metadata capture:** A managed ingestion process allows governance rules to be set that can capture the metadata on all of the data before the data enters the raw data zone.

- **Data cleansing:** Setting up data quality standards that are applied or evaluated against the data as the data is ingested helps to ensure that only data in a reasonable state transitions into the data lake for end-user access.

Additional aspects of data governance are discussed in Chapter 7.

Data Storage and Retention

A data lake portion of a data topology is not intended to be another data warehouse but a mechanism to provide capabilities found previously lacking, along with cost-effective data storage. After all, with a data warehouse schema-on-write model, data storage is relatively inefficient, even when a data warehouse's data is stored in the cloud.

In a data warehouse, large amounts of disk space can be wasted due to database page layouts and the problems associated with sparse tables. For example, imagine having a spreadsheet that combines two different data sources. One data source uses a spreadsheet with 200 fields, and the other data source uses 500 fields. To combine the two data sources, 300 new columns would need to be added to the original spreadsheet with 200 fields. The rows of the original spreadsheet would not possess any data for the 300 new columns. The net result of the table is that it contains many empty cells.

With certain technologies, wastage can be held to a minimum, and large volumes of data can be stored in less space than would otherwise be required for even a relatively small conventional database. This is because many technologies are based on being able to record data as an attribute/value pair such as those that follow JavaScript Object Notation (JSON) data formats, which means only attributes with actual values need to be written.

When considering the data storage for a data topology, one aspect that should not be overlooked is the incorporation of policy-based data retention—even if the retention goal is postulated by your organization as being *forever*! For example, some organizations can use portions of a data topology as an active-archival that can be queried without needing to leverage a tape management system.

Some organizations are obligated by law to keep certain types of records for a minimal period of time. For example, in the medical field within the United States, state and federal laws require mandatory record retention for hospitals rather than each physician practice to manage their own retention capability.

The Medicare Conditions of Participation (COP) requires hospitals to retain records for five years, but six years for critical access hospitals, whereas the Occupational Safety and Health Administration (OSHA) requires an employer to retain medical records for 30 years for employees that have been exposed to toxic substances and harmful agents. The privacy regulations for the Health Insurance Portability and Accountability Act (HIPAA) require records to be retained for six years from when the record was created.

The Colorado State Board of Medical Examiners Policy 40-07 recommends that medical records are to be retained for a minimum of seven years after the last date of treatment for an adult and for seven years after a minor has reached the age of majority (which is 18 years old). The California Medical Association recommends a retention period of at least 10 years but would prefer that all medical records be retained indefinitely.

One reason an organization may decide to remove data after the retention period has expired is to remove any exposure or liability due to possible litigation. Optionally, an organization may choose to sufficiently redact or obfuscate data that is held past a formal retention requirement.

However, should storage space become an issue for an organization, there has to be a process in place to readily determine which data can be removed, and if the data is to be further archived, where that data is to be archived. In this way, the data can be an active component in a tiered archival system. An archival capability would leverage different data zones than those specified in the starter set, such as a data zone that is explicitly and solely used for archival purposes. Within the data topology, the archived data zone may also be preserved in a different topography or topographical layer.

NOTE   Data might be moved from one cloud node to another or from a fog node to the cloud, for example.

Technology for data storage may include the following:

- **Db2 Big SQL:** Big SQL is a SQL engine for Hadoop that concurrently exploits Hive, Hbase, and Spark using a single database connection. Db2 Big SQL acts as a hybrid engine.

- **Db2 Warehouse**: Db2 Warehouse is a relational database that IBM provides to enable organizations to gain insights by leveraging in-database analytics and massively parallel processing.

- **Cloudant**: Cloudant is a NoSQL JSON document store by IBM that is used to optimize handling heavy workloads of concurrent reads and writes.

- **HDFS:** HDFS is a Java-based filesystem that provides scalable and reliable data storage. HDFS is designed to span large clusters of commodity servers.

- **Hive:** Hive is a data warehouse system for querying and analyzing large datasets stored in Hadoop.

- **HBase**: HBase is a nonrelational, distributed database written in Java. HBase has been modeled after Google's BigTable. HBase runs on top of HDFS and provides BigTable-like capabilities.

- **MongoDB**: MongoDB is a distributed database and stores data in JSON-like documents, meaning that fields can vary from document to document and that the data structure can be changed over time. The document model maps to objects in an application. Ad hoc queries, indexing, and real-time aggregation are used for access and analysis of data. MongoDB is intended to be high availability with support for horizontal scaling and geographic data distribution.

- **PostgreSQL:** PostgreSQL is an enterprise-class relational database that supports both structured query language (SQL) and JSON querying, which means that it supports both relational and nonrelational query access. PostgreSQL provides for a highly stable database management system with high levels of resilience, integrity, and correctness. PostgreSQL can be used as a primary data store for many types of web, mobile, geospatial, and analytical applications.

- **ElasticSearch:** ElasticSearch is a RESTful search engine built on top of Lucene. ElasticSearch is Java-based and can search and index document files in diverse formats.

As the volume of data held by an organization grows, storage must be scalable, reliable, and cost-effective. The data can be spread across the entire data topography to promote resiliency, to minimize latency, and to allow data to reside close to where the data is processed.

Data Processing

While data can be offered in a raw state, most business users are still best served when data is transformed and uniformly standardized. As opposed to the traditional data warehouse, any transformation or standardization in a data lake can be actively deferred. In many situations, the transformation can occur at the time of the read. At that point, a business user can exercise a variety of tools by which to standardize or transform the data.

Different business users can perform different standardizations and transformations, depending on their unique needs. Unlike a traditional data warehouse, the users of a data lake are not limited to a single set of standardizations and transformations associated with enterprise models tied to the schema-on-write approach.

For example, a sales department business user can transform *NYC* to New York City; a legal department business user can transform *NYC* to the City of New York; and a travel department business user can transform *NYC* to JFK.

Processes can occur in either batch or near real-time use cases that harness streaming. Batch use cases can make use of Pig, Hive, Spark, and MapReduce, while streaming use cases can leverage Spark-Streaming, Kafka, Flume, Storm, or Streams. By provisioning workflows, repeatable data processing is enabled.

Technology for processing data into the data lake may include the following:

- **Streams:** Streams is an advanced stream processing platform that is offered by IBM to correlate massive volumes of continuous data streams. Streams provides a programming language and an integrated development environment for applications, a runtime system that can execute applications on a single or distributed set of hosts, and analytic toolkits to speed development for ingesting data.

- **MapReduce:** MapReduce is a programming model and an associated implementation for processing and generating large datasets with a parallel, distributed algorithm on a cluster.

- **Hive:** Hive provides a mechanism to project structure onto large datasets and to query the data using a SQL-like language called HiveQL.

- **Spark:** Spark is an engine developed specifically for handling large-scale data processing and analytics.

- **Storm**: Storm is a system for processing streaming data in real time. Storm adds reliable real-time data processing capabilities to a data lake. Storm can be used with YARN for scenarios that require real-time analytics, machine learning, and continuous monitoring of operations.

- **Drill:** Drill is a framework that supports data-intensive distributed applications for interactive analysis of large-scale datasets.

Dark data is data that is never accessed. The lack of access might be because the data is not adequately cataloged and remains hidden because the data cannot be readily discovered for processing. Dark data can also refer to data that is being neglected because the data has ceased to provide value or utility to the organization.

But no matter how much data is actually stored across the data topology, the data must be suitable and oriented toward providing value and utility for consumption and access.

Data Access

There are various modes of accessing data: queries, tool-based extractions, or extractions that need to happen through an API. Some applications need to source the data for performing analyses or other transformations downstream. Application access to the data is provided through APIs, message queues, and database access.

Visualizing data is an important gateway into working with data. Visualizing data can be as simple as using text-based values or involve something much more elaborate, with charts and other forms of graphics that can aid comprehension and consumption. Business users can also use dashboards. A dashboard is a type of visualization that is used to provide at-a-glance views of relevant KPIs.

A dashboard can show static or dynamic data. With static data, the data values are those that existed at the time the dashboard was created. With dynamic data, the data is constantly being updated in real time on the dashboard. For example, a dashboard may show details across the time horizons past, present, and future.

For example, in a manufacturing process, the dashboard numbers could be related to productivity, such as the number of parts manufactured or the number of failed quality inspections per hour. Similarly, a dashboard used by a human resources department may show numbers related to staff recruitment, retention, and composition.

Technology for accessing data may include the following:

- **Cognos Analytics:** IBM's Cognos Analytics is a self-service analytic platform that integrates cognitive computing technology, including AI and machine learning, which had been originally developed for Watson Analytics. The platform incorporates cognitive technologies to automate data preparation, and the system can learn about the data over time. Cognos Analytics is able to generate recommendations for data joins and visualizations and is intended as an all-in-one platform to provide analytics functions ranging from the creation of dashboards to reporting and exploration.

- **Brunel:** Brunel is a high-level language that describes visualizations in terms of composable actions. Brunel drives the D3 visualization engine that is used to perform the actual rendering and interactivity.

- **R:** R is a highly extensible language and environment for statistical computing and graphics. R provides a wide variety of graphical techniques and statistical techniques (such as linear and nonlinear modeling, classical statistical tests, time-series analysis, classification, and clustering).

- **RESTful APIs:** This is an API that uses HTTP requests to GET, PUT, POST, and DELETE data.

- **API Connect:** IBM's API Connect is an integrated API management capability that can perform all of the steps and actions across the API lifecycle that includes creating the API, running the API, managing the API, and securing the API.

- **Kafka:** Kafka is a scalable, durable, and fault-tolerant publish-subscribe messaging system. Kafka is often used in place of message brokers like JMS and AMQP because of Kafka's throughput, reliability, and replication.

- **Java Database Connectivity (JDBC):** This is an API for the programming language Java, which defines how a client may access a database.

While the goal of an analytical environment is to promote access to the data for purposes of analytics and AI, the access cannot go untethered. Access must be appropriate and purposeful. For that reason, the environment and its access must be managed and monitored.

Management and Monitoring

Unified data governance helps ensure that the needs of business users and data scientists are consistently met. Data governance can serve to help track data lineage and data access and take advantage of common metadata to capitalize on the enterprise's data resources. Data governance encompasses managing data ingestion, data inventory, data enrichment, data quality, metadata management, data lineage, workflow, and self-service access.

Data governance approaches can blend a top-down approach with a bottom-up one. A top-down approach takes best practices from the organization's data warehousing experiences and attempts to impose governance and management from the moment the data is ingested into the zone map. A bottom-up approach allows users to explore, discover, and analyze the data with degrees of fluidly and flexibly that are often surfaced through self-service capabilities.

With a top-down approach, data governance policies are defined centrally—potentially by the chief data officer's office—and are enforced by all of the functional capabilities in the data topology. These capabilities include having data quality and data security practices that equally encompass both data as well as metadata; developing disciplines that serve to identify and classify systems used for provisioning data along with their update frequencies (which can be incorporated into the management of operational metadata); capturing and maintaining all metadata (including business metadata, technical metadata, and operational metadata); annotating critical data elements; and establishing processes (including waiver or dispensation processes) that can be driven by an authorized and accepted data authority.

In a bottom-up approach, collective input from the organization's users helps to decide which datasets are valuable and useful and have good-quality data. These datasets are shared with other peers through collaborative software.

To help make the managing and monitoring possible through data governance, the collection and management of metadata is vital to your efforts.

Metadata

As mentioned in Chapter 2, "Framing Part I: Considerations for Organizations Using AI," metadata is commonly viewed as one of three types: business metadata, technical metadata, and operational metadata. However, other forms of metadata also exist to provide for formatting, to help navigate decision trees, to provide guides for orchestration, etc.

In fact, the majority of business data is itself metadata, as the vast majority of all business data—cryptocurrencies are an exception because they exist only virtually—consists of descriptions of something in the physical world: a person's name, a person's height, a purchase order, an item, etc. The data is actually data about something from the real world. As such, that makes data another form of metadata.

Viewing data as metadata affords the opportunity to develop a single set of practices and procedures for managing the quality and integrity of any type of data, regardless of its perceived classification.

A pragmatic data governance strategy requires that you have the right metadata in place. With accurate and descriptive metadata, policies and standards can be set for managing and using the data. For example, policies can be created to force users to acquire their data from certain places; identify which users own certain datasets and are therefore responsible for the data; identify which users can access the data; how the data can be used; and how the data is protected.

A unified data governance strategy must also specify how data needs to be audited to ensure that compliance and regulatory needs are being met. As diverse datasets can be combined and transformed, the data's lineage and provenance take on additional value.

WHITE BOX, GRAY BOX, BLACK BOX

An organization is a blend of custom-built systems and prepackaged solutions. While organizations may have full visibility and control into a system (white box), other systems will limit how much can be known (gray box and black box). A zone can be identified, leveraged, and exercised regardless of how much control an organization ultimately has over the data assets.

Summary

To enable the data zone, the ability and means to master a series of disciplines are critical:

- Ingesting data for reoccurring feeds and one-off feeds
- Providing a data governance practice
- Storing large volumes of data
- Retiring and removing data that is no longer needed or results in a liability to the organization
- Remediating and processing the data
- Enabling access to the data through a series of capabilities
- Managing and monitoring all access to ensure that data use and access are always appropriate
- Possessing all of the relevant metadata

However, before a data zone can be enabled, the use of multiple zones must be established. More important, a data topology must be created that can produce an appropriate zone map that includes and identifies all of the necessary data flows. Additionally, because of the complexities of the modern business world, a data topography must be defined, as not all of the organization's data is likely to live in one place.

Having multiple data zones means that there is not a single version (or source) of all data. In all likelihood, there will never be a single version of truth—because of complex organizational structures with numerous lines of business and departments, there is not a single source of enterprise truth because of all the unique needs across the organizational and enterprise boundaries.

When there's a need to align truth to a business need, the need for multiple data zones will be manifest. Developing a data topology as part of an information architecture becomes part of enabling AI to benefit the organization, not as a whole, but for each line of business and based on each specialized need.

While a data topology is part of an initial plan to manage data for analytics and AI, there are other considerations to be addressed to building and sustaining an AI environment. Some of these other topics such as DevOps/MLOps, DataOps, and AIOps are addressed in the next chapter.

CHAPTER 6

Addressing Operational Disciplines on the AI Ladder

"Not only are there no silver bullets..."
—Frederick Brooks
The Mythical Man-Month: Essays on Software Engineering

This chapter explores scenarios that organizations may encounter on their journey toward leveraging artificial intelligence (AI) for predicting, automation, and optimization.

The scenarios are viewed across the contexts of various xOps approaches as a means toward continual operational improvement.

xOps is a shorthand way to indicate various types of operational disciplines that are helpful for managing robust analytical platforms for AI and other forms in an agile and sustainable manner. These operational disciplines are as follows:

- DevOps and MLOps—development and IT operations
- DataOps—data operations
- AIOps—AI for IT operations

DevOps and MLOps involve a combination of software development practices with IT operations to help shorten the amount of time to develop and release software and ML/AI models into production. DataOps focuses on the processes that improve the speed and accuracy of analytics, including data access, quality control, automation, integration, and model deployment for AI. AIOps combines DevOps with machine learning and AI to help drive faster root-cause analysis and accelerate the mean time to repair. AIOps uses longitudinal operational data to help identify signals that can indicate a negative situation.

Each xOp is going to embrace its own nuanced methodology. The Ladder to AI can accommodate the adoption of multiple specialized methodologies, but the collective should be complementary to avoid conflicting priorities and drivers. Scaffolding and ladders can both be used to climb, but they can create conflict if not used appropriately in a coordinated effort. As such, there are often multiple methods or means to accomplish an outcome, but aligning to a consistent interpretation and approach can improve the chances that you'll reach a successful outcome consistently.

The challenges presented in this chapter are meant to further highlight the need for an underlying information architecture.

A Passage of Time

The vast majority of IT-based solutions that are created for solving business problems are also required to provide certain economies of scale. The solutions must be able to perform continually, transaction after transaction, and day after day. AI-infused solutions are no exception. The passage of time presents a challenging dilemma. Over time, data can decay, products and services can change, and societal preferences can shift. The passage of time is not a problem solely anchored in the past; the passage of time can apply to future time as well.

It's been decades since the father of the IBM 360 computer, Fredrick Brooks, wrote about the absence of silver bullets—that you're unlikely to find "a quick solution to a difficult problem"—in his software engineering book, *The Mythical Man-Month* (Addison-Wesley, 1975). A mythical man-month is a hypothetical span of time to accomplish work. It represents the amount of work that can be accomplished in a month (or in agile terms, a *sprint*). Brooks found flaws in measuring output for computer projects in rigid passages of time.

While modern agile and lean practices can be considered to promote efficiencies and effectiveness, pragmatically speaking, they are still likely to fall short of the ultimate quick solution to a difficult problem. Even when combined with faster machines, higher-level languages, self-service tooling, productivity tooling, and the schema-less-write, practitioners ostensibly still find themselves, many decades after the publication of the *Mythical Man Month*, fighting a similar fight: the need to rapidly deliver more effective and capable applications with higher levels of quality control across a complex and distributed technology infrastructure. Moreover, there is an implication that a data topology must compensate and address many of the aspects that have contributed to the faltering of an organization's analytical environment. A data topology, because of the potential expanse of the organizational data that can be encompassed, is likely to have its own set of issues to address, especially in the absence of a well-honed information architecture discipline.

While many organizations have stumbled attempting to create a data repository to support organizational reporting, analytics, and AI, organizations look toward alternative approaches in helping to achieve success. Organizational success with supporting analytics has potentially also been hampered by a shift in developing analytics to support a system of record against the need to provide support for analytics with a system of engagement.

A *system of record* is typically a large software application that accommodates one or two annual releases for increasing functionality or enhancing capabilities. These applications tend to be relatively reliable and are usually designed to support heavy transactional workloads. While on the surface, these systems appear to be functionally stable, organizations often have a backlog of changes that cannot be incorporated into the system quickly.

With the popularity of smart devices and mobile communications as well as the evolution of web-based applications, systems of record are being complemented with systems of engagement. In a *system of engagement*, a customer (not the traditional end user) has the ability to readily access the system to interact with the business. Applications designed for system of engagement interaction must be easy to use such that a user training manual—beyond a list of basic FAQs—is not required. The system of engagement must also be high-performing and require the incorporation of rapid changes to address changing business needs and evolving market forces.

Organizations must be prepared to tackle the development and operational issues that are anticipated or those that have caused concerns in the past. A data topology can provide for a conceptual framework for thinking about how to organize, store, and provide access to large volumes of disparate organizational data across a complex multicloud environment, which includes fog and mist computing.

The ability to produce a report or to perform some descriptive analytics is no longer sufficient for an organization wanting to engage in real-time awareness of their business or in seeking to proactively sense and adjust to real-time demands. Sensing can involve more than just the use of sensors and actuators, leading to the development of a discipline known as *sensemaking*. According to organizational theorist Karl Weick, "Sensemaking is tested to the extreme when people encounter an event whose occurrence is so implausible that they hesitate to report it for fear they will not be believed" (*Sensemaking in Organizations*. Sage Publications, Inc., 1995).

Weick's concept of sensemaking asserts that organizations operate in environments of chaos and flux and that people develop conceivable interpretations of their environments by noticing and bracketing out certain pieces of information. To "bracket out" is to position something that is unfamiliar in a known context ("Organizing and the Process of Sensemaking," *Organization Science*, vol. 16, no. 4, 2005).

Fostering a partnership between AI and employees through the use of augmented intelligence creates significant opportunity. Augmented intelligence includes the notion that both the machine and the employee are included in the decisioning loop to help make interpretations orderly and better understood. If you are using sensemaking with augmented intelligence, you are more likely to meaningfully address the situation if there are ambiguous elements.

Making sense of something is always subject to disruption and therefore must be continually reevaluated. The key to operating in a real-time situation is the ability to continually address smarter data science questions such as "What is going on?" and "What can be done?"

Situations of crisis, forcing change, adapting to change, and promoting foundations of customer-centricity can be unsettling. Humans tend to respond to unfamiliar situations with unease—AI can play a partnering role in decision-making in these situations. In an augmented role between AI and the employee, both must be trained to operate in fairness, and both must operate with transparency such that all decisions can be equally traced, fully understood, and lessons learned.

Analytics is no longer an isolated back-office function. Moving advanced analytics into the organization as a ubiquitous function requires time for adjustment. Employees of an organization will have to think about their work in a new way, yet that new way may not have a point of reference to facilitate the adjustment.

The development of an information architecture is likely to be built via trial and error, as technologists seek to find ways to complement an organization during transitional phases. Of course, the modern organization is likely to remain in some type of transitional phase.

An information architecture must be able to address a highly distributed and, to a large extent, a fragmented deployment environment, but the information architecture must also address the needs of every person's job. As such, AI's ability to support prediction and diagnostics along with other forms of automation and optimization are essential.

Challenges are likely to be encountered with a data topology as the organization learns to adjust to the supply chain of data, value chain of data, and lifecycle of data. See Figure 6-1 for the challenges associated with creating, executing, and operating an analytics capability within the data topology.

The longevity of the data topology, of which a data lake may be a component, is likely to be tied to how well an organization overcomes the challenges that are encountered in trying to drive value. This includes creating and executing new activities and realizing business value generated by advanced analytics.

Keeping track of all the data in the data topology is one of the more difficult challenges to address. The need to embrace agile processes is an imperative, but so too is the imperative to perform all aspects of data management with prudence and mastery. Without a way to holistically manage the data topology, the data may become fractured and splintered and promote the use of isolated silos of data.

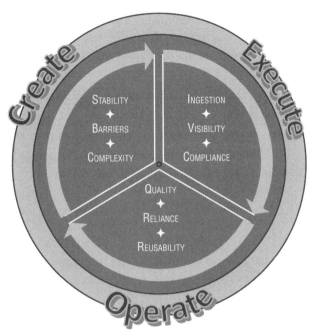

Figure 6-1: Challenges

Agile processes foster improved collaborations and practices that often follow a lightweight framework. Agile disciplines can help organizations function and maintain focus on rapid delivery while helping to minimize risk.

The use of iterative design and receiving feedback is an essential part of developing a data topology and building an information architecture. First and foremost, the information architecture must adequately serve all of the applications and AI models that need data in a timely and consistent manner.

Some of the general principles associated with agile processes include the following:

- Help curate data so that systems, AI models, and end users get the data they need.

- Use appropriate design abstracts so as to facilitate change. The target goal addressing change with data assets is the ability to incorporate new or modified data in near zero time at near zero cost.

- Concentrate on delivering catalogs and lineage profiles that are automated and accurate so as to foster the discovery of all data assets.

- Architects, developers, and businesspeople must always work together to create a sustainable data topology and functional distributed deployment environment.

- The tools to support a data topology are varied and so too are the underlying technologies that are used. Architects should be given a tool suite that can support the broad organizational needs.

- While collaborative software is useful, face-to-face communication can often be the best way to transfer information to and from a team, especially when the finer points of a direction or a discussion need to be played out. With successful deployments, the devil is often in the details.

- Secured, accessible, and accurate data are the primary measurements of progress.

- Agile processes will promote the development of data practices that are sustainable.

- Continual devotion to technical excellence should enhance agility.

- Drive for simplicity to create completeness.

- Self-organized teams often lead to designs that can iteratively evolve to incorporate new needs.

- At regular intervals, teams should reflect on evolving the practice of agility and fine-tuning their methods and behaviors accordingly.

As previously mentioned, the following abilities cannot be cherry-picked: ingesting data from either internal data sources or external data sources, providing data governance practices, successfully moving and storing large volumes of data, remediating and processing the data, enabling access to the data through a series of capabilities, managing and monitoring all access to ensure that data use and access are always appropriate, and sufficiently having all of the underlying metadata that can drive all that needs to be accomplished. An information architecture, and the associated disciplines required from design to implementation, for AI is an all-or-nothing proposition so as not to end up with a fragmented and uneven deployment.

In the context of agility and teaming, the ability to create is really about the ability to collaboratively create (co-create). The ability to execute is the ability to collaboratively execute (co-execute), and the ability to operate is to collaboratively operate (co-operate). Co-creating means the ability to help envision and pave the way for the future with ideas and designs; co-executing is about iterating to the next minimally viable product, and co-operating is about addressing the need to scale an outcome to meet the needs of the market.

NOTE   A minimum viable product (MVP) is a product with just enough features to satisfy the needs of customers for a short period of time before the next MVP is delivered to add on to the existing features.

Create, *execute*, and *operate* each share seven fundamental practices, as shown in Figure 6-2.

- **Culture:** Transform an organization by combining business, technology, and process innovations to help teams learn from market experiences.

- **Discover:** Delve into a domain area where an opportunity exists. Important practices are to help align everyone on common goals and to identify potential problems and bottlenecks that can be removed.

- **Envision:** Incrementally deliver data and AI capabilities using design thinking and related design practices to establish a repeatable approach for rapidly delivering innovative user experiences.

NOTE   IBM's *design thinking* is a scalable framework used to help teams continuously understand and continuously deliver. Design thinking begins by making a conscious commitment, as a team, to prioritizing business concerns. To move fast, design thinking encourages that a well-rounded and multidisciplined team is put in place that is empowered to commit or reject ideas in real time. Design thinking also encourages everything to be thought of as a prototype. With design thinking, teams are encouraged to restlessly reinvent and rethink about how a problem can be solved.

- **Develop:** Produce high-quality code and models that are in support of data that you can confidently drive toward delivering insights. Time-to-market is accelerated by leveraging continuous integration, continuous delivery, and automation to deliver fully trained and monitored AI models.

- **Reason:** Build a robust information architecture to help turn data into knowledge and actionable insights. AI models should also be considered for integration into solutions that can extend a system's capabilities.

- **Operate:** Ensure that operational excellence is achieved with continuous AI monitoring, high availability, and fast recovery practices that expedite fairness, problem identification, and resolution.

- **Learn:** Continuously experiment to test or evaluate hypotheses, using clear measurements to inform decisions and drive findings.

Figure 6-2: Seven practices

ADAPTIVE OVER AGILE

Being adaptive is different from being agile. In addressing the impact of time on an organization, time to value is the essential measure. Being able to respond to something next month has value. Being able to respond next week would be better. Responding today? Even better. Responding in real time is the gold standard. Reducing time requires an ability to adapt rather than an ability to be agile, especially in terms of changing IT assets.

Gary Hamel, in *The Future of Management,* 2007, Harvard Business Review Press, wrote this: "To thrive in an increasingly disruptive world, companies must become as strategically adaptable as they are operationally efficient." Reference data is an example of how IT can use adaptive practices. A new value can be added to a system as needed (an adaptive approach) without the need to write new code for the system (an agile approach).

When reference data is associated with effective and expiration dates, a concept (or value) can be primed ahead of time and automatically go into effect when needed. The same value can be retired or deprecated automatically as well.

Create

Create is about planning for the future by defining business initiatives that can use analytics and AI to drive new insights into an existing idea or to help to establish something that is altogether new.

During the process to co-create is a drive to explore and rationalize how insights can be leveraged from the breadth of data assets across the data topology. The need to democratize certain data assets or the necessity to curate a new data asset might materialize. However, as many organizations now make use of open source assets, maintaining a stable environment can present a moving target.

Stability

The data topology is likely to blend a multitude of database technologies, from those that operate on a smart device to those that support highly available transactional systems to those that make use of Hadoop. All must provide for stability. For example, the Hadoop ecosystem is large, complex, and constantly changing. Trying to keep up-to-date with the open source community developments can involve a significant time commitment. Each component continually evolves, and new tools and solutions are constantly emerging.

NOTE See `hadoopecosystemtable.github.io` for an example of the vastness of the Hadoop ecosystem.

With such a large cadre of technologies to choose from, an organization should be careful not to embrace too many technologies so as to create a barrier when a point in time is reached when the organization no longer has the appropriate skills to support the technology.

Barriers

As technology emerges, advanced skills are required to create and sustain the assets and platforms incorporated into the information architecture. An information architecture is never developed in isolation, and the deployment of an information architecture does not mean the architectural activities have come to an end. Supporting analytics and AI is a continuous activity for developers, data scientists, data analysts, and architecture professionals.

While money, corporate culture, business alignment, the appropriate use of technology, the rate of business change, and business relationships can all serve as barriers to success, the gap in skills continues to be prevalent and should be addressed by the information architecture. Each iteration of the information architecture should be something that the organization can fully support.

While IT departments should always push themselves to add value to the organization, they should avoid getting *too far out over their skis*—getting too far ahead of their ability to adequately support because of inherent complexities.

Complexity

An information architecture is realized through a compendium of products. The complexities involved in the integration of hardware, software, and applications cannot be wished away, and the activities associated with integration at all levels becomes a to-do item for many organizations. Even when using cloud-based SaaS platforms with known release compatibility, integration efforts can still exist, especially around the security of each interconnected component.

Once an environment is viable, the means to develop assets can begin.

REDUCTION

As the volume of collected data climbs, how best to visualize and draw inferences from that data becomes ever more perplexing. Being able to methodically reduce the number of features or dimensions in a model can become a necessity.

Reduction can be accomplished by the following:

- Keeping the most important variables from the sourced dataset. Feature reduction is the inverse of feature selection.

- Finding a smaller set of new variables, where each variable is a combination of the input variables, containing similar information to the input variables. This technique is called *dimensionality reduction*.

The following are the benefits of applying reduction:

- Reducing the amount of space that is required to store data
- Reducing the amount of time that is needed to train a model
- Reducing the amount of time to compute values
- Increased performance, as some algorithms perform better with fewer dimensions
- Avoiding multicollinearity variables that only yield the same level of prediction
- Adding the ability to visualize data

Execute

To *execute* is to build a complete solution through the use of a series of minimally viable products (MVPs). An MVP must always be a product or a capability that is 100 percent complete—regardless of the amount of functionality—and is distinct from building an increment. Figure 6-3 illustrates the difference between an incrementally built solution and the same solution built through a series of MVPs.

Incrementally Influenced Build

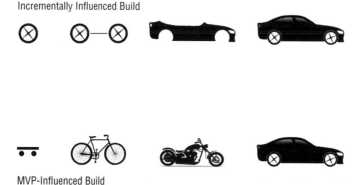

MVP-Influenced Build

Figure 6-3: Building to an MVP

Therefore, an iteration or a sprint is different from that of an MVP if the iteration or sprint is not directly associated with outcomes that can be moved to production and experienced by a user community, an AI model, or an application. Iterations and sprints are terms associated with incremental delivery techniques that address building out a capability.

In Figure 6-3, the incrementally influenced build results in a car that can be used and driven. However, each iterative creation is not 100 percent usable by the end consumer. The initial wheel is not usable. The two wheels connected by an axle is not usable; even the chassis is not fully usable. Only when everything is assembled is there an MVP or a production-ready version usable by the consumer.

On the other hand, the MVP-influenced build has something that is fully usable by an end consumer in each instance. While the skateboard is not the end state of a car, the skateboard does represent a minimally viable product that (if defined and agreed to by the consumer) has utility. Each MVP adds capabilities until the final version is produced. The objective is that the consumer is always provided a fully usable and viable version.

A core initial need for any build is to incorporate data by one means or another.

Ingestion

Ingestion is the process of moving data into a database within a data zone. Deploying a solution that can help with managing ingestion is critical, as data can be sourced from many different types of technologies, including streamed data from sensors or transactional systems, files that have been landed on an edge node, or data that has even been entered via a user interface, etc.

The data's point of entry is where data quality checks should be ideally performed. As data quality is often associated with a business rule and as business rules are subject to change due to new market demands, regulatory requirements, etc., what passes for quality can vary over time. As part of the data provenance, the version of the rules that contributed to the instantiation should ideally be captured.

Visibility into what data exists within the data topology leads to an appreciation that no data is equal in value and utility to an organization. Governance rules need to take the inequity into account in order to be flexible and based on the type of data that is being incorporated into the data topology.

Some data should be internally certified within an organization as being accurate and high-quality. Other data might suffice with less accuracy and precision, and therefore different governance rules should apply. As indicated with the description of Figure 2-3 (Chapter 2, "Framing Part I: Considerations for Organizations Using AI"), a basic grading scale can be established for the levels of data quality. The diamond grid pattern indicates poor data. The diagonal stripes pattern indicates moderate quality, which means the information may be unreliable. The square grid pattern indicates high-quality, reliable information.

> **NOTE**   For example, different governance rules might apply when a date of birth and national identifier might be required to be exact. However, a person's height, weight, and hair color might be permitted to approximate in their represented values.

When ingesting data into the data topology:

- Ensure that the incoming data is defined from a business perspective.
- Document the context, lineage, and frequency of the incoming data.
- Incorporate data provenance even to which business rules were triggered to ensure the data's business viability.
- Classify the security level (public, internal, sensitive, restricted) of the incoming data.
- Document the creation, usage, privacy, regulatory, and encryption business rules that apply to the incoming data.
- Identify the data owner or sponsor of the ingested data.
- Identify the data stewards charged with monitoring the health of the specific datasets.
- Continuously measure data quality across each zone of the data topology.

While data may be assigned to an internal owner, not all of the data within a data topology is actually owned by the organization. For example, employee or customer records may be associated with a national identifier. However, should the prevailing national government change the nature and formatting of the national identifier, the organization must respond by changing their data accordingly. In this way, an organization is a custodian over their data, but not necessarily its owner.

The organization must use data governance and data catalogs to manage the visibility into each aspect of the data asset, including ownership.

Visibility

Without the proper tools, an organization may lack visibility and transparency into the data topology and fail to understand how data can be meaningfully replicated to support hyper-personalized experiences, instead mistakenly manufacturing data silos. Ideally, a solution should organize and catalog data as the data arrives. Having a user-friendly search mechanism is an imperative for all instantiations of data for each replicated or moved copy, so as to appropriately maintain discoverability and to ensure appropriate levels of security are being applied.

Compliance

An enterprise's data can often be a sensitive nature and must address a series of compliance needs. The compliance needs may be associated with privacy, industry edicts, or government mandates, etc. Masking and tokenizing sensitive data such as national identifiers, birthdates, and telephone numbers can be important capabilities.

Protecting the data so that the information can be viewed only by authorized users and addressing the increasing number of privacy rules and regulations can only be accomplished through forethought. Managing an organization's exposure to risk should not be treated as an afterthought when establishing an information architecture.

By itself, data is an inert asset. Data always needs software code or an AI model, in which the algorithms are themselves software code, in order to accomplish anything. Ensuring that code can operate on the data helps to sustain data quality, build reliance, and promote reusability. Therefore, considerations for compliance must take software, models, and data into account to ensure compliance is viewed holistically.

MVP

A measure as to what is viable can require the need for context. Alternative approaches to an MVP include the following:

- Minimum marketable release (MMR)
- Minimum marketable product (MMP)
- Minimum marketable feature (MMF)
- Minimum desirable product (MDP)

Other minimum types that could be used include loveable, delightful, awesome, etc. But whatever style of MVP you drive toward, acceptability is drawn by the needs of others and not from your own interpretation.

Operate

Operate is the ability to take work with numerous MVPs at scale in a production environment. It's essential that a production environment is reliable and easy to monitor. The use of continuous integration and continuous delivery (CI/CD) might mean that most production environments are rapidly evolving. CI refers to an automation process for developers and means that new code changes are regularly built, tested, and merged into a shared repository. CD typically refers to continuous delivery, but the initials can also mean continuous deployment. Both continuous delivery and continuous deployment refer to the automation of subsequent stages in the lifecycle pipeline.

Continuous delivery can often mean that a developer's changes are being automatically tested for defects (bugs) and then uploaded to a repository such as GitHub, where the code can be deployed to a live production environment by an operations team. Continuous delivery helps to promote communication between development squads and business teams to help expedite deploying new capabilities.

> **NOTE** GitHub is based on an open source version control system called Git. Git assists with organizing changes that have been made to software code. GitHub provided an easier interface on top of Git to help store source code for software projects as well as provide additional capabilities, such as allowing for discussions and sharing materials about a given project.

Continuous deployment can refer to the automation of releasing developer changes from a repository to production, where the code is executed. Continuous deployment addresses the problem of overloading operations teams with manual processes that can slow down the delivery of new capabilities into production. Continuous deployment builds on the benefits of continuous delivery by automating the next stage in the lifecycle pipeline.

Should the CI/CD fail to be adequately applied, the data quality can be adversely affected.

Quality

Data quality issues have correlations with business impacts. Data quality as a discipline is often described as having multiple dimensions.

- **Completeness** is a determination to understand if certain data points are missing.

- **Conformity** is an understanding of uniformity in representation.

- **Consistency** is a demonstration that the data values representing a concept are repeating.

- **Accuracy** is an association between the data value and its representation of the real world.

- **Integrity** is a means that data can be correlated between datasets and data sources.

Understanding key data quality dimensions can be a first step in establishing a data quality improvement program. Being able to isolate data flaws by dimension or classification allows data scientists and data architects to apply data quality improvement techniques. Through the use of data quality tools, goals for improving information and the processes that create and manipulate information can be established.

Data is subject to decay. Over time, data that was once correct can cease to be correct, resulting in a degradation in the level of data quality, even though the data itself has not changed. Decaying data can have a huge impact on AI and the insights that are perceived to guide predictive patterns, such as offering to refinance an asset that is no longer owned.

> **NOTE**   Data decay refers to the gradual loss of data quality and can impact any type of data, including contact information for customers. Data decay is the result of the data becoming outdated. The outdated data is then often invalid, adversely affecting the level of data quality. As the human-created aspects of our world are constantly changing, data is not immune to that change. Data can only reliably reflect the point in time in which it was ingested.

Reliance

Repeatable processes and adherence to governance practices are an initial step in addressing the frequency and significance of decay. As previously mentioned, not all data being created equal also means that the impact of decay varies on a case-by-case basis.

A strong reliance on IT departments to perform many of the day-to-day functions of data governance is a potential indicator that the AI models may not yield the necessary utility that the business anticipated. Both data and metadata are subject to variances in levels of quality, and both should have some level of oversight from the business.

In addressing decay and other aspects of data quality, all processes should be designed to take advantage of reusability where and when appropriate.

Reusability

Automating the many aspects associated with ingesting, storing, and processing data produces a set of reusable assets. Without reusability, many of the steps required to maintain and oversee the data across the entire data topology are going to be subject to continuous reinvention (as a wordplay on CI/CD). As the overall data topology and the number of applications that make use of infused AI models grow ever larger, not just in terms of volume but also in terms of data sources, designing repeatable processes through automation is critical to avoiding some of the challenges associated with a complex data environment.

An information architecture should be able to guide how a single rule or policy can manifest into building an entire workflow, for example, the steps or workflow to provision data for an internal application within a given data zone. In this case, each workflow should be reviewed to determine how the asset can be reused across different datasets and different data zones.

Being able to co-create, co-execute, and co-operate for AI and a data topology requires the developing disciplines for xOps.

ADAPTIVE

When it comes to explaining bizarre AI outcomes, a lack of understanding is not going to be a tolerated excuse. A lack of transparency in AI can leave users uncertain about the validity and accuracy of their results. When AI projects are inexplicable, it could be that the models are wrong, or it could have something to do with the data. The bottom line is that troubleshooting an AI result can be really difficult.

To help combat the black-box aspects of AI, data scientists can explore using open source algorithms and other proprietary methods.

■ **LIME (Locally Interpretable Model-Agnostic Explanations):** LIME is an open source algorithm developed by the University of Washington and was designed to help explain predictions made by AI systems by comparing an explanation to an easily interpretable model.

■ **MACEM (Model Agnostic Contrastive Explanations Method):** ACEM was a proprietary method developed by IBM that identifies pertinent features that are present in a piece of data and those that are absent, enabling the construction of contrastive explanations.

As society moves toward regulating algorithms used in AI and machine learning, the right to an explanation dictates how certain models are established. The move toward explainable AI (XAI) is to enable your organization and your customers to understand, appropriately trust, and manage their engagements.

The xOps Trifecta: DevOps/MLOps, DataOps, and AIOps

DevOps, along with its machine learning equivalent, MLOps, are business-driven software delivery approaches that make use of lean and agile approaches in which people from multiple parts of the organization meaningfully collaborate. Business owners, along with teams from development, operations, and quality assurance departments, work together to deliver software in a continuous manner of continuous integration and continuous development. Rapid integration into a production environment enables the business to seize market opportunities quickly and can help in reducing the time needed to collect customer feedback.

As many organizations leverage multiple technologies, databases, and analytical tools, and embrace a multicloud deployment strategy, DevOps can be used to manage business operations that are dependent upon a broad and heterogeneous technology landscape. Ideas for new or enhanced business capabilities can be taken from design thinking all the way to a production deployment, providing business value to customers in an efficient manner and capturing feedback as customers engage with each capability. In addition to active participation from stakeholders and other teams associated with the software lifecycle pipeline, an information architecture must accommodate DevOps and MLOps for AI to be sustainable and impactful.

Because systems of engagement are used directly by customers, this type of system requires design and development efforts that focus on the user experience, but the designs and the real-time experiences can be enhanced through the use of real-time analytics with AI. In addition, the system of engagement must incorporate the means to vastly improve upon the speed of functional delivery. Therefore, the traits required by a system of engagement must be lean and agile and naturally point toward adopting a strong DevOps approach.

Systems of engagement should be designed with interoperability in mind, as many will need to integrate with a system of record. A change to a system of engagement may have a ripple effect to requiring a change be made to a system of record. DevOps can help toward providing for the rapid cross-system delivery of innovation.

Innovation can be driven by emerging technology trends, such as multicloud computing, mobile applications, Big Data, social media, and AI, resulting in the need to apply agile and lean principles across an entire software supply chain. While DevOps/MLOps address the software supply chain, DataOps addresses agile and lean principles across an entire data value chain.

DevOps/MLOps

DevOps is a disciplined approach to help improve the way that a business delivers value to its customers, suppliers, and partners. It's an essential business process and not just a capability of IT. MLOps has corollaries to DevOps for developing machine learning and AI models for business-centric applications. DevOps/MLOps can help drive utility around these areas:

- **Enhancing the customer experience:** To build customer loyalty and increase an organization's market share, DevOps can be used to provide a continuously improving, differentiating, and engaging customer experience. To meaningfully improve the experience, an organization must obtain and respond to feedback.

- **Increasing the capacity to innovate:** A practice in lean practices is *A-B testing*, which would involve an organization working with a small group of users to test and rate two or more sets of software that have different capabilities. The capability set that fares better is rolled out to all users. DevOps processes accommodate realistic A-B testing practices because of the efficient and automated mechanisms facilitated by the diagram in Figure 6-4, where the DevOps emphasis is placed on moving certain operations closer to the front of the software delivery cycle. Part of the ability to innovate is to reduce the scrap and rework associated with software designs and builds.

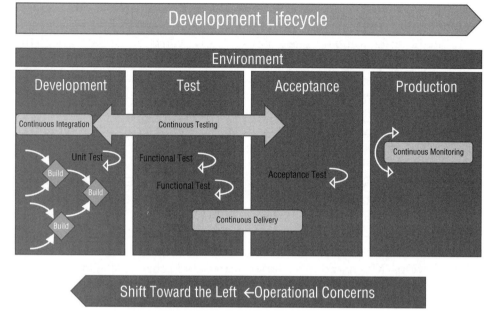

Figure 6-4: DevOps shift-left approach

- **Driving faster time to value:** Increasing time to value involves automation and the development of a complementary culture and set of practices that accommodate fast, efficient, and reliable software delivery into a production environment.

The term *shift left* refers to a practice in software development in which teams focus on quality and seek to work on problem prevention instead of problem detection. Shift left requires two key DevOps practices, namely, continuous testing and continuous deployment. These practices also apply to machine learning in the need to address *concept drift* and to detect any untoward bias.

Figure 6-5 helps to illustrate the core capabilities DevOps and MLOps must provision.

DEVOPS	MLOPS
Plan and measure	Plan and measure
Develop and test	Feature selection and model training
Release and deploy	Infused model deployment
Monitor and optimize	Model management, monitoring, and outcome explanation

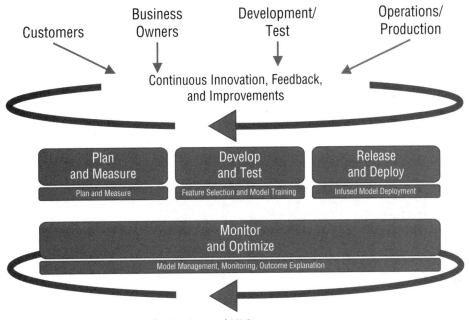

Figure 6-5: Core capabilities for DevOps and MLOps

In *planning and measuring,* organizations leverage customer feedback to test and adjust the business vision or value. To help achieve the organizational goals, key performance indicators (KPIs) are used to determine what customers really need, allowing the organization to update their business plans accordingly.

The practical purpose of *developing and testing* is to infuse quality assurance (QA) capabilities into each tangible deliverable. By using collaborative development, key parties can be involved in a cross-functional team, and continuous testing helps to ensure that code is integrated with other components to ensure intended outcomes.

Release and deploy is a software delivery pipeline established to facilitate continuous deployment in an efficient and automated manner, while *monitoring and optimizing* involves providing data and associated metrics to all cross-functional teams. Through the use of feedback, systems can be optimized and adjusted.

DataOps

While DevOps primarily focuses on software and not data, data is addressed through a practice known as DataOps. The purpose of DataOps is to accelerate the creation of data and analytics pipelines, automate the execution of data workflows, and deliver analytical solutions that address the needs of the organization. With DataOps, the approach orientates toward delivering data and analytics by using a combination of automation, testing, orchestration, collaborative development, containerization, and continuous monitoring.

DataOps stems from the underlying ideas that are associated with DevOps. With DataOps, stakeholders from across the enterprise are brought together, as shown in Figure 6-6, and can include data scientists, architects, analysts, engineers, and IT operations. DataOps is used to drive collaboration between these stakeholders and help to align them with the organization's requirements for data and analytics.

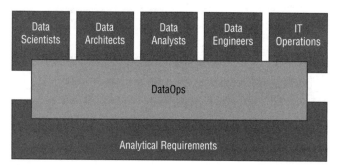

Figure 6-6: Identifying DataOps stakeholders

Sometimes, stakeholder activities and interests are going to vary, so a successful implementation of DataOps requires the following:

- Fostering a culture where all stakeholders are willing to work together and feel responsible for the entire DataOps process
- Incorporating a series of well-defined processes, roles, guidelines, and metrics to reinforce objectives and goals
- Leveraging software tools and infrastructure to support automation, testing, and orchestration, as well as collaboration and communication across all stakeholders

Like DevOps, DataOps borrows heavily from agile and lean practices. DataOps emphasizes the use of self-organizing teams with business involvement and short development sprints that deliver verified assets. Version control systems and code repositories are used for efficiencies and for code and model reuse. Principles for DataOps can include the following:

- Realizing that data is not an end in itself but that data is a means of delivering insights that add and drive value to the business
- Learning from mistakes and continuously reviewing and updating processes

- Knowledge is shared and feedback is provided at every stage of the analytics lifecycle.
- Automation occurs wherever possible, and existing artifacts are reused to avoid unnecessary rework.
- Data, schemas, software tools, and software code are orchestrated throughout the information architecture and the data topology.
- Releases are iterated in short cycles via an MVP to adapt to new and evolving needs quickly.
- Data artifacts such as AI models and data visualizations are generically viewed as code and therefore make use of version control, automated testing, and continuous deployment.
- Quality and testing are priorities such that no untested asset is implemented into production.
- Processes are monitored as a means to enhance performance and value.

Many data pipelines follow an orderly progression that includes the following:

- Collecting data from various sources and then validating and loading the data into a data zone
- Organizing data through cleansing, enriching, integrating, and modeling to support a target data zone
- Analyzing data and refining and packaging data models that can help drive organizational insights
- Infusing AI into applications to help with predictions and to facilitate optimization and automation

By addressing a complex data topology spanning cloud, fog, and mist computing, DataOps can contribute in the following areas:

- Speeding up processes and increasing quality by providing streamlined data analytics pipelines via deep levels of automation and testing
- Increasing the value proposition of data and analytics through the adoption of rigorous processes
- Establishing a culture of continuous improvement and collaboration
- Supporting the management and orchestration of data flows within the data topology
- Operationalizing data science to improve AI value to the business

DataOps is a pragmatic approach for helping an organization make use of data and analytics more efficiently and for paving the way for continuous improvement to drive value and support an organization that must itself continuously evolve to remain viable. As software, data, and analytics must always be accessible within a production, the applied use of AIOps can help address availability needs.

AIOps

AIOps is distinct from the previously discussed MLOps, involving the use of machine learning and AI, along with big data, to make use of data-driven insights in automating decision-making for IT operations. AIOps uses machine learning to detect relationships across entities and to process millions of events to detect patterns and sequences that may be associated with an operating anomaly.

AIOps can be used to improve productivity and to help reduce operational costs. For example, based on sequences of a repeating event with a business impact, AIOps could detect the repeating pattern and predict that a business outage might occur at a given point in time. As IT environments can be heterogeneous with dynamic workloads distributed across public clouds and private data centers (fog computing), machine learning and AI techniques are suitable for handling the various operational activities. Figure 6-7 shows some of the progressive building blocks that are critical for AIOps.

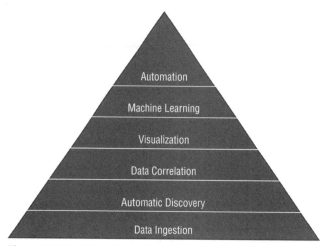

Figure 6-7: Building blocks for AIOps

AIOps can involve the following types of activities:

- The collection of data and telemetry information from data sources that include performance metrics, log alerts, trouble tickets, etc. The data should be accessible to establish an accurate and real-time view of an IT environment that includes all of the topographical layers across the cloud, fog, and mist computing nodes.

- Because of the dynamic nature of an IT environment, automated data discovery processes can aid in the collection of data across all infrastructure and application domains, including on-premise computing, virtualized computing, and cloud deployments.

- Data must be correlated to determine any relationships between an application and its infrastructure and between business transactions and the applications.

- Data must be presented in an easy-to-use visual format that can help to pinpoint issues that require corrective action.

- Uncovering the root cause of a problem is a necessary capability for AIOps as too is determining recurring patterns and predicting future events. AIOps are intended to make use of supervised and unsupervised machine learning models to determine patterns of time series events.

- As anomalies are detected, a series of remediation actions should be executed to address the situation.

- Automating predictions about the future, such as how user traffic is likely to change at a given point in time, and then reacting in an appropriate manner

- To fully support operations, any alert that is raised must be contended with in a timely manner.

- The use of automation is preferred over the use of human operators when working to drive closed-loop remediation.

- Machine learning models are used to detect anomalies from expected behaviors and thresholds and to predict outages and signal potential performance issues.

- AIOps helps to automate operational IT tasks that can help improve customer satisfaction by reducing the meantime to repair, which is a maintenance metric that measures the average time that is required to troubleshoot and repair failed equipment, the network, or an application. As a calculation, the meantime to repair is used to reflect how quickly an organization can respond to an unplanned breakdown or failure.

The general processes by which AIOps functions can be described across the previously described create, execute, operate flow.

- **Create:** Potential data sources would be identified and planned to be collected through data discovery in near real time so as to be able to detect patterns that can be used as insight. Designs for discovery algorithms should have the capabilities to extract meaningful data from infrastructure elements and application relationships from virtual machines, containers, and hypervisors, etc.

- **Execute:** Orchestration services are required to be built across key operational domains that may include multicloud environments and involve asset management, change management, and incident management. AIOps can be built to update configuration management databases by leveraging the configuration information about the environment and the environment's state.

- **Operate:** AIOps should operate in an automated manner by using machine learning to clean log files, free up space, or restart applications as necessary. Automation can also be used, for example, to change application traffic policy on a router as warranted.

Tackling an evolving IT ecosystem over a complex multicloud environment that supports cloud, fog, and mist computing requires the use of machine learning and AI to meaningfully aid IT operations, especially as IT infrastructures must be regarded and treated as being highly dynamic. By recognizing that the use of AI in business applications is only going to grow, the use of DataOps fills the data-centric gap left by DevOps. All three xOps are fundamental to succeeding with AI and must be taken into account within an information architecture.

> **ADAPTIVE**
>
> Change can be difficult to handle because it can be associated with fear. Metathesiophobia is the term for a phobia that acknowledges the fear of change. DevOps/MLOps, DataOps, and AIOps are all predicated on change being persistent, and that change is going to be part of our day-to-day work. As automation is a core part of xOps, using robust tools and defined processes should help to address phobias associated with the constant change that team members might experience.

Summary

As applications morph from a system of record to a system of engagement, organizations need to be more critical of how people engage with an application. Using AI to help improve the user experience, as well as tracking the user's experiences, becomes an important dynamic in how AI responds to the needs of users and serves as a core analytic with sensemaking.

In moving toward a cloud-native paradigm, with cloud, fog, and mist computing, organizations must delve further in agile and lean practices and collaboratively co-create, co-execute, and co-operate on deploying successful applications, based on the next iteration of an MVP.

The combined use of DevOps/MLOps, DataOps, and AIOps promotes automation and the speed to delivery for software development and data-centric applications that take advantage of machine learning and AI as part of the deployed analytic capabilities across the organization. As the organization is likely to have a complex topography, the use of AI helps keep the environment operationally viable with predictive failures and automated repairs.

The next chapter builds on the disciplines outlined in this chapter and begins to look at the capabilities that are needed to provide adequate support for the use of AI in both operational and analytical environments.

Maximizing the Use of Your Data: Being Value Driven

"Ah, but who do you think created the chaos?"
—Grady Booch
Object-Oriented Analysis and Design with Applications

For many years, a doctrine known as the *single version of truth* (SVOT) permeated how organizations approached the deployment of their data for analytic-based implementations. In 2004, Bill Inmon wrote the following:

There are many reasons why a single version of the truth is so appealing:

- *There is a basis for reconciliation;*
- *There is always a starting point for new analyses;*
- *There is less redundant data; and*
- *There is integrity of data, etc.*

The appeal of the single version of the truth is valid and strong. It is a worthy goal for organizations everywhere.

"The Single Version of the Truth" (`www.b-eye-network.com/view/282`)

While an SVOT did not mean that an organization must implement only a single data store, it did mean that multiple data stores should not contain the same, or overlapping, data. In recognizing the disparate needs of an organization, an SVOT does not always align with the way a business does business. This chapter delves into the drivers that require the support of multiple versions of data—even when the data may conflict with the ideals of an SVOT.

Managing multiple versions provides improved capabilities to support the needs of the organization and to provide the necessary contexts for solving business problems using AI, in both operational and analytical environments. The awareness of signals and triggered events are critical in ascertaining the correct set of features to use within an AI model, especially with the use of AI to support real-time situations.

Broader awareness creates an understanding of what type of data should be procured, maintained, and accessed so as to ultimately influence the creation of an information architecture and components that must also be addressed through the architecture.

Toward a Value Chain

Data and *information* are words that are typically used interchangeably within an organization. But when addressing an organization's data strategy, the terms *data* and *information* are distinct. The famed management consultant Peter Drucker once described information as "data endowed with relevance and purpose" ("The Coming of the New Organization," *Harvard Business Review*, January 1988). Drucker further expressed that "converting data into information thus requires knowledge. And knowledge, by definition, is specialized." The organizational theorist Russell Ackoff stated that the difference between data and information is "functional [and] not structural" (*Ackoff's Best*, John Wiley & Sons, 1999).

Figure 7-1 shows how data, information, and knowledge can form a progressive hierarchy of inferred utility. The progression through the hierarchy is an enrichment process captured by Ackoff's pyramid for data, information, knowledge, and wisdom (DIKW). Data is foundational. Having information is better than just having data. Likewise, knowledge is better than just having information, and wisdom is better than knowledge.

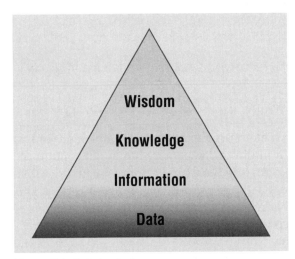

Figure 7-1: Data to wisdom

Prior to Drucker and Ackoff, poets and songwriters had surmised the existence and importance of the relationships between information, knowledge, and wisdom. In 1979, singer-songwriter Frank Zappa wrote in a song titled "Packard Goose":

Information is not knowledge,
Knowledge is not wisdom,
Wisdom is not truth

songmeanings.com/songs/view/78874

The macabre, dour point of view that Zappa established was because the song was associated with a dystopian society. If the lyric had been written for a utopian society, Zappa might have inverted the sentiment. In 1934, the poet T. S. Eliot also wrote about the lost opportunities from failing to learn from experience:

Where is the wisdom we have lost in knowledge?
Where is the knowledge we have lost in information?

Collected Poems, 1909–1962. Harcourt Brace Jovanovich, 1991

The economist Milan Zeleny extended DIKW by adding enlightenment as the pinnacle, which he saw as being that of truth and insight (www.milanzeleny .com/Files/Content/Madeira%20Zeleny.pdf). But Zeleny's clarity was to associate a series of *know* tags to each layer in the hierarchy. Beyond any inherent definition, each tag phrase served to clearly denote distinguishable aspects between data, information, knowledge, and wisdom:

Data ⇨ Know nothing

Information ⇨ Know that

Knowledge ⇨ Know how

Wisdom ⇨ Know why

The progression reveals why building an information architecture is a goal, as opposed to a goal of building a wisdom architecture. *How* and *why* (in terms of the tags *know how* and *know why*) need to be innately contextual in order for the progression to work and yield value. Need and circumstance are required to help form a context, and establishing context can be infinite. Information, therefore, forms a plane of observation upon which context can be added.

NOTE Many IT professionals often have a trite answer for questions that are nuanced. That answer is "it depends." When asking a question about how to establish a context, the answer may very well start out, "it depends." Therefore, a conclusion can be drawn that organizing data out of context can be an easier starting position than organizing data in context. Creating data in-context from data that is out-of-context can be a repeatable model to rapidly respond to contextual needs.

Further, in 1739, under the pseudonym Poor Richard, Benjamin Franklin, one of the Founding Fathers of the United States, published a version of the proverb "For want of a nail" in *Poor Richard's Almanack* to demonstrate correlation:

For want of a nail the shoe was lost;
For want of a shoe the horse was lost;
For want of a horse the rider was lost;
For want of the rider the battle was lost;
For want of a battle, the kingdom was lost;
And all for the want of a horseshoe nail.

In the mid-1700s, Franklin used the proverb to warn the colonists not to become too complacent and neglectful about their British adversaries. This is akin to Eliot's question, "Where is the wisdom we have lost in knowledge?" While the proverb's series of correlations begins "For want of a nail," can *the want of a nail* be regarded as the root cause for such an unsavory outcome—the loss of the kingdom?

Consider that:

For want of an apprentice, the blacksmith was lost;
For want of a blacksmith, the shop was lost;
For want of a shop, the hammer was lost;
For want of hammer, the nail was lost. . .

These correlations imply that the means to discover data is an essential aspect of the data scientist's role in building AI models. Feature selection and feature engineering require the ability to establish correlation and context to help drive an understanding. Ultimately, the understanding should be regarded as being holistic.

Referring to Chapter 2, "Framing Part I: Considerations for Organizations Using AI," Rudyard Kipling's poem, *The Elephant's Child*, was discussed for his insight that a set of six English interrogatives formed the primitives that can help guide a person to form a holistic viewpoint:

I keep six honest serving-men: (They taught me all I knew)
Their names are What and Where and When and How and Why and Who.

Subsequently, the interrogatives provided the basis for Zachman to build his framework. The Zachman Framework, also mentioned in Chapter 2, is regarded as an ontology because the framework represents "a theory of the existence of a structured set of essential components of an object for which explicit expressions *are* necessary and perhaps even mandatory" in formulating and demonstrating a complete (holistic) understanding (`www.zachman.com/16-zachman/the-zachman-framework/35-the-concise-definition`).

Whether the object in Zachman's quote is a nail, a horse, a rider, a kingdom, or something else altogether, the essential components navigate forward or backward along a value chain of data. Suffice to say that a *value chain of data* is a correlation of facts that are offered within a given context.

To provide utility and guidance for moving forward or backward along a data value chain, the Zachman Framework provides an iterating metamodel for each of the six interrogatives. The metamodel can be used by data scientists to explore the data's narrative to the beginning of the value chain or to the end of the value chain.

The metamodel for each of the interrogatives is as follows:

- **For the interrogative what:** relationship-thing-relationship
- **For the interrogative how:** input-transform-output
- **For the interrogative where:** link-location-link
- **For the interrogative who:** role-work product-role
- **For the interrogative when:** event-cycle-event
- **For the interrogative why:** ends-means-ends

The iterative or recursive aspect of each metamodel implies an unending chain of inquiry that can be established, such that:

- **What:** relationship-thing-relationship-thing-relationship-thing. . ., and so on
- **How:** input-transform-output/input-transform-output/input. . ., and so on
- **Where:** link-location-link-location-link-location. . ., and so on
- **Who:** role-work product-role-work product. . ., and so on
- **When:** event-cycle-event-cycle-event-cycle. . ., and so on
- **Why:** ends-means-ends-means-ends-means. . ., and so on

In addition to the recursive property of the metamodel, it also contains fractal properties. Therefore, for every binary relationship that is associated with an object, the correlations can change orientation. The change in orientation is somewhat akin to a drill-up, drill-down, or drill-across capability that is associated with business intelligence analytics.

Drilling up can help to correlate or link a given object to a higher-level object or concept. Drilling down could help to correlate or explore the decomposition of an object into a smaller object that retains meaningfulness to a business (in this case, meaningfulness for a business is always defined by establishing a context). Lastly, drilling across would help to correlate an object to a peer object.

An example of drilling up from one object to another is a CPU that is used in a laptop computer. A drill-down example could be that the CPU contains a given number of cores. A drill-across might be that the laptop is associated with an externally connected storage device.

Regardless of the granularity associated with a given object, the metamodel retains its fractal nature. The metamodel pattern to explore an object always remains consistent. The recursive nature of the metamodel, both forwards and backwards, is likely to possess a finite number of endpoints because an organization only manages a quantifiable volume of data. However, through extrapolation and interpolation processes that can be performed on the quantifiable data points, an organization can investigate the means to explore infinite endpoints.

> **NOTE**   In terms of granularity, an individual amount for a sales transaction could be regarded as fine-grained. The amount (or total) for all transaction sales for a given year can be considered coarse-grained.

Chaining Through Correlation

To discover or explore possible correlations beyond those that may be self-evident or empirically derived, the metamodel provides the underpinning to guide exploration. For each digital asset, the "what" metamodel indicates that there is likely to be a preceding relationship to another digital asset (the "thing" in the metamodel). If a relationship to another digital asset does not exist or cannot be found, the digital asset represents the earliest discoverable value in the value chain and can potentially be a value associated with any root-cause analysis or diagnostic. Additionally, the relationships can contribute toward the data scientist's approach toward feature selection for a model.

Exploring the relationship forward, the digital asset is potentially itself a dependency on another digital asset (the recursive nature of the metamodel). If there are no other digital assets that are related, the value chain is potentially at its current endpoint.

> **NOTE**   A "current endpoint" is a reference to a point in time. The use of the word *current* infers that a future event may generate additional data points that result in negating the digital asset as an actual endpoint—other than an endpoint in a temporally related point-in-time context.

If the information and knowledge being gained from exploring the relationships both forward and backward appear to tell an incomplete or disparate story, the data scientist might infer that other sources of data need to be considered for which the data can be further correlated.

The "how" metamodel correlates the known transformations and processes that are directly or indirectly associated with a digital asset. Often transformations and processes leave their own wake in terms of digital assets such as audit logs, operational metadata, and parametric data, etc.

"Where" is the foundation to form correlations associated with geometry. The use of the term geometry would incorporate digital or communication networks, data centers, and any type of location—whether stationary or mobile, real or virtual, terrestrial or extraterrestrial. "Who" correlates actors, whether a person or a machine, that are involved in the creation of a work product. "When" recognizes the existence of time between events. The aspect of time represents a given cycle. Finally, the "why" metamodel helps to understand motivation by correlating broad outcomes and causation: an ends and a means.

Each primitive metamodel is, therefore, the basis for examining each aspect of "For the want of a nail," whereby the aggregate examination is holistic. However, each metamodel can be combined with one or more of the other metamodels to establish a composite metamodel that can be used to develop complex lines of inquiry and understanding. For example, combining "who" and "when" provides a correlation and an understanding of work products over time.

For a data scientist, the primitive metamodels provide a means to understand data through analysis, while composite metamodels provide for a means to understand data through synthesis. Synthesis is then the means to draw upon more than one viewpoint of understanding to form additional correlations and to establish or build context.

AI is part of the contextual progression that can be realized from an underlying information architecture. AI can be correlated to being part of the knowledge layer, where the knowledge comes from uncovering patterns from across the data for which AI models have been given visibility and access. Knowing why, a reference to wisdom in Zeleny's know-tag model, can in part require feedback for which an information architecture must be able to preserve if and when captured.

Information is the organization of data where data is enriched through the use of definitions, relationships, and provenance. As mentioned previously, data is inert—but so too is information. Neither data nor information is self-organizing nor self-aware. Making information operable requires a computer program or a model. AI can provide both and can also surmise inference based on a given context.

Enabling Action

Any action that is taken through the use of a machine or by a person reflects a level of observation from which the action was deemed appropriate and relevant. For example, if an AI model is calculating a score based on uncovering a pattern, a computer program can take the next appropriate step based on that score. The score and the next step are acts associated with knowledge.

AI is therefore providing additive value and transcends the value of information alone. Plain vanilla data, such as sales figures and customer retention rates, can be meaningless if solely analyzed as standalone figures. But once data is enriched by combining it with other data, the data can be transformed into something with higher value (e.g., information). AI is a vehicle (a means) to generate value (an ends).

Sales figures from a single month would not provide an organization with any significant knowledge as to how the organization is actually performing. By providing some historical context, such as the inclusion of financial figures from preceding months, the information possesses utility. This utility enables the organization to uncover insights and act appropriately.

AI models have the ability to correlate and combine ever-increasing volumes of data to yield even greater insights. An underlying information architecture fosters an ability to make the data discoverable and to organize the data in such a way as to drive affinity.

Discovery becomes an important topic, as no organization functions with a single database for the enterprise's data. Furthermore, no organization could exist with just one single database for the enterprise's data.

The needs of an organization, when combined with real-world physics, make seeking a single version of the truth (a single database for a single fact) a misplaced ideal. Should a single version of the truth be possible, an information architecture would not be necessary. The basis of an information architecture is therefore predicated on the fact that multiple versions of data exist and that supporting multiple versions of data is, in fact, desirable. The key use of an information architecture is to help enforce integrity specifically because a single version ideal cannot be achieved.

A single version of the truth concept relies on achieving one unchallengeable source within an organization to deliver all of the crucial data and information required to run a business. The crucial data may include customer details, supplier details, product information, service contracts, and so on. By using a single version of truth, the perception of control is achieved.

The single version is viewed as being reliable and can be used by every department and line of business. The single version is not specific to any one part of the business and therein lies the rub: an inability to directly support personalized needs. Personalization was a topic covered in Chapter 3, "Framing Part II: Considerations for Working with Data and AI."

Not having or not striving for a single version of truth can be considered as a means to promote a discombobulated and chaotic proposition for an organization. However, within the ability to architect a solution lies the innate opportunity to meaningfully manage and sustain a solution to avoid any untoward side effects and outcomes. As such, an information architecture affords the ability to manage multiple versions of the truth and to sustain a viable solution over time.

While deploying multiple sources for what is supposed to be the same data can lead to confusion and mistakes, the outcome does not have to be that way. Organizations that seek to manage a deployment based on multiple versions of the truth are not subscribing to the overt creation of alternative facts—whether intentionally or unintentionally.

Expanding the Means to Act

Multiple versions of the truth accommodate data value chains and recognize that not everyone within an organization needs to consume data in precisely the same way. Specialized data assets provide the opportunity to align information to a person's job for the purposes of promoting efficiencies. For example, certain tasks can be made easier when information is organized in a graph database, such as fraud detection, whereas a graph database is not necessarily the appropriate repository for all types of analytics.

Taking an architected approach to building a multiple-version data topology allows the data scientist to discover and explore the features associated with each instantiation of data, because the adoption of a multiple-versions-of-truth approach does not dictate that each version must be an exact mirror. Each version represents data that is in accordance with the data's place in the value chain and organized within a specific schema. A schema in one version may be a fully denormalized flat file, another might use a relational model organized around the principles of third-normal form, and another schema might be based on a dimensional model, a graph model, a document store, etc.

Consider the way in which a data scientist might prepare models for an organization's marketing department and an organization's accounting department related to marketing spend. The models built for the marketing department might be oriented toward certain predictions relating to campaign effectiveness and marketing expenditures. The models for the accounting department might focus on features for predicting cash flow and predicting when invoices are actually going to be paid.

The outcomes from the models for the marketing and accounting departments are different, and the difference does not imply that one or both are incorrect. Having data stores that are oriented toward the requisite features relevant to a given department can help the data scientist in building a model as well as helping the individuals who query the data stores for self-service analytics.

Within the context of the DIKW pyramid, both the single version of truth and the multiple versions of truth represent information. However, as knowledge and wisdom represent higher levels of attainment from the use of data and information, the multiple-versions-of-the-truth paradigm can help to directly organize data and information that is closer to its contextual use. Therefore, the creation of information architecture helps the architect to think through design concepts for managing multiple versions of the truth, and multiple versions of the truth can be a practical device for establishing contextual versions of the truth.

The pathway from data to wisdom provides a line of sight for the creation of a data-centered value chain through the use of multiple versions oriented toward contextual use. The insight generated from a specialized data store is likely to be greater than the sum of the parts. Being able to curate data is a core practice in building an information architecture that supports multiple versions of the *same* data. Curation is not an act of gathering as much information as possible; curation is about providing sufficient information as to drive knowledge. And, knowledge requires context. Curation provides a general bounding scope that makes the search for knowledge practical.

IT'S ALL JUST METADATA

The vast majority of the data captured for business purposes reflects some occurrence from the real world. As such, data is used to describe something that is of interest to the business. Any data that is used to describe or represent something else is meta-data (data about data). You can, therefore, conclude that in a business context, data doesn't really exist. It's all metadata.

Realizing that data is just a form of metadata can help you understand the data in the context of the value chain. Fundamentally, being able to qualify how representative the data (or, in this case, the metadata) is in describing an entity, object, or event from the real world can provide a sense of its richness, depth, or value. In moving from one point in the value chain to the next, the data (the metadata) should either provide some quantifiable enrichment to what is knowable or provide sufficient insight about how the entity, object, or event has changed.

In many organizations, IT departments set up one set of practices for managing data and a separate set of practices for managing metadata. Understanding that it's all metadata can help to simplify and coalesce the management of all digital assets.

Curation

Curation is a field of endeavor that involves assembling, managing, and subsequently presenting some type of collection. To curate, you generally need someone or something to act as a curator because data is not, as already mentioned, self-organizing (self-assembling, self-managing, or self-presenting).

For example, a curator in a museum will research, select, and acquire pieces for the institution's collections and will oversee interpretation, displays, and exhibits. When a person visits a museum, not everything that is on display is representative of everything that the museum has acquired or can possibly access for its display. Overall, curation is an ability to dutifully subselect—to cherry-pick and to meaningfully arrange.

A curated set of data is chosen so as not to overwhelm or to mislead. Curated data can provoke interest, improve understanding, and foster efficiency. Curated data is not data that is randomly placed and interspersed. Data curation is an activity that has historically been ignored, due to constraints involved with cost, storage, and processor speeds, and with organizations preferring to create encompassing homogenous datasets for general-purpose use.

The ability to curate data for discrete communities of interest helps to avoid having a logical or physical central melting pot for every piece of data—the mythical single version of the truth. "Logical" is used in the sense that the data itself may be spread over multiple locations and across multiple technologies.

NOTE   A community of interest represents a group of people or teams that share a common purpose or mission within an area of specialization.

Data is a digital asset. As such, it is easily replicated without any loss of precision. Therefore, the same data asset within a data topology may appear in more than one data zone. This is an essentially different task from that which is afforded to a museum curator, who must pick only one place to showcase a tangible artifact. Data curation and data topologies are not constrained to finding the *best home* for a single piece of data, but rather, the *best homes* (i.e., the most applicable data zones) to place the data, so as to maximize the data's potential to drive value—via a person, piece of code, or a model.

Curated data affords the user an ability to access assembled and managed data for a broad spectrum of uses while being focused on supporting the user's needs—creating a set of data that supports a personalized work experience. For example, curation is a process that can make separating raw data from cleansed and standardized data that is repeatable and straightforward for a data scientist. If the data scientist just requires current production records, those records can be curated from a data store that also includes historical records. If the data scientist needs an end-to-end view of a supply chain, the end-to-end view can be curated to make navigation easy and reliable. If the data scientist needs to seek observations to help improve support for *knowing-your-customer* (KYC), irrelevant data can be separated from the curated set.

Within the capabilities of a given set of data-oriented technologies, a data topology promotes data curation to support enterprise views, line-of-business views, departmental views, group views, and even the discrete views for an individual businessperson—where each represents a personalized subset.

Establishing a data topology is the starting point to allow for data curation. As discussed in Chapter 5, "A Look Forward on Analytics: Not Everything Can Be a Nail," a data topology is organized around data zones and includes a series of data flows and the data topography. Collectively, the data zones comprise a zone map, much like a museum map with all of the different viewing rooms based around themes and topics. Each data zone is themed and provides the basis for assembling, managing, and presenting digital assets—something that data or information cannot achieve without aid.

Data zones are created based on an area of business interest. The data zone represents a subset (or a collection) of data that is reasonably aligned to an area of interest but loosely enough so as not to constrain insight.

Data curation is an exercise of a control. Controls can be viewed as foundational toward building trustworthy data for use in business-critical situations. Controls are normally added through the use of data management and data governance. As an example, consider a bank looking to perform risk data aggregation across different lines of business into a common risk-reporting platform that is in accordance with the Basel Committee on Banking Supervision (BCBS) 239 standard (www.bis.org/publ/bcbs239.pdf). The data needs to be highly accurate and accompanied by the correct data lineage to help ensure that all of the reports are acceptable. Banks rely on their ability to produce compliant reports for key decision-making regarding how much capital to carry. Without the data lineage, there would be little assurance that the data is, in fact, accurate. Curating the data can help meet the needs of the users and help work toward ensuring compliance.

By using data governance and integrated data management capabilities, organizations can manage, automate, and execute operational tasks that can make offering curated data at a personalized level to make an employee's job easier to perform and more efficient.

FIT FOR PURPOSE

When you send mail to someone in New York City, the initials NY will suffice for the city name in a dataset. However, someone from a company's in-house counsel may want to see the legal name for the city: the City of New York. A person in corporate travel may prefer to use one of the airport codes such as JFK or LGA in lieu of the city name.

When curating data, elements that are fit for purpose must be taken into account. Fit for purpose implies that the data is good enough for its intended use. As an organization is comprised of many actors, what is good enough is, as we have previously discussed, going to vary. Curating data can involve content from a general perspective and then representation from a more specific perspective.

> As the example of NYC shows, many different departments can make use of an address (the general perspective), but how individuals in those departments can best leverage the information can vary (the specific perspective). A curated dataset takes into account the need for data and the representation of that data.

Data Governance

As discussed in Chapter 3, data governance is an essential element for organizing data and can be used to provide mechanisms to perform the oversight necessary to ensure that the data is appropriately used for decision-making. To that end, data governance is both a tools-based process and a human-based process. Some of the human processes can be as simple as assigning a data steward or a data custodian to a new dataset.

Data governance practices can be formalized through the creation of a data governance council, a group that can establish data definitions and standards and ensure that the needs of the organization are taken into account when designing a data topology.

Here too, the tooling for data governance can assist by recording the assigned person or team that is acting as the data steward, providing a dashboard to the data council, and seeking to leverage AI-based automation through cognitive classification that can assist with standards.

When considering goals for a data governance initiative, the following factors should be taken into account:

- **Quality and consistency:** Being able to ascertain the level of quality and consistency in the data so that the data can prove useful to business users and data scientists alike while making important discoveries and decisions

- **Policies and standards:** Ensuring that the policies and standards can be adequately stated for ingesting, transforming, and using data and that, subsequently, they are observed or enforced uniformly throughout the organization

- **Security, privacy, and compliance:** Even with digital democracy, limiting access to those with need and justification

- **Data lifecycle management:** Making provisions for data to be off-boarded (archived or hard-deleted) as well as onboarded. In addition, this includes being able to understand how data decays over time so that the appropriate datasets are accessed.

Figure 3-5 in Chapter 3 illustrated how data governance could be applied proactively or reactively by an organization. The factors listed here can be incorporated into Figure 3-5's controls lifecycle: ensure, assure, insure, and reassure.

The effectiveness of data governance depends on how a governance body decides to react and adapt to the cultural environment within the organization. To that end, data governance may have to continually adjust its *modus operandi* or help to influence a change in the organizational behavior. In either case, data governance must manipulate or tweak its operations. In Figure 7-2, this tweaking is called *dialing*.

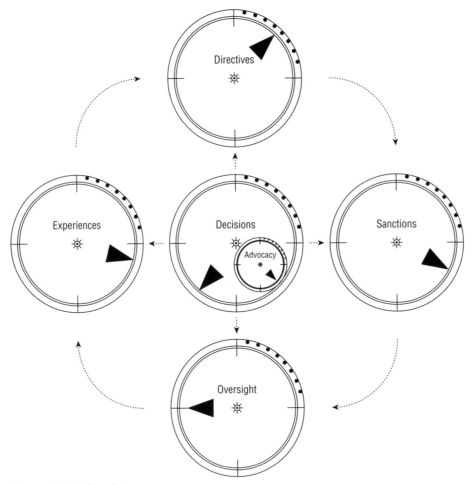

Figure 7-2: Dialing data governance

The model in Figure 7-2 gives an overview of the data governance operational adjustment process. The process consists of five primary dials with one subdial. The dials are named as follows: Experiences, Directives, Sanctions, Oversight, Decisions, and Advocacy.

The collection of dials identifies core operations that can be tuned to meet the cultural style and objectives for data governance within an organization.

- **Experiences** are related to the evaluation of operational experiences for deployed solutions and are to ensure that quality and integrity are preserved and sustained. In addition, compliance and regulatory requirements are intended to be met.

- **Directives** include the development of policies and guidance, as well as the interpretation of other sources of influence, both internal and external.

- **Sanctions** can involve licensing or certifying that data stores are trusted and being used as intended. Additionally, data consumers and data providers are authorized so that an inventory is maintained to assist in tracking the provenance of all data.

- **Oversight** relates to the activities that are necessary to ensure that integrity, compliance, and consistency are achieved and sustained.

- **Decisions** are ones that result from performing research on data-related issues, holding meetings to address any concerns that a community of interest may have, and working with other governance bodies within the organization to ensure symmetry in decision-making.

- **Advocacy** is to promote the successes achieved by the organization to the organization as a whole. Advocacy becomes the promotional arm of data governance.

The dials are impacted and adjusted as the data governance body strives to improve its processes in these five areas by assessing need and determining risk. Within data governance, risk combines the probability of noncompliance with the consequence of noncompliance and, finally, how to optimally mitigate an issue should noncompliance occur.

In many cases, a deployed environment provides the context for data governance to fully rationalize the synergies or outcomes between intention and practice. As such, the data management underpinnings are extremely important to a data governance practice.

WAIVERS

An essential component in building a successful governance practice is to avoid falling into an autocratic-style trap—attempting to force everything you touch to comply with a self-imposed regulation. Sometimes it makes sense not to be so regimented. Developing a process to manage waivers should be instated as a primary governance capability.

A waiver process is used to provide dispensation to deviate from a preferred course of action. A formal waiver process becomes a preventative measure against certain managers taking their initiatives into stealth mode: flying unseen and under the radar from oversight. There is nothing more detrimental to a governance practice than not having knowledge about what is going on in the organization.

> Whether it's to meet a critical short-term deadline, to leverage a database technology that is to be sunsetted, or to use a model from a deprecated AI library, a waiver process can authorize activities that would otherwise be regarded as being internally out of compliance. Of course, the process should also have the ability to deny a request as well as support an appeals process.
>
> Along with an authorized waiver, the governance protocol should include work efforts to build a plan with stakeholders for bringing waivered efforts into compliance based on time, cost, resources, and access to technology.

Integrated Data Management

In the discussion of the value chain earlier in this chapter, the progressive hierarchy DIKW was used to illustrate that how you choose to organize business facts can have a significant bearing on how useful those facts are when they're being used. The usefulness for how facts can drive action from insight was illustrated through Zeleny's *know* tags, specifically, the tags for *knowing how* and *knowing why*. The *how* and *why* know tags aligned to knowledge and wisdom in the DIKW hierarchy.

To illustrate an example of data, we can use a person's vital signs, which represent measures for essential body functions, such as the heart rate. Other vital signs would include the breathing or respiration rate, body temperature, and blood pressure. Blood pressure is an interesting data point as it is made up of two separate facts: a systolic reading and a diastolic reading. Depending on your design preferences, you may choose to store blood pressure in a multitude of ways, including whether to use a single feature or two features.

Systolic blood pressure is a measure of the pressure in your blood vessels when your heart beats, while diastolic blood pressure is a measure of the pressure in your blood vessels when your heart is resting between beats. If the systolic and the diastolic readings are stored in a single feature, it would be essential for most users that the systolic reading appears ahead of the diastolic. Blood pressure is generally captured in terms of millimeters of mercury (mmHg)—but it is possible that other units of measure could also be used.

Blood pressure may be stored as a single value such as "120/80." Possible alternatives may include "120 80," "120|80," "120-80," "120/80 mmHg," and "120/80 mm Hg." Normally, the data's metadata would include a description as to how to decipher the reading. But if data is being collected from multiple points of origin, the format may turn out to be nonstandardized. Standardizing disparate formats and the metadata would be one way that information can be produced (relative to the DIKW hierarchy). If you are storing blood pressure readings as two separate and distinct values, the name of the feature or the metadata should clearly delineate which reading is which.

If individual vital signs represent data, information would be the result of correlating the measures with an identifiable individual and other pertinent facts. The information could be further enriched if a series of vital signs were collected over time as part of a longitudinal comparison for the individual.

By adding context, knowledge (in terms of DIKW) would result if a practitioner or a model could synthesize data points so as to understand whether or not some form of an intervention is likely to be required, while wisdom (per DIKW) would be a demonstration in the accuracy of selecting an appropriate intervention. Furthermore, accuracy should be incorporated as additional data points that are captured as part of a feedback loop and to further support aspects of wisdom.

Understanding value, as well as the contexts for which facts will be used during the course of business, will serve to significantly influence your design choices. Realistically, you'll want to serve data in a multitude of forms, which is also why data curation and data governance must be considered important topics of consideration for building an information architecture for artificial intelligence at the scale of the enterprise.

The activities for value recognition/generation, curation, and governance are to a large extent optional, while data management activities can be considered more mainstream. Each decision point or each design point regarding value, curation, and governance will make use of the set of data management activities.

The use of an integrated platform for managing all aspects of a data topology is often preferable over stitching together a series of different point products. As data is ingested, metadata can be captured. As the data is transformed, the data is refined. As the data flows, the data lineage can be automatically captured.

Rules can be applied to inspect the data for quality so that whatever data becomes available for consumption, the information has gone through a series of data quality checks such as the data's perceived accuracy and the precision by which the data represents its real-world corollary. Other data quality checks can include the data's legitimacy, validity, reliability, consistency, timeliness, relevance, completeness, comprehensiveness, availability and accessibility, granularity, and uniqueness.

To be effective, a data management platform requires data. Before the data can be consumed, the data must first be acquired or ingested. As acquisition may not always be as straightforward as pulling data from an SVOT, an integrated data management function must work in tight coordination with a data governance practice.

Onboarding

A managed data ingestion process helps to simplify the *onboarding* process for new datasets, and subsequently, a repeatable process has a positive impact on the development of new use cases and applications. Managed data ingestion also serves as a well-defined data pipeline throughout all of the zones across the data topology.

There are various options for incorporating data into a data zone. These options may be based on whether the information is being acquired internally via the completion of a transaction, externally acquired via a data stream, simply through the movement from one data zone to another, and so on. Incorporating data in a managed way means that you have control over what data is actually ingested, where the data originates, when the data arrives, and where in the zone map the data is stored.

Using the concept of the data zone means that certain data is intentionally duplicated. This feature is regarded as *controlled redundancy* because the use of data governance provides insight as to where the data is located. Controlled redundancy is the means to create multiple versions of the truth that are adequately managed to ensure integrity.

A managed ingestion process can be used to raise notifications and capture log entries so that the environment can be adequately diagnosed should an ingestion process fail. These capabilities can aid in remediation and help with restarting a process.

Additionally, over time, streaming workloads are likely to be increasingly used as data feeds. Service level agreements (SLAs) via policies can be used to determine whether the stream payload is exhibiting acceptable behaviors. An SLA is a vehicle to make explicit acceptable terms and conditions between multiple parties. Typically, one party is providing something, and another party is receiving something. Both parties may be internal to an organization. The SLA often outlines both the conditions that are used to identify or interpret a failed condition and the actions that are necessary to remediate a failed condition.

Metadata needs to be captured through a batch process or a streaming process regardless of data being presented to any of the data zones. A batch process is an interchange of data that normally occurs at a prescribed time based on a schedule. A streaming process is an interchange that is continuous. Data quality checks are also a requisite need for streamed data. Record formats, as appropriate, need to be validated for correctness and that the content values conform to range checks, specific values, or referential integrity checks.

Data zones follow a prescribed data flow for distributing and moving data. While the data flow itself can be agnostic to the organization of data, the receiving data zone receives data for a given purpose, and that purpose often requires the data to be organized.

Organizing

When data is stored, data encryption for added security may be a requirement to consider. In addition, data may need to be redacted (masked) or obfuscated (tokenized) and then protected with the appropriate level of access control.

The implication for services such as security is that they need to be provided enterprise-wide across the entire zone map and that there has to be inherent support for multiple business groups.

Multiple business groups need to coexist and gain access to cataloging aspects for their business data. While this can be efficiently accomplished, time must be spent to make sure the governance team fully understands the permission levels required.

For example, protected health information (PHI) will legally require privacy controls for an organization operating in the healthcare industry. Violators—organizations that do not respect PHI—can be financially penalized. The European General Data Protection Regulation (GDPR), mentioned in Chapter 2, also seeks to enforce not only what information is kept but also how that information is used.

The data preparation stage, which is further described later in this chapter, is often where sensitive data, such as financial and health information, is manipulated. Sensitive or private data can be completely removed through a process known as *redaction* or masking.

Alternatively, sensitive or private data can be converted to an innocuous value in a process known as *obfuscation* or tokenization. The technique to obfuscate should be unidirectional and not subject to techniques of reverse engineering. Unidirectional obfuscation helps to safeguard the data by ensuring that a mathematical process cannot uncover the original values.

Determining the best format to store data must be considered. Data may need to be held in a raw format, the format by which the data was first collected within the data topology. Depending on the user community, the raw format is not always going to lend itself to being in a readily usable state for consumption—a topic previously covered in the discussion of personalization (Chapter 3) and multiple versions of the truth and controlled redundancy earlier in this chapter.

For example, data scientists, as well as citizen data scientists (individuals whose primary job function is outside of the field of statistics but who are able to create or generate a machine learning model or an AI model), may require features organized in a certain manner to complement the algorithms that are being used. An example is separating (parsing out) an embedded county code from a telephone number. (The telephone number +1.212.555.1212 would become two features: +1 and 212.555.1212.)

NOTE   For more information about citizen data scientists, see `www.gartner.com/en/newsroom/press-releases/2017-01-16-gartner-says-more-than-40-percent-of-data-science-tasks-will-be-automated-by-2020`.

Analytical queries that are performed on a columnar data store can often return results faster than those using a traditional row-oriented data store. Data compression is also another consideration when storing large volumes of data.

Many unstructured datasets that are not text-based may enter a data zone in a format that is already compressed, such as those that are used for audio and video.

Automating aspects of the data lifecycle management process can be required, for example, to help address SLA needs in supporting certain queries. If fast data access may be required for data that is less than 30 days old, a memory-resident data store may be required.

Additionally, the scenario for managing data that is 31 to 90 days old may permit slightly slower response times and may require the use of solid-state flash drives. Beyond 90 days, the SLA might tolerate even slower data access times, and the data might be migrated to slower commodity disks for a period of up to 7 years. After 7 years, the data may then need to be physically removed or archived to a data zone that has been explicitly designated for archival purposes.

A designated archival zone may also be mapped to another part of the data topography within the data topology whereby the pre-archive zones are associated with an on-premise fog computing node, and the archival data zone with a public cloud provider.

As data can be managed across the zone map, an indexing mechanism for the data topology is warranted. Many indexing capabilities are incorporated into data catalogs.

Cataloging

A *catalog* helps data scientists and business users quickly discover data assets that can be accessed, categorized, and shared. Data assets can include business data, and it can also include analytical models.

A catalog as a function of data governance helps users understand what exists within the data topology. Users also need to know the data's properties, lineage, provenance, ingestion histories, the level of data quality, and other KPIs associated with the life history of data.

Data scientists and other data professionals often experience a situation where their time is disproportionately consumed during problem solving. Instead of working on the core problem, they burn significantly more time on finding and preparing the appropriate data. As a result, data scientists may feel pressured to rush through important activities such as model building, visualizations, and reporting.

A core part of an information architecture includes the ability to control data and to prevent it from becoming invisible or unmanaged. Often organizations encounter situations where the more data that is added to the data topology, the harder the data becomes to find, store, and govern. To help thwart any potential problems, a catalog becomes a vital tool. A data scientist or a business analyst must always be able to determine the following:

- Where exactly is the organization's data?
- What does the data truly represent?

- Where did the data originate?
- How accurate is the data?
- Can the data be trusted for the purpose for which the data is needed?
- Can the data be used for purposes other than which the data was originally intended?
- How should the data be accessed?
- Do I have permission to see the data?

The profile of the data, including the meta-triad attributes for business metadata, technical metadata, and operational metadata, should be readily accessible. This information needs to be abstracted so users can understand it and use that data effectively for insight. This is the role of the data catalog within the data topology.

The data catalog needs to be searchable, whether for the source system, schema attributes, subject areas, or time ranges. A cognitive search is essential for business users to maximize the use of the data topology in a swift and agile way.

With a data catalog, users can uncover datasets that have already been curated so that they do not have to spend time cleaning up and preparing the data all over again. Being able to select datasets required for model building without having to involve an IT department shortens the analytics timeline.

While a catalog can provide many features, the information that makes up the catalog is metadata.

Metadata

Metadata is extraordinarily important in the efforts to manage a data topology effectively. Metadata helps to avoid *data dumping*, which is a situation where persisted data results in consuming disk space without ever providing any business value.

Metadata is critical for ensuring data is leveraged to its fullest extent. Whether the data is manually collected or automatically created during the ingestion process, metadata allows users to locate the data they need to analyze. Metadata also provides clues for future users to help with understanding the contents of a dataset and how the underlying data can be leveraged and reused.

As the data topology grows and more information is flowed across the zone map, the use of metadata becomes intrinsic to conducting daily business and decision-making. Metadata becomes a vital asset.

The meta-triad consists of business metadata, technical metadata, and operational metadata.

- Business metadata is used to capture the definition of what the data means to the analytics user and includes business names, descriptions, tags, data quality measures, and masking rules.

- Technical metadata is used to capture the form and structure of each dataset and includes the type of data such as text, JSON, Avro, and the structure of the data in terms of fields and their types.

- Operational metadata is used to capture lineage, data quality, profile, and provenance of the data and includes source and target locations of data, the dataset size, the number of records, and the data lineage associated with all data flows.

Without all of these types of metadata being created and actively curated, the data topology may result in a failed information architecture. Metadata can also be used to capture the contextual use of data within a data zone. As such, metadata can provide a basis for data-driven data preparation approaches to organizing and enriching data.

Preparing

While raw data has utility and use, the term *raw* implies that refined data must either exist or be required. *Data preparation* refines the data, making it easier for business users to access. Ideally, refinement can be carried out without the need to rely on IT to perform an activity.

While access to raw data can be vital, the data scientist can also benefit from access to prepared data. Data preparation is required as part of delivering contextual data assets to each business community within the organization. Inevitably, data can arrive into the data zone with various types of errors, corrupted formats, or duplications. Often the imperfect data is contextually associated with the next series of data points, which are associated with the value chain and should be remediated.

Adequately preparing and cleansing the data is necessary and should be accomplished with the understanding of data security, data quality, and data visibility.

Data preparation activities can include the following:

- Data tagging to aid searching and organizing the data

- Converting data formats so that queries are easier to create and potentially faster in their execution

- Completing complex workflows to integrate updated or changed data

Data preparation should generate metadata for data lineage, transformations, and exercised queries as a byproduct of the preparation. Additionally, when generating refined data from any raw data, fields for data provenance should be created. The data provenance helps trace individual records or fields back through the data lineage to the source. Additionally, format conversions may be required as part of the data preparation such as transforming data from a row-wise organization to a columnar data format.

Other issues can also arise. Source systems are not immutable and may change over time, potentially frequently. Datasets may need to be managed as a time series over a period of time.

Not every data store is preplanned. Certain data stores are dynamically provisioned, but the data should still be prepared for use.

Provisioning

Self-service consumption can be an essential part of a successful data topology. Different types of users consume data in different ways and look for different things. The need to access data in different styles should be self-evident based on the number of different job roles and responsibilities that exist within an organization. Overall, *provisioning* provides for empowered users to gather data of their choosing and recognizes that different users may want to work with data in different formats from various sources of data.

Take, for example, the simple activity of reviewing quarterly company revenue. The CFO's office may want to look at the fiscal quarter's physical revenue (monies that have been deposited into a corporate bank account or a line of credit that has been drawn down). The sales department may want to look at revenue for purchase orders that have been received during the quarter, while marketing may want to look at the revenue associated with the quarter's business pipeline. Each need looks for comparable things differently and in a different manner. But each user and even the data scientist would prefer to access the data in a self-service manner, without the formal aid of IT.

Several personas are attributed to the analytical users of a data topology.

- A **senior manager** may seek trends or aggregations to make an important business decision and might look at the predictive analytics of sales based on history and analytical models that were built by a data scientist. Within the data topology, the data could be ingested from numerous data sources including both streamed and batched data. The data would have been massaged through the data zones as a series of data flows to help produce a final dataset with insights that can be presented in a visual format.

- A **data scientist** typically consumes data to develop and build a model. By performing discovery or exploratory ad hoc analysis, the data scientist can iterate on their models to prove or disprove a hypothesis. Data scientists who build and test their models find utility in having access to complete datasets from the relevant part of the value chain for which they are interested. A data scientist is likely to write scripts in Python or other appropriate languages to further manipulate the data and generate engineered features.

- A **business analyst** may try to correlate multiple datasets together to manufacture an aggregated or holistic view of a scenario. A materialized view can be sliced and diced using transitional business intelligence approaches or other visualization tools. With self-service capabilities and tools, a business analyst can be given a data zone to curate data for their needs and take control of their own requirements. For example, a business analyst might need to investigate the impact of severe weather on projected sales. Based on historical data from public datasets and combined with in-house datasets from the data topology, the business analyst can search the data catalog to see what datasets have been cleansed and standardized and then run queries against that data.

- Another persona type is the **downstream system**, such as an application or another platform that receives either raw or refined data via an extract or an API. For example, if the downstream application is a database, a data zone can send the final aggregated data to the downstream system for subsequent processing.

Multi-Tenancy

With many persona types in an organization, *multi-tenancy* allows for one or more logical software instances to be created and executed on top of primary software. Multi-tenancy provides for multiple personas to work in a software environment at the same time, each with their own separate user interface, resources, and services.

A managed approach to data topology can help avoid the need for separate business units to sponsor discrete business-unit-owned data topology environments. A data topology should be established, from the onset, with multi-tenancy in mind. A multi-tenancy topology will exhibit characteristics that can address overarching integrity through lineage, contextual use/understanding, metadata, and any transformations that have been applied.

- Tracking the source and lineage of any data loaded into the data topology provides traceability. The lineage can help an organization determine where the data came from, when the data came to the data topology, how many records were contained in the data, and if the dataset was created from other datasets. These details help establish accountability and can be used to perform impact analysis on the data.

- Context can be attributed to the data if the purpose for which the data was collected is tracked and augmented with any employed sampling strategies or business glossary entries. Collecting provenance and context can provide productive alternative types of insight during the analytical lifecycle as users seek to derive insights from the actual data.

- Each time new data is loaded into a data zone from the same source, an operational metadata entry should be produced. Operational metadata would also apply as a means to record any changes from the original data that have been introduced via an update. If a large organization had many retail stores and each retail store had many point-of-sale terminals, any upgrades would likely take place over a period of days or weeks. During the transition period, a data zone could receive mixed formats. Some might be associated with the old terminals, and the others might be associated with the upgrade. Keeping track of the versions and the metadata is part of the logging.

- As changes occur, operational metadata should track when the data was changed, by whom, and by what method the change was accomplished.

- Driving transformations through the use of metadata (such as the technique of using a decision table) can significantly help with streamlining. Transformations may involve converting data from one format to another. For example, machine learning algorithms are easier to assemble when working on a completely denormalized record.

- While performing a transformation is a necessity when producing refined data, the type of transformation should subsequently be discoverable. Tracking the data lineage should also expose how individual fields were transformed.

- Managing all of the metadata requires an independent metadata data store. The data store should be able to manage all forms of metadata, including business metadata, technical metadata, and operational metadata.

Within an integrated data management platform, multi-tenancy can make upgrading software easier as a central application or codebase can be updated instead of multiple instances needing to be updated, and the changes can be made instantly available to all users. Additional layers can also be incorporated to provide for customizations while still maintaining an underlying codebase that can remain constant for all users. Multi-tenancy can also benefit because dedicated resources are not required to be reconfigured after an upgrade has taken place.

FEATURE ENGINEERING

Integrated data management is iterative. Some facts are derived later. In AI, feature engineering is an example of a fact that may be determined only after the original data has been cataloged, organized, prepared, provisioned, etc.

A number of different techniques can be used in feature engineering and may include the following:

- Interpolation and extrapolation

- Binning

- Logarithm transformation

- One-hot encoding

- Grouping and aggregating

- Splitting

- Scaling

Techniques for interpolation and extrapolation involve generating additional or missing values between data points and can help to avoid having to drop entire records. Adding missing values can affect the performance of machine learning models. For interpolating or extrapolating values, determining whether you want to preserve a uniform distribution, use an acceptable min/max value, or use the most frequently occurring value are options that you can consider.

With binning, data is created to help improve the data groupings to avoid small observation errors. Binning can make the model more robust and prevent overfitting. Logarithm transformation is a common mathematical transformation in feature engineering as it helps to address skewed data. Log transforms also help to decrease the impact of outliers on the model.

One-hot encoding is a method to spread values that exist in a single column and *pivot* to multiple flag columns and then to assign the flag columns with a value of 0 or 1. The binary values are used to express the relationship between the grouped and encoded columns. For example, if a column contained the values *right* and *wrong*, two flag columns would be created, one for each value in the column. The binary values assigned to the flag columns would uniquely be associated with the original values.

When datasets are orderly and consistent, they can be referred to as being *tidy* and have an affinity to Chapter 4's, "A Look Back on Analytics: More Than One Hammer," discussion on third normal form. Many transactional datasets can be untidy as the transactional values are discrete, and the data is often organized to aid the collection of data rather than its analysis. The use of grouping and aggregation can help to make certain facts conform and improve ML results.

Splitting features by extracting discrete parts can be beneficial for machine learning. Split features can improve binning and grouping and can help to improve the overall performance of a model through uncovering hidden information. Splitting may also prove useful for dates or times by splitting a date into month, day, and year features and splitting a time into hour, minute, and second features.

Numerical features within a dataset are not expected to have consistent ranges. It would not be normal for a person's age and their income to have the range. By applying a scaling process, the ranges would be comparable and useful to machine learning.

NOTE   For more information about tidy datasets, see Hadley Wickham's article "Tidy Data" in the *Journal of Statistical Software*, vol. 59, no. 10, August 2014.

Summary

This chapter identified how the pyramid for data, information, knowledge, and wisdom could provide the logic to understand the separation between data and information, followed by the necessary contexts for knowledge and wisdom. The pyramid helps to shape why information architectures are developed rather than wisdom architectures.

To support knowledge and wisdom, the use of multiple versions of the truth helps to promote curated data stores for personalization and organizational efficiencies. But to ensure integrity, data governance is required to make the information architecture plausible.

The use of an integrated data management platform must also provide a basis to provide a practical environment for which to deploy the information with considerations for onboarding data, data preparation, data cataloging, metadata support, provisioning, and organizing data along with the support for multi-tenancy. Data should be deliberately organized so as to turn as much *data* as possible into *information*. Information becomes the natural bedrock to insight and to driving *knowledge*-based decision-making and *wisdom*-based action.

In the next chapter, various organizational needs are accessed for addressing democratized and nondemocratized data for purposes of performing analytics and AI that support prediction, automation, and optimization.

Valuing Data with Statistical Analysis and Enabling Meaningful Access

*"There are thousands of ways to mess up or damage
a software project, and only a few ways to do them well."*
—Capers Jones

Applied Software Measurement: Global Analysis of Productivity and Quality

A business organization is not set up to be egalitarian. Certainly, when it comes to social interactions in the workplace, we should always show respect and be courteous to everyone. But organizationally, distinct roles and areas of responsibility require that boundaries be set. Regarding data access, organizational boundaries dictate appropriate permissions and privileges for each employee, determining what can be known and what can be acted on.

This chapter introduces approaches for accessing data determined by your role and responsibility. This includes data that has been valued and intentionally democratized or data that, by design, is not intended to be used as a democratized asset. Performing analytics and artificial intelligence (AI) drives the need for accessing data that is in direct support of the organizational demands for prediction, automation, and optimization.

Deriving Value: Managing Data as an Asset

While data, information, knowledge, and wisdom (DIKW) (discussed in Chapter 7, "Maximizing the Use of Your Data: Being Value Driven") addresses the formation of a value chain, each point in each chain should be measurable so as to demonstrate value. If the data is to be regarded or treated as an asset, you'll want to apply some type of metric to the asset. Each point in the value chain is an asset in its own right. Return on investment (ROI) is often a default measure of value for organizations.

The purpose of calculating an ROI is to measure, per period, the rates of return on money that has been invested or spent. Using an ROI in casual business conversation is often a means to justify a *qualitative* benefit over a *quantified* measure. Calculation of an ROI can be lax, reflecting a sentiment that the ROI expresses a generalization rather than a definitive measure.

NOTE   Return on investment is calculated as:

(**current value of an investment − the cost of investment**) / **the cost of investment.**

For example, suppose $1,000 was invested in some machine learning algorithms. One year later, the algorithms had generated $1,200 in new client sales. To calculate the ROI, the profits ($1,200 − $1,000 = $200) would be divided by the investment cost ($1,000), for an ROI of 20 percent, or $200/$1,000.

Alternatively, $2,000 could have been invested in monitoring and remediating bias in AI models. Three years later, monitoring and remediation helped to generate $2,800 in additional client sales. The ROI on the monitoring and remediation software would be 40 percent, or ($2800 − $2000)/$2,000.

While the second investment yields a higher percentage, when averaged on a per-year basis, the return is 13.3 percent (40 percent/3 years). This would make the first investment more valuable. ROI is used in this type of *lax* manner when time frames and other indirect costs are ignored.

Another type of measurement is *return on assets* (ROA). ROA is a metric that can be used to provide an indication as to how efficiently assets are helping to generate earnings. ROA is calculated by dividing an organization's annual earnings by its total assets. As with an ROI, an ROA is presented as a percentage.

In the era of advanced analytics, organizations will want to demonstrate tangible benefits from using data to drive efficiencies through predicting outcomes, providing automation, furthering the optimization of resources, increasing earnings, or expanding presence or market share. Stating the derived value from data should be formalized in a measurement. A *return on data assets* (RDA) is one such measure.

RDA can be used as a measure for how efficiently an organization is able to generate gains from its data corpus or inventory of data. Because data is inert, data cannot derive its own value. Data cannot be associated with value generation without a deliberate means to provide insight that can be acted upon (value) for the organization.

The term for information within the data topology that is not accessed, or for information that has been rendered inaccessible, is *dark data*. Dark data is a cost to an organization and yields no value. Additionally, not all data is created equal. This means that certain preserved facts contribute more heavily toward an outcome than other preserved facts. For instance, the date of a customer's last placed order is likely to yield more value to an organization than the middle initial of a customer's name.

Calculating the value of a data asset can be complicated and potentially made more complex by the fact that not all data is created equal, but also because the value of data can change along its value chain. Exposing a formal data value chain can be a good starting point to establish asset values for data (as well as the data's accompanying metadata).

Along the data value chain, data is part of a lifecycle, and each point in the lifecycle represents a tangible resource for the organization. Assessing the data's value is one thing, but knowing how to grow that value can be another organizational challenge altogether. While data has value, data is also a cost and accrues ongoing costs.

The often-used analogy between data and crude oil illustrates how both materials can be used for a diversity of applications as the respective materials are refined and gain in value over the original value of the base raw product. The comparison also brings to the forefront that, like oil, data needs to be considered a tangible asset and be measured as such.

To create value, data typically goes through many steps, from ingestion to integration and from correlation to consumption. The aspect of consumption is where the analogy between data and oil falters as data is an asset that is not depleted upon consumption. Data is an asset that is not depleted upon consumption. Data can be eternal, and while an organization may be able to control certain aspects of the data's longevity, digital derivatives can persist without incurring generational loss outside the auspices and control of the organization.

NOTE   Generational loss is a degradation in the quality or atomicity of data between subsequent copies of data. Techniques such as aggregation and compression can reduce the granularity or the overall quality when making a derivative copy, but a derivative that represents an exact copy would not be subject to generation loss.

As an asset, data is fully reusable versus being depletable or renewable. However, over time, data can be subject to a type of decay, which means that given a current context, the values are no longer representative. In all cases, it's the reusability of data as an asset that enables data to participate in a value chain. Understanding the value chain is crucial to building an information architecture that provides an organization with the capability to continually solve business problems with agility, scalability, and AI. As shown in Figure 8-1, smarter data science incrementally adds to the value of data, and every step in the data value chain is vital. While the quality of data does not have to be pristine, a lack of quality can place a negative impact on the value or even negate all value.

ATTENTION TO DETAIL

For instance, the failure and ultimate destruction of NASA's Mars Climate Orbiter in 1999 resulted from a data quality issue. One team of engineers used imperial measurement units while another engineering team used the metric system. The discrepancy resulted in an outcome that generated zero value.

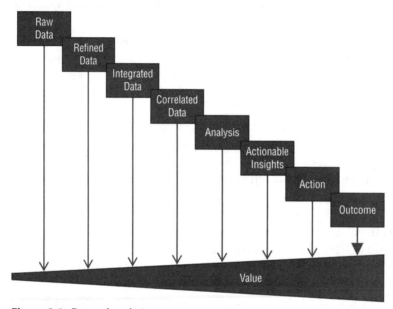

Figure 8-1: Data value chain

As a raw material, an intriguing aspect of data is that value can be derived from another organization's data (raw material) and, in some cases, without the need to purchase usage rights or be associated with the normal costs that are attributed to internal data generation.

A use of a data topology can help with providing a general map (vis-à-vis the zone map) for the value chain to overlay. As just explained, not all data zones would need to be organizationally internal data assets. A data zone can, for example, cover external data that is virtualized by the organization. Here, the use of virtualization ensures the external data remains in place and is not formally copied or replicated into another data zone.

NOTE   Virtualized data is data that can be accessed from a source without needing to first relocate it.

The value chain implies that value is further increased by harvesting and processing data that can be repurposed. As such, derivative data products from the raw material are likely to be materialized, and those materialized assets are likely to be incorporated into a data zone that is internal to the organization.

All data sources, internal or external, need to be discoverable, located, and evaluated for cost, coverage, and quality. The ingest pipeline, or data flow, is fundamental to enabling reliable operation throughout the entire data topology, especially as the data flows from one data zone to another. There are diverse file formats and network connections to consider, as well as considerations around frequency and volume.

Following ingestion, the data can be refined. Refinement can condition the data and make it generally usable for the organization. Later, the data can also be transformed into a format that facilitates reuse, or the data can be curated in a manner that provides efficiency through personalization to individuals or teams across the organization.

Distributed storage provides many options for persisting data over the data topology, along with the choice of format or database technology in a leaf zone. The choice of format or technology is often influenced by where in the value chain the data is likely to reside and be consumed. For example, certain formats and technologies are chosen for operational uses versus those that are made for analytics and AI.

Increasing the value in data can often be achieved by combining a variety of data sources together to search for new or previously obscured facts or insights. Integration is a nontrivial but valuable step in the value chain and enables correlation processes to occur. Analytics is dependent on every other step in the value chain.

Data scientists often spend more time in the earlier stages of the value chain because the data is not readied for their activities. The results of advanced analytics and the data that is exposed to the organization's users represent a final point-in-time step in deriving interim value from data. The value does not have to dissipate as the data itself has not been depleted.

> **NOTE** Time can change the value of data. For example, a real-time stock price has a certain point-in-time value. The immediacy of the price can be used by an AI model to make an immediate buy or sell decision. That same data point (price) if consumed a year later does not carry the same weight (value) in making a buy or sell decision. This is why historical stock price data only reflects a given day's opening price, closing price, intraday high, and intraday low. All of the other prices no longer hold the same value as when they reflected the real-time point in time.

Each insight can be evaluated and acted upon. The outcomes that are a result of the action also produce data points that can be fed back into the chain to further improve the value of the data asset.

A decision not to act is also a type of action that can be recorded for feedback. The feedback for nonaction can be used to understand why an action was not taken. The data point could be useful for future understanding and optimization.

As organizations grow their data estates and add to their AI capabilities, evaluating the asset value must be performed so as to ensure an organization can accelerate the means to increase the value of data. Developing a standard RDA metric could prove a useful measure.

> **NOTE**   A data estate is a broad concept and can represent a collection of data storage locations that natively occur across the data topography of cloud, fog, and mist computing.

The data valuation chain can help illuminate how raw data begets many intermediate forms as it is collected, processed, integrated, correlated, and transformed with context to produce actionable insights, which can lead to an action with a discernible and measurable outcome.

An Inexact Science

Valuing the data asset may be an inexact science due to a multitude of reasons. The data's value can increase or decrease as it moves through the data valuation chain. For example, knowing a customer's home address can have a certain value. However, should the customer no longer reside at that home address, the data may have less value if the current home address remains unknown. If both the old address and the current address are known, additional value can be derived through a better understanding of the longitudinal aspects of the customer.

> **NOTE**   Longitudinal data provides the ability to track or understand observations for an entity, such as a person, over time. This might include a person's home address over time. Does the address remain the same, or does the address change?

In this regard, data is measured on a value-based system with regard to the potential value on business action that can be taken. As data progresses through the chain, the value increases or decreases in relation to the ability to act and the end-product value. Data's valuation can depend on where in the chain the data actually lies. Separating the intermediate value of a data asset from the overall value of a completed chain can vary from one chain to the next. Correlating multiple datasets can be worth much more than the linear sum of their combined individual values.

A machine learning or statistical model can exponentially increase the value of a data source, but valuing such analysis must also be predicated on the type of action and the expected outcome.

The valuation of the chain must be completed to aid in realizing the value from the data. In economics, goods can be described as being rivalrous because the consumption of a good can prevent others from consuming the same good. As data is not depleted, the data itself is nonrivalrous.

The initial costs of manufacturing data as a raw material can be expensive, but the marginal costs can decline as the data is refined and flows across the data topology. Deriving value from data can be risky when the value of any resulting business action and outcome is not definite. Quantifying that risk for the data's value can also be difficult.

The same raw data can be a common origination point for multiple value chains. As with the analogy to crude oil, the oil goes through a value chain with the intent of producing a viable product. However, crude oil has a relatively small number of possible end products whose market values are well defined and that are driven by the demand and supply in the global market.

Raw data has the potential to have an indefinite number of possible end-product uses. Each end-product for data can depend on the user and intention and purpose for which the data can be applied, all of which are subject to change over time and possibly frequently.

A retailer may decide to use aggregated GPS information to ascertain which location to use for a store expansion initiative but could subsequently use the same GPS information to determine efficiencies for offering in-home delivery to customers. This can make it difficult to value data in monetization terms through income-based methods. The number of possible uses of data—and, therefore, the potential income associated with the data—can change drastically.

Ultimately, the valuation chain could be completed only to result in yielding no value at all. In economics, goods are viewed as transparent because the buyer typically knows what they are getting before they agree to purchase a good. Data and other information goods can be deemed experience goods. With experience goods, value may not be fully determined until after the goods have been used.

Many different data chains can be established from the same original raw data. As previously noted, persisted data is not a resource that is depleted, and in addition, the data is nonsubtractable. *Nonsubtractable* means that the use of data does not detract from being applied to other uses. You could use the same data source for multiple forms of analytics and decisions by many different users. So, the value of data may prove highly variable across multiple uses.

While regulations such as the General Data Protection Regulation (GDPR) may limit or even prevent data access for subsequent business purposes, many data assets can continue to be disseminated for additional decision-making.

Different valuation chains might require different levels of data quality. Data quality is multidimensional and can be measured using different means such as accuracy, completeness, breadth, latency, granularity, etc. Different types of analytics may require different levels of quality for each dimension. Data that is regarded as being high-quality data for one use may be regarded as being low-quality data for another use. For example, stock exchange data that has been cleansed and has had its outliers removed may be extremely valuable to long-term financial modelers but inappropriate for data scientists working in the area of fraud detection.

Raw data from completely different sources could provide the same insight and result in the same business actions. While data fuels key business processes and decisions, where the actual data came from is often less important than the actual insight provided. GPS data that is aggregated by telephone providers could provide information on population density that can guide decisions about where to locate a new store, but satellite photographs could potentially provide comparable information.

The derivable value from a data source depends not only on its potential end use but also on whether a substitute data source can be made available. The alternative data source may have differing cost factors as well.

The purpose of providing analytics to an organization is to provide value to the business by serving the organizational analytical delegates. From an analytical user perspective, the following factors are important to understand or to discover:

- The type of content that is accessible
- The level of data quality regarding the accessible data
- The profile of the data that is accessible
- The business metadata, technical metadata, and operational metadata associated with accessible data
- The means by which self-service is available to enrich, cleanse, enhance, and aggregate the accessible data
- The means by which to annotate and tag the accessible data

In this context, accessible data implies the range of data a single user has permission to consume. What data is accessible can vary by user, and being able to understand or discover each of the preceding items is dependent on the information architecture along with the provisioning of unified data governance and the appropriate security rules.

FROM THE BEGINNING

Fat fingering—a situation that occurs when you mistakenly press an unintended key on your keyboard—has caused more than a few people to generate a devastating faux pas. In one such incident, Japan's government reprimanded the Tokyo Stock Exchange and one of the biggest brokerage firms in the country after a fat-fingered error by an employee from Mizuho Securities caused the company to lose more than 40 billion yen on a stock trade. The ripple effect from the fat fingering caused the Nikkei index to drop significantly and forced the president of the Tokyo Stock Exchange to resign.

The trouble started when Mizuho sold 610,000 shares at the price of 1 yen. The Mizuho employee had actually intended to sell 1 share at 610,000 yen. The error represented a sales order that was 41 times larger than the number of outstanding shares (Fackler, Martin. "President of Tokyo Stock Exchange Resigns." *The New York Times*, December 21, 2005).

Although Mizuho attempted to cancel the order, the stock exchange had a policy not to cancel transactions even when they are executed in error. However, with a reasonable set of controls surrounding the data entry process, the data could have been better managed to avoid a negative consequence. Managing data as an asset begins the moment the data is created.

Accessibility to Data: Not All Users Are Equal

In previous chapters, we noted that not all data is created equal; certain data will yield significantly more benefit to the organization than other pieces of data. Aspects of inequality can also apply to other organizational assets, including employees. Because an organization designates that each employee is given a discrete set of roles and responsibilities, we can infer that the data privileges afforded to each employee might also vary from one employee to the next; *not all employees are created equal.*

By virtue of each unique role and responsibility, there can be a shift in what information an employee is entitled to view or manipulate and what information they are not entitled to view or manipulate. Curated data stores, as discussed in Chapter 7, can be a means to ensure an employee not only receives the data they are entitled to use but also receives it in a format that promotes work efficiencies.

Furthermore, what data is made accessible to one user and what data is made available to another user can impact derived insights. While it is easy to understand that through implemented security measures a single user should see only what they are entitled to see, how business results can be impacted can be a little bit more subtle.

Suppose a data zone has three datasets: Dataset A, Dataset B, and Dataset C. If one user has access to all three datasets and another user has access to only two of the datasets, different results (or insights) can be gained or lost depending on the privilege to access. If both users need to correlate data, a scenario could play out in this manner:

- User 1 has permission to access Dataset A, Dataset B, and Dataset C. In Dataset A is a record for Eminem. Dataset B has a record for Marshall Mathers, and Dataset C has a record for Slim Shady. When correlating the three datasets, Dataset C has the requisite data points that enable combining all three persons together as a single individual. The result is a single person record with three name aliases.

■ If User 2 does not have permission to access Dataset C, the ability to correlate some of the data between Dataset A and Dataset B is lost. The result is two distinct person records with no known aliases. There is now a true sense of irony to the question, "Will the real Slim Shady please stand up?"

While accessibility to data is always in accordance with security and permission, accessibility has another dimension in terms of whether the information is accessed on your behalf or whether the data can be self-accessed.

HIDDEN BY NECESSITY

Security necessities can drive the need to establish a mixed-box model management for AI. For certain employees, the model will be managed as a white box, and each feature will be identifiable and observable. For others, the model will be managed as a black-box model where only the inputs and the outputs can be observed.

A black-box model is not risky by default, but a black box can raise governance and ethics questions. Whether a corporate organization chart is designed around functional themes, divisional themes, matrixed, or flat, not all information is fully shared all of the time. For instance, a public entity will carefully guard *numbers* associated with quarterly performance prior to public announcements to prevent insider trading. Likewise, a model may use features that are not broadly shareable outside their use within a model that is broadly shared.

Providing Self-Service to Data

Self-accessed or self-service implies that either a technical professional or a nontechnical business user can access and analyze data without involving others from an IT department. Self-service means that all users can—regardless of their job responsibilities—access data without the need for formal assistance from an IT department. Data scientists and citizen data scientists alike are trusted with the tools to achieve their mission within the organization.

In a self-service model, users gain access to the metadata and data profiles to aid them in understanding each attribute or feature in a dataset. Captured metadata should provide enough information for users to establish new data formats from existing data formats, using a combination of enrichment and analytics.

The data catalog is a foundational tool for users to discover data or to discover machine learning models. Users should also be able to look for any kind of feature. Examples include searching across a timeframe such as February 1 to February 28 and searching on a subject area such as marketing or finance. Users should also be able to locate datasets based on included features, such as finding datasets than contain features for a 30-year bond or a feature that contains a percentage.

Discovery should also include the means to uncover data based on classification, quality levels, the data's lineage, the model's provenance, which assets have been enriched, or which are in need of enrichment. Cognitive-driven discovery would also enable the recommendation of assets to further aid the users in driving insights.

The accumulation of business metadata, technical metadata, and operational metadata is critical for maintaining a data catalog. Users may also want to see the historical activity for all of the ingested data. If a user is looking at streamed data, a search might be conducted for days when no data came into an organization. The intent of the user would be to ensure that those days are not included in the representative datasets for campaign analytics. Overall, access to data lineage, the ability to perform quality checks, and view ingestion history can yield a good sense of the data, so users can begin their analytic tasks.

A catalog is essential for maximizing the accessible data in the data topology. The data topology represents an enterprise-grade approach to data management as the data topology is not necessarily constrained to serving just one aspect of the organization. In support of self-service, the catalog also needs to provide an enterprise-grade view. As organizational users collaborate, a catalog can leverage credentials so that collaboration can be meaningful by applying data protection policies to protect sensitive data through either redaction or the anonymization of data and to ensure controlled access.

AVOIDING VAGUE OR AMBIGUOUS METADATA

Metadata is vital to enable self-service. All too often descriptions that are created for metadata are overly concise and terse and may prevent a thorough understanding. Lackluster definitions can contribute to misused features or to ignoring features.

A description for a customer might read "a person or organization that buys goods or services." While the description is not necessarily wrong, it is probably incomplete. As stated, the definition limits the concept of a customer to being solely attributed to the person who physically procures a good or service. Within an organization, that could be a person from the purchasing department who arranges the purchase on behalf of the organization. The description, as stated, misses the aspect of the person or organization that actually consumes the good or service.

An organization is likely to have internal customers as well as external ones. There will be customers who purchase and customers who receive. There will be customers who request a need and ones that articulate a need. While some customers will act as a proxy for the actual customer.

A customer is a type of relationship between people or organizations. The nature of the relationship often gets lost in a short definition. Many definitions recorded in metadata are intentionally dumbed down to try to be universally correct to every faction of the organization as a whole. Extreme generalization can work against those seeking to self-serve.

Access: The Importance of Adding Controls

When providing various users with the tools they need, security over the data remains a critical capability. Setting and consistently enforcing the security policies is essential for the long-term viability of the data supported through the information architecture. Security features should not be restricted to the consumption data but also include the data zones that might be exclusively used for data preparation and data enrichment.

Because data scientists may need more flexibility, with less formal governance, an exploration and discovery data zone is often established for them. In general, data scientists must be practiced in the management of sensitive data. A data catalog should be able to indicate data that is sensitive, but don't assume that the catalog is always used. Data must always remain tightly controlled.

With security policies in place, users should have access only to the datasets assigned to their security profile or level of privilege. However, because the data afforded a data scientist may be untethered or unmonitored, the data may be susceptible to leakage.

Data leakage is the distribution of private or sensitive data to someone who is not authorized to view the data. The delivery of leaked data can be unintentional. Data from the discovery and exploration data zone can be vulnerable to leakage, especially if a data scientist is given open access to that data.

Data leakage can be exacerbated by the fact that data might not follow the data flows indicated by the data topology for both inbound and outbound data. An information architecture must ensure that data flows do not go unregulated and unmonitored.

The adverse consequences of a data leakage incident can be classified as a direct loss or an indirect loss. Direct losses are generally tangible and can be easy to measure or estimate quantitatively. Indirect losses are associative and may be more difficult to access in terms of cost, place, and time. A direct loss can include violations of regulations resulting in fines to the organization, settlements or customer compensation fees, litigation involving lawsuits, loss of future sales, costs of investigation, and remedial or restoration fees. Indirect losses can include reduced share prices for publicly traded companies as a result of negative publicity, damage to an organization's goodwill and reputation, customer abandonment, and the potential exposure of intellectual property.

Access controls also enable collaboration. For example, a user might find a dataset that is important to a project and be able to interactively share findings with other colleagues, while in turn those colleagues provide various enrichments.

While many controls are enacted top-down through security and data governance, certain usage can be garnered in a bottom-up approach as well.

LYING

Invariably, an AI model will have access to a large corpus. Ultimately, the model can know and infer. Ask a chatbot a question, "Am I under an investigation for committing internal fraud?" And, what should be the answer, assuming that you are, in fact, being investigated for suspicious conduct regarding fraudulent acts? Should it be "yes"?

As part of the overall approach to controlled access, teaching an AI engine how to lie must become part and parcel of its capabilities. An answer that provides the information that you are not authorized to look at your own suspicious activity file would, in essence, be the equivalent of a "yes" answer. Therefore, contexts exist for a chatbot to provide answers that are contrary to what it knows.

Ranking Datasets Using a Bottom-Up Approach for Data Governance

The bottom-up approach to data governance enables the ability to rank the usefulness of datasets by asking users to rate the value of a given dataset. The ranking can greatly assist cognitive-driven discovery capabilities that are used to further recommend assets.

An ability to rate a dataset leverages crowdsourcing techniques from an internal group of users. Internal-based crowdsourcing can help to establish a preferred source to access data rather than being directed to the source via top-down governance.

Tools are required to help create new data models from existing datasets. An example is taking a customer dataset and a transaction dataset to create a customer dataset based on predictions for total lifetime customer value (LCV). Performing these types of enrichments and transformations is important in providing a holistic framework for delivering advanced analytics, especially by the citizen data scientist, regardless of their associated industry.

DATA QUALITY APPLIES

A ranking system can stymie teamwork and favor a competitive work environment. Some may choose to use a ranking system to demonstrate their productivity by ranking as many datasets as possible. Some may worry that by not ranking assets, they may be flagged as a low performer. As with all types of data, information, and metadata, quality plays a vital role in ranking. Any information gathered for ranking must become subject to a data quality assessment.

How Various Industries Use Data and AI

In Chapter 7, we discussed how design choices can be influenced based on your understanding of the value of data and the value chain for serving different points of the business, e.g., order intake versus order fulfilment versus order completion, etc. Across different industries, within an industry, and across the different lines of business, products, services, and customers, the orientation as to what types of models can provide significant business impact can vary.

As a common foundation, an information architecture can prove to be an enabler for providing value for many different vertical industries that seek to benefit from AI. Here are some examples:

- Healthcare providers can maintain millions of records for millions of patients, encompassing structured, semistructured, and unstructured data from electronic medical records, radiology images, and doctors' notes. Leveraging advanced analytics can be performed to enable payments, mitigate instances of fraud, predict readmissions, and help frame future coverage. Raw data helps preserve the data in an untampered state, and lifecycle management practices enable data offloading after a prescribed period of time.

- Financial service organizations must comply with various fiscal regulations depending on the country in which they operate. The data zones can aid reconciliation, settlement, and regulatory reporting.

- Retail banking also has important use cases where advanced analytics can help reduce first-party fraud, anti-money laundering (AML), and other financial crimes.

- Retailers can help improve the customer experience by positioning the correct products to up-sell and cross-sell. Advanced analytics can be used to provide timely offers and incentives.

- Governments can help improve citizen experiences by ensuring that citizens receive the services they need when they need them.

- Telephone companies can seek to reduce churn and to also understand the demographic concentration of certain areas by monitoring call times and call durations. Cellular companies can detect cell tower issues by associating dropped calls.

- Manufacturers are always sensitive to increasing efficiency. By using designated data zones to serve as a gateway between connected devices and the Internet of Things (IoT), AI can help to provide predictive analytics to connect factories and optimize the supply chain.

In each of the industry use cases, there are likely to be outliers and exceptions. Statistics can provide the requisite insight to fine-tune AI models or, with the establishment of a series of ensemble models, to create a desirable outcome.

BOUNDARIES

Every organization must be able to understand the boundaries of its own enterprise, which can affect the information architecture and data topologies that are laid out. The boundaries of the enterprise can be impacted by the industry in which the enterprise plays—whether for regulatory, competitive, or other reasons.

In the gig economy, does an organization include the workforce as part of the enterprise or simply part of a broader ecosystem? Should the ecosystem be tightly or loosely coupled into the architecture? Does the ecosystem just represent a legal divide to the enterprise rather than an operational one? For an organization with many subsidiaries and each operating as independent companies, what does the notion of an enterprise mean? Can an enterprise be decomposed to where, a level down, another enterprise is revealed? Where is the natural boundary for an enterprise?

At any point in time, boundaries affect what can be known and what is knowable. Boundaries serve to affect approaches practitioners make toward establishing an information architecture. Allowing for shifting boundaries should be a principal tenet when approaching the creation of an information architecture for AI.

Benefiting from Statistics

As data will be accessed and used across the value chain and whether provisioned by IT or self-served, statistically interpreting the data can be beneficial. Not only will statistics help you with how to rank a data asset, you'll also find ways that will provide greater insight into placing a value on the data too. And, depending on which industry you're working in, you may be oriented to specific statistical methods that you'll want to apply.

In statistics, a *normality test* is often used to determine whether the data reflects what could be considered a normal distribution. There are many statistical functions that are used in conjunction with AI that rely on the data's distribution to be regarded as being normal or nearly normal. Statistically, there are two numerical measures of shape that can be used to test for normality in data. These numerical measures are known as *skewness* and *kurtosis*.

Skewness represents a measure of symmetry or, more precisely, a measure that can represent the lack of symmetry. A distribution is symmetric if the data point plots look the same to the left and to the right of the center point. A *kurtosis* is used as a measure to show if the data is heavy-tailed or light-tailed, relative to a normal distribution.

As shown in Figure 8-2, there can be a positive skewness and a negative skewness. A fully symmetrical distribution has a skewness of zero, and the mean, mode, and median will share the same value.

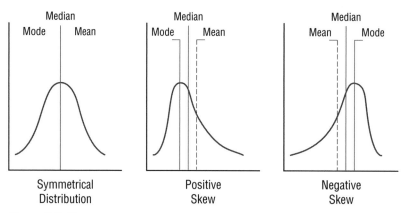

Figure 8-2: Skewness

The *mean* is the average number that is calculated by summing all of the values divided by the total number of values. So, the mean for the values 1, 10, 100, and 1000 would be 1111/4, which is equal to 277.8.

The *mode* is the most frequent value that occurs in a set of data. If the values for a given set are 1, 5, 2, 6, 2, 8, 2, and 34, the most frequently occurring value is 2. The number 2 as the most frequently occurring value can be readily seen should the values be sorted in ascending sequence: 1, 2, 2, 2, 5, 6, 8, 34.

In a list of sorted values, the *median* is the middle number. If our values are 1, 2, 3, 4, 5, 6, and 7, then the middle number is 4.

A positive skewness means that the tail on the right side of the distribution is longer, and the mode is less than both the mean and median. For a negative skewness, the tail of the left side of the distribution is longer than the tail on the right side, and the mean and the median are less than the mode. When calculating the skewness, know the following:

- A result that is between 0 and –0.5 (a negative skewness) means that the data is reasonably symmetrical.

- A result that is between –0.5 and –1.0 (a negative skewness) means that the data is moderately skewed.

- A result that is between –1.0 or higher (a negative skewness) means that the data is highly skewed.

- A result that is between 0 and +0.5 (a positive skewness) means that the data is reasonably symmetrical.

- A result that is between +0.5 and +1.0 (a positive skewness) means that the data is moderately skewed.

- A result that is between +1.0 or higher (a positive skewness) means that the data is highly skewed.

Suppose house prices ranged in value from $100,000 to $1,000,000, with the average house price being $500,000. If the peak of the distribution was to the left of the average value, this would mean that the skewness in the distribution was positive. A positive skewness would indicate that many of the houses were being sold for less than the average value of $500,000.

Alternatively, if the peak of the distributed data was to the right of the average value, that would indicate a negative skewness and would mean that more of the houses were being sold for a price higher than the average value of $500,000.

The other measure regarding the normality of the distribution is kurtosis. With kurtosis, a resulting value describes the tail of the distribution rather than the "peakedness." A kurtosis is used to describe the extreme values and is a measure of the outliers present within the distribution.

Data with a high kurtosis value is an indicator that the data has heavy tails or excessive outlier values. For AI, a high kurtosis might require a separate model to address the outliers to improve how a particular cohort is handed. A low kurtosis is an indicator that data has light tails or a lack of outliers. Potentially, you'll consider data with a low kurtosis preferable over a high kurtosis.

Figure 8-3 illustrates three types of kurtosis curves: leptokurtic, mesokurtic, and platykurtic.

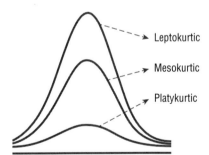

Figure 8-3: Kurtosis

Leptokurtic curves have a kurtosis value that is greater than 3. The leptokurtic distribution is longer with tails that are fatter. Additionally, the leptokurtic peak is higher and sharper than that of the mesokurtic curve, which means the data is heavy-tailed or has an abundance of outliers. Outliers cause the horizontal axis of a visual histogram graph to be stretched, which makes the bulk of the data appear within a narrow vertical range.

Mesokurtic distributions have a kurtosis statistic that is similar to that of the normal distribution and implies that the extreme values of the distribution are similar to that of a normal distribution characteristic. The mesokurtic distribution has a standard normal distribution and a kurtosis value of 3.

Platykurtic distributions are shorter, and their tails are thinner than the normal distribution. The peak is lower and broader than with the mesokurtic distribution. A platykurtic distribution means that data are light-tailed and have a lack of outliers. The lack of outliers in the platykurtic distribution is because the extreme values are less than that of the normal distribution.

Being able to calculate the skewness and kurtosis allows data scientists to create specialized models to handle certain portions of the data rather than through a single generalized model. The skewness or kurtosis calculation allows for specific data points to be identified. Figure 8-4 plots a data population that includes a number of extreme outliers.

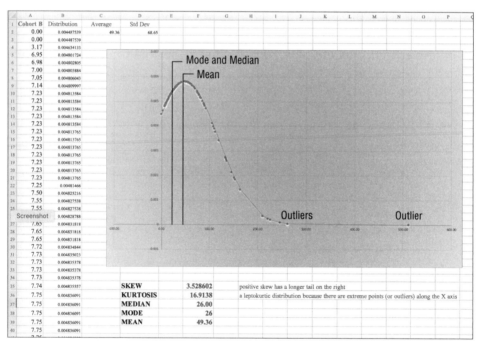

Figure 8-4: Identifying outliers

Understanding skewness and kurtosis means that a data scientist can more readily recognize that an answer to a question can more than likely yield a variety of acceptable answers. In preparing a model, the data scientist is not necessarily expecting one answer, but a range of all different options, and the distribution provides a tendency toward potential answers. This is especially useful when seeking to draw a conclusion about the population of data from a particular sample set.

While exploring various features for a model, data scientists must use statistics to infer values. Should a data scientist have access to a complete dataset, then an exact average known as the true mean can be calculated. If a sample is chosen at random rather than observed, then the expected mean could vary from the true mean. A sampling error is the difference between the sample mean and the true mean.

A standard error refers to the standard deviation of all the means. The sampling error shows how much the values of the mean of a bunch of samples differ from one another.

In Figure 8-4, column B is named "Distribution" and is the normal distribution value of the data in the column named "Cohort B." The distribution is associated to the shape the data has when represented as a graph. The bell curve that is calculated in the figure is one of the better-known distributions of continuous values. The normal distribution in the bell curve is also known as the *Gaussian distribution*.

The Python code shown in Figure 8-5 can create an idealized Gaussian distribution.

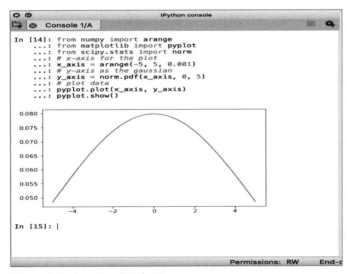

Figure 8-5: Gaussian distribution

In Figure 8-5, the x-axis represents the observations, and the y-axis shows the frequency of each observation. The observations around 0.0 are the most common, and observations around –5.0 and +5.0 are rare.

In statistics, many methods are dedicated to Gaussian type distributions. In many cases, business data that is used in conjunction with machine learning tends to fit well into a Gaussian distribution. But not all data is Gaussian, and non-Gaussian data can be checked by reviewing histogram plots of the data or using statistical tests. For example, too many extreme values in the data population can result in a distribution that is skewed.

Data cleansing can be used to try to remediate or improve the data. Cleansing activities may involve the need to remove all of the outliers. Outliers must be identified as special causes before they are eliminated. Normally distributed data often contains a small percentage of extreme values, and that can be expected to be *normal*. Not every outlier is caused by an exceptional condition. Extreme values should be removed from the data only if the extreme values are occurring more frequently than expected under normal conditions.

The collected data is referred to as a *sample*, whereas a population is the name given to all the data that could be collected:

- A *data sample* is a subset of observations from a group.

- A *data population* is all of the possible observations from a group.

The distinction between a sample and a population is important because different statistical methods are applied to samples and populations. Machine learning is more typically applied to samples of data. Two examples of data samples encountered in machine learning are as follows:

- The train and test datasets

- The performance scores for a model

When using statistical methods, claims about the population are typically inferred from using observations in a sample. Here are some examples:

- The training sample should be representative of the population of observations so that a useful model can be fitted.

- The test sample should be representative of the population of observations so that an unbiased evaluation of the model skill can be developed.

Because machine learning works with samples and makes claims about a population, there is likely to be some uncertainty. The `randn()` NumPy function in Python can be used to generate a sample of random numbers drawn from a Gaussian distribution. The mean and the standard deviation are two key parameters used for defining a Gaussian distribution.

The `randn()` function in Python can be used to generate a specified number of random numbers. The scenario shown in Figure 8-6 creates 100,000 random numbers drawn from a Gaussian distribution. The mean and standard deviation are scaled to 50 and 5. To prevent the histogram from appearing too blocky, the option "bins=140" has been added to the plot for the histogram.

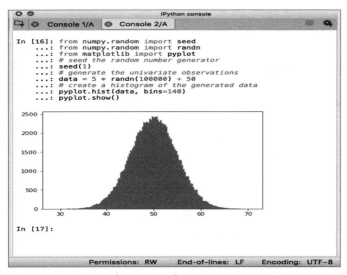

```
In [16]: from numpy.random import seed
    ...: from numpy.random import randn
    ...: from matplotlib import pyplot
    ...: # seed the random number generator
    ...: seed(1)
    ...: # generate the univariate observations
    ...: data = 5 * randn(100000) + 50
    ...: # create a histogram of the generated data
    ...: pyplot.hist(data, bins=140)
    ...: pyplot.show()
```

Figure 8-6: Gaussian histogram plot

The nonperfect curve results from the fact that the numbers were randomly chosen and that a degree of noise was introduced into the data sample. Noise is often expected in a data sample.

The central tendency of a distribution refers to the middle value in the distribution, which is the most likely value to occur in the set. In a Gaussian distribution, the central tendency is called the *mean* and is one of the two main parameters that define a Gaussian distribution. The mean of a sample is calculated as the sum of the observations divided by the total number of observations in the sample. In Python, the mean can be calculated as follows:

$$Result = mean(data)$$

The mean calculated from the random data sample in Figure 8-6 is 50.026 and is an estimate of the parameter of the underlying Gaussian distribution. As an estimate, the number is reasonably accurate, as the true mean would be 50.

The mean is influenced by outlier values, and the resulting mean may be misleading. With outliers or a non-Gaussian distribution, an alternative central tendency can be based on the median. The median is calculated by sorting all data and then locating the middle value in the sample. For an odd number of observations, this is quite straightforward. If there are an even number of observations, the median is calculated as the average of the middle two observations. In Python, the median can be calculated as follows:

$$Result = median(data)$$

The median calculated from the random data sample in Figure 8-6 is 50.030. The result is not too dissimilar from the mean because the sample has a Gaussian distribution. If the data had a non-Gaussian distribution, the median may be very different from the mean and could be a better reflection of the central tendency of the underlying population.

The *variance* in a distribution refers to how much, on average, the observations are varying or differing from the mean value. The variance measures the spread in the distribution. A low variance has values grouped around the mean and exhibits a narrow bell shape. A high variance has values that are spread out from the mean and produce a wide bell shape.

Figure 8-7 shows an idealized Gaussian with low and high variances. The taller plot is the low variance with values grouped around the mean, and the lower plot is the higher variance that has more spread. In Python, the variance can be calculated as follows:

$$Result = var(data)$$

The variance calculated from the random data sample in Figure 8-7 is 24.917. The variance of a sample drawn from a Gaussian distribution is calculated as the average squared difference of each observation from the sample mean.

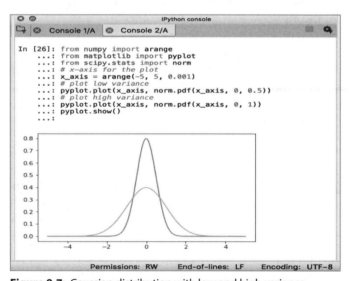

Figure 8-7: Gaussian distribution with low and high variance

When a Gaussian distribution is summarized, the square root of the variance is used. In this case, the square root of 24.917 would be 4.992. This is also called the *standard deviation* and is very close to the value of 5 that was used in the creation of the test samples shown in Figures 8-6 and 8-7. The standard deviation and the mean are required to specify a Gaussian distribution. In Python, the standard deviation can be calculated as follows:

$$Result = std(data)$$

In applied machine learning, the estimated skill of the model on the output-of-sample data results needs to be reported. The report often reflects the mean performance from a k-fold cross-validation, or some other repeated sampling procedure. When reporting, model skill reflects the summarization of the distribution of skill scores.

NOTE   Cross-validation is a resampling procedure that is used to evaluate machine learning models on a limited data sample. The resampling procedure has a single parameter called *k* that refers to the number of groups into which a given data sample can be split. Therefore, if k = 10, k-fold cross-validation becomes 10-fold cross-validation.

In addition to reporting the mean performance of the model, the median and the standard deviation should also be included along with the size of the sample.

MISAPPLIED

In his book *Chapters from My Autobiography*, 1907, North American Review, Mark Twain helped to popularize this sentiment: "There are three kinds of lies: lies, damned lies, and statistics."

Sam Savage, a consulting professor at Stanford, has illustrated how something as simple as an average can lead to misleading insights. Using a hypothetical life sciences company selling a perishable antibiotic, Savage described incurred costs when historically an average monthly demand has been 5,000 units.

One day, the boss appears. "Give me a forecast of demand for next year," he says to his product manager. "I need it to estimate inventory cost for the budget." The product manager responds, "Demand varies from month to month. Here, let me give you a distribution." But the boss doesn't want a "distribution." "Give me a number!" he insists. "Well," the manager says meekly, "the average demand is 5,000 units a month. So, if you need a single number, go with 5,000."

The boss now proceeds to estimate inventory costs, which are calculated as follows: If monthly demand is less than the amount stocked, the firm incurs a spoilage cost of $50 per unsold unit. On the other hand, if the demand is greater than the amount stocked, the firm must air-freight the extra units at an increased cost of $150 each. These are the only two costs that depend on the accuracy of the forecast.

The boss has developed a spreadsheet model to calculate the costs associated with any given demand and amount stocked. Since the average demand is 5,000 units, he plugs in 5,000. Since the company always stocks 5,000 units, the spreadsheet dutifully reports that for this average demand, the cost is zero: no spoilage or airfreight costs.

From "The Flaw of Averages" in *Harvard Business Review*
(hbr.org/2002/11/the-flaw-of-averages)

However, the use of a monthly average can miss the impact of fluctuations. The average cost won't be zero, and the company will incur costs as the demand for the antibiotic shifts up or down.

Summary

This chapter focused on the importance of and difficulties associated with providing a quantitative value for data. If an organization wants to treat data as an asset, then the asset needs to be given a valuation. The data value chain illustrated that value is not static, and depending on whether the data is in its raw state, refined, or correlated with other data assets, the value can change. Potentially, the value increases as the data moves through the data value chain.

Data is not always fully democratized, and differing security profiles mean that the value different users can extract from the data can also cause complications in the valuation of a data asset.

Data needs to be accessible, and to be accessible, the data must be discoverable. Data assets that are exposed through the use of a catalog also have the opportunity to support the self-service needs of an organization. The ability for datasets to be rated for usefulness can help steer self-service and further improve the benefits of providing a cataloging capability.

As an asset to the organization, data always needs to be protected and secured. The trust afforded to the data scientist can expose weaknesses in a security plan as data can be subject to leakage.

Statistical literacy, with a core facet being anchored to data awareness, helped to showcase how some fundamental statistical knowledge could promote a data scientist's awareness of results from machine learning and deep learning models. The awareness would come from identifying and addressing data that potentially falls outside that of a normal distribution.

In the next chapter, a number of issues that can serve to promote the long-term viability of an information architecture, as well as a deeper dive into data literacy, are explored.

Constructing for the Long-Term

"A design that doesn't take change into account risks major redesign in the future."
—Erich Gamma
Design Patterns: Elements of Reusable Object-Oriented Software

The metaphor surrounding the Ladder to AI involves a progressive climb to hone one's skills. But its real purpose is to ensure that artificial intelligence (AI) projects are not tackled tactically and independently as a relentless series of one-off enablements. For decades, IT shops have tried to undo the effects of siloed, standalone applications and databases: those applications that are not integrated—or readily integrated or even capable of integration—with other IT systems. The disintegration often places a burden on the enterprise in terms of cost and addressing new business requirements.

If data and AI efforts are tactically defined and deployed as independent efforts, they are likely to become disenfranchised and fractured. They will ultimately serve to place another IT burden on the enterprise. The Ladder to AI is ultimately a journey for technical continuity: driving sustainable business benefits from AI for short-term gains and long-term utility.

This chapter addresses a number of issues that can inhibit the long-term viability of an information architecture and AI. The goal is to help you achieve a program of smarter data science that can sustainably support mission-critical processes over time. An information architecture must promote across the enterprise full support for developing and driving insights derived from any type of data across disparate AI use cases. Although the use cases can be disparate, the means and the approach to the deployment should be uniform and additive.

The Need to Change Habits: Avoiding Hard-Coding

Hard-coding is a programming technique that often requires a change to a program's source code any time a characteristic from the outside world changes. In other words, the program code is so tightly correlated to the requirements of a business that the program code reflects an anchoring of the business to a point in time. When the correlation is so tightly coupled, a resulting ripple effect requires that changes be made to program code.

Hard-coding programming techniques can be prevalent across all aspects of preparing data associated with the data value chain discussed in the previous chapter: data ingestion, refinement, correlation, etc.

For example, many computer programs and their associated data stores that are written for users in the United States are written to support a single currency and a national identifier that is based on nine numerical digits. If another currency is added to the U.S. economy, such as a cryptocurrency, or the national identifier is extended or altered to allow alphabetic characters, many programs are likely to be negatively impacted.

The change to a computer program's source code may be for new logic, a new variable, a new value, a new length, and so on. The affinity or tight coupling between the programming style and the speed of business (with regard to change) manifests its own butterfly effect.

> **NOTE**   A butterfly effect is associated with chaos theory whereby a localized change in a complex system can result in large effects elsewhere.

Hard-coding is considered an anti-pattern and you should consider it to be highly undesirable. These days, the desire to hard-code programming logic is often used under the duress to meet a delivery date.

> **NOTE**   An *anti-pattern* is a response to a recurring problem that is often regarded as being ineffective, and the response risks being counterproductive in both the short and the long-term.

While today's practitioners occasionally delve into the dark art that is hard-coding, the practice is generally (and rightfully) frowned upon. As far back as the early 1970s, organizations such as the Association for Computing Machinery, an organization that dates back to the 1940s, published magazine articles that cried foul on the use of hard-coding techniques.

Mitigating the need to hard-code involves some level of abstraction and the use of techniques that can dynamically use a method to perform some variation of late binding.

> **NOTE** *Late binding* or *dynamic binding* refers to bindings that occur at the runtime of a program. Early or static binding refers to bindings that occur at the time that the computer program is compiled.

Overloading

To mitigate forced changes associated with data, some organizations have resorted to overloading. Take, for example, the International Organization for Standardization (ISO) currency codes standard: ISO 4217. As one might expect in an international standard that is titled currency codes, the standard provides a list of countries and their respective currencies—and is actively used by many international organizations. For purposes of financial reporting when revenues are collected in multiple currencies, an organization will use a currency exchange rate to convert from one currency to another. To eliminate the constant fluctuations in exchange rates, an organization might choose to use an accounting technique such as a constant currency to establish a fixed exchange rate for a given fiscal year.

> **NOTE** In programming, overloading refers to the ability to use a single identifier to define multiple methods that differ in their input and output parameters. Overloading is a concept used to avoid redundant code where the same method name is used multiple times but with a different set of parameters. In a data store, overloading is when a single field or feature has multiple meanings and the meaning is derived from determining the appropriate use.

Within the ISO 4217 standard, the United States is listed as using the U.S. dollar with an alphabetic currency code of USD. Each alphabetic currency code also has an accompanying numeric equivalency code. The numeric equivalency for USD is 840.

The country of El Salvador also uses the U.S. dollar. However, prior to 2002, El Salvador used a different currency called the Salvadoran colón. The colón was assigned the currency codes SVC and 222. The United Kingdom uses pound sterling as its currency. Pound sterling has the currency code GBP (for Great Britain Pound) and has 826 as the numeric equivalent code. Germany, Italy, France, and The Netherlands all use the euro, which has the currency code EUR and a numeric equivalent of 978. So far, so good.

Within ISO 4217, there is a currency code XXX with a numeric equivalent 999. XXX is a formal currency code that happens to represent *no currency* and *no country*. Another noncurrency code is XTS, which is reserved for some type of testing. Currency code XDR and the numeric equivalent 960 is also not a currency and is used by the International Monetary Fund (IMF) to exchange certain assets.

XBD is used by the European Unit of Account 17, which happens to be defunct. But when XBD was active, XBD represented a portfolio of selected currencies, much like the relationship between mutual funds and stocks.

Of significance to the computer science technique of overloading is the currency code XPT. XPT represents a metal: platinum. Platinum is not a currency and is certainly not the primary currency of any sovereign country. The ISO standard is overloaded in that it doesn't just represent currencies. ISO does maintain a side rule for overloading in that overloaded currency codes must start with X. As a rhetorical question, why are codes being overloaded in the currency codes table anyway?

If the cryptocurrency Bitcoin was given a currency code, would or should that start with an X or some other letter? Unofficially, Bitcoin has been assigned the currency code XBT. While the X indicates that XBT is not a traditional currency, this currency code does represent a currency in the form of a cryptocurrency.

While Bitcoin is not a sovereign-based currency (with the associated risk mitigation controls), most people are likely to regard Bitcoin as a currency, which means the ISO X designation and implied meaning could appear to be a little wishy-washy. Interestingly, the U.S. Internal Revenue Service (IRS) recognizes Bitcoin for purposes of taxation. The IRS taxes Bitcoin as though it were an asset and not as a currency. As an asset, taxes can be applied on any realized gains from exchanging the currency.

Locked In

A common worldwide business concept that can be used to showcase the dilemmas associated how hard-coding negatively locks you in is a vehicle identification number (VIN). VINs are attached to road vehicles such as cars and trucks. The modern 17-digit VIN uniquely identifies a particular vehicle but also contains information that describes the vehicle itself.

VINs are a global concept used by automobile manufacturers, insurance companies, government agencies, law enforcement agencies, vehicle distributors, banks, identification and credentialing verification service providers, and others.

The VIN structure was designated by the Society of Automotive Engineers (SAE) and is currently controlled by ISO. Therefore, a VIN is not owned by any particular community that has an actual business operation involved in creating or maintaining the number.

Historically, the VIN structure has never been outrightly stable. Prior to 1980, different manufacturers used different formats, and in October 1980, the SAE published a standard to guarantee unique numbers for a period of 30 years. Why 30 years? Back in 1980, 30 years and infinity *felt* closely linked, so 30 years seemed a sufficient duration of time. Today, generating a concept that has a limited or restricted lifespan is better understood to be shortsighted from a business perspective.

SIMPLE ISSUES MAY NOT ALWAYS BE SIMPLE TO MITIGATE

Y2K was another outcome of the hard-coding debacle involving data, where developers chose to save the last two digits of the Gregorian year instead of the full four digits. The choice was made to give the appearance of saving disk space, but other alternatives to preserve the full fidelity of the year without consuming more space were unilaterally ignored.

Soon after, the year 2000 the SAE was obliged to re-address its standard because, starting in 2010, automobile manufacturers would have been able to generate duplicate VIN numbers. Duplicate VIN numbers are unacceptable to many organizations, especially insurance companies and law enforcement agencies (for obvious reasons—it's problematic and a safety issue to law enforcement officers to have multiple vehicles on the road with the same number).

The 1980 VIN standard was organized around a 17-byte composite field. A composite field means that a concept is not atomically defined. While exploring options to revise the standard for 2010, the SAE discovered that extending the length of the VIN was not a viable option, not even by a single character or a single byte. The change in length was determined to be insurmountable.

An ensuing ripple effect of the originally proposed change to the computer program code halted a change from occurring in the real world. A substantial number of organizations were confronted with too many systems to change. The astronomical price tag associated with the remediation made a change far too expensive.

The resolution adopted by the SAE involved adjusting some of the embedded characteristics of the 17-byte composite field. The adjustment extended the VIN life span for only another 30 years. In the lingua franca of information technology, the SAE simply applied a "temporary patch." Ultimately, the VIN problem remains unresolved—a technology-centric time bomb that waits to disrupt organizations worldwide during the 2030s with a considerable expense.

Historically, whenever an organization's data administration group or data governance council would listen to the business need for something like a VIN, the analytical response was fairly quick and straightforward.

"So, you say we need a VIN. It's an identifier. Seventeen bytes long. Okay then. This is what'll we do. Call it "VIN_ID" and make it a 17-character string. Done. Next item..."

The result is a hard-coded concept with hard-coded characteristics—two things that are really difficult to change once a database-centric system has been built. Data scientists follow this type of practice for engineering features that go into a machine learning model.

Ownership and Decomposition

Many organizations fail to recognize that lots of business concepts, like VIN, are not owned or controlled by the organization. Other examples of data items that organizations don't directly control include person names, location addresses, dates of birth, national identifiers, etc. The list is long. There are dangers in designing to concepts that an organization cannot explicitly control. These are things that many data scientists, data stewards, data owners, and data governance councils have failed to adequately recognize.

Exacerbating this problem is the decomposable nature of certain types of data. A person's name can be decomposed into a first name, a middle name, and a last name. A last name, especially, can be further decomposed by cultural associations (paternal last name, maternal last name, and in which sequence, and so forth). Addresses can be decomposed into a house number, a street name, a town, a postal code, a county, a country, etc. Dates of birth can be decomposed into a day, a month, and a year.

VINs, as previously mentioned, are also decomposable. In fact, VINs have three levels of decomposition. The first level, or the root level of the VIN, is the VIN in its entirety—all 17 characters. The second level, or nonleaf level, has three elements: a 3-byte world manufacturer identifier, a 6-byte vehicle descriptor, and an 8-byte vehicle identifier section. The third level, or the VIN's leaf level, contains the country of origin, the manufacturer, various vehicle attributes, a check digit, the vehicle model year, the assembly plant, and a sequential number. For organizations that need to work with the decompositions, those too are often hard-coded.

Design to Avoid Change

People have often complained that traditional data design techniques used in operational and analytical systems use rigid and inflexible data structures. The complaint has always been aimed at the technology rather than the design technique itself.

Ultimately, the real problem has been with the *humans* who made the decisions to hard-code business concepts. One means of resolution is to use meta-driven techniques. All of the problems just mentioned can be avoided with techniques that avoid unnecessary hard-coding and that can still be leveraged by SQL and NoSQL users alike. While XML and JSON structures can make it easier to accommodate fluctuations in the dynamics of a business concept, the surrounding metadata to help make the dynamic truly understandable over time is often missing.

While the schema-less-write helps to avoid issues associated with hard-coding, the read side of the data needs to embrace methods to prevent breaking the analytics process when change does occur to the concepts persisted through data.

Importantly, any business concept and its representation within a data store should serve to help remove any inherent volatility within a concept. If a concept is subject to change over time, an alternative representation should be adopted to minimize or altogether remove the need to make any change to the data store or a program that processes the data store.

Additionally, with regard to future needs, how likely are new concepts going to be needed, and can the areas that might be affected be anticipated? Even if future needs are entirely unknown, understanding how the organization has historically changed over time can be leveraged to provide insights into the types of changes that may occur in the future.

Anticipating and accommodating change is the best way to protect the value of data as an asset.

OSAPI

OSAPI is a heuristic intended to assist in remediating how a business concept is developed for feature selection and long-term storage in a data zone. OSAPI (pronounced "oh-sap-ee") is an acronym for ownership, stability, abstraction, performance, and interfaced. These are five characteristics that you can interrogate to avoid any unnecessary hard-coding.

Each characteristic can be evaluated against a simple yes or no question. For every "yes" answer, a cumulative total would be incremented by 1. For every "no" response, the cumulative total would remain unchanged. If preferred, weightings can be added to the characteristics to accommodate different types of high-value or lower-value business data. The resulting cumulative total provides a score that can be compared to a cutoff point. At or below the cutoff point, it would be recommended to explore options to soften the hard-coding to mitigate any impacts from future business changes.

The characteristic *ownership* explores an organization's control over all aspects of an attribute or column. For example, dates, times, national IDs, etc., would not be owned by an organization. *Stability* inquires into the mutability of the feature's domain over time. *Abstraction* explores the degree of modeled generalization. For example, a last name is a concrete concept, and a party name that accommodates both people and organizations would be an abstract concept. *Performance* analyzes latency issues, and *interfaced* is used to look at how broadly a feature is shared across the organization.

The OSAPI questions are phrased as follows. The term *concept* covers elements, attributes, columns, fields, and features.

- **Ownership:** Is the concept owned, controlled, and governed by our organization?
- **Stability:** Has the domain set for the concept been stable over time (past, present, and the anticipated future)?
- **Abstraction:** Is the concept represented using an abstract representation?

- **Performance:** Does this concept have distinct performance requirements?
- **Interfaced:** Is this concept shared beyond this model, system, application, or topography?

The closer an OSAPI score is to zero, the stronger the recommendation is to mitigate certain aspects of hard-coding to the concept or to the values that are attributed to the concept.

Extending the Value of Data Through AI

Data is an asset—at least, that is the drumbeat message. Caesars Entertainment is a company that runs many casinos, including the world-famous Las Vegas casino Caesars Palace. In 2015, the company found itself inconvenienced by a messy bankruptcy case regarding allegations of deficient anti-money laundering controls.

Creditors fought for the most valuable of the individual company-owned assets, which turned out to be the data from the casino's Total Rewards data collection initiative (`ftalphaville-cdn.ft.com/wp-content/uploads/2014/12/1st-lien-complaint-1.pdf`). Figure 9-1 shows the conservative estimated equity value for assets, as listed in the bankruptcy documents.

Date of Transfer	Asset Transferred	Conservative Estimated Equity Value	Equity Value Attributed	Equity Valuation Shortfall – $	Equity Valuation Shortfall – %
August 2010	Trademarks	$45MM	None	$45MM	100%
2011 – 2013	Caesars Interactive Entertainment *Online gaming business*	$635MM	Likely none	$635MM	100%
October 2013	Linq / Octavius *Two Las Vegas properties*	$942MM	$134MM	$808MM	86%
October 2013	Planet Hollywood	$633MM	$134MM	$499MM	79%
October 2013	Horseshoe Baltimore	$236MM	$80MM	$156MM	66%
May 2014	Cromwell, Quad and Bally's *Three Las Vegas properties*	$1.6BN	$1.4BN	$213MM	13%
May 2014	Harrah's New Orleans	$855MM	$660MM	$195MM	23%
May 2014	Total Rewards	$1.0BN	None	$1.0BN	100%
TOTAL		**$5.9BN**	**$2.4BN**	**$3.6BN**	**60%**

Figure 9-1: Caesar's Entertainment operating company asset values

Caesars had gathered a lot of data through the organization's Total Rewards loyalty program, amassing many years of bits and bytes spanning millions of customers. At the time, Caesars had a reputation as a pioneer in big data-driven marketing and customer service. This led one of the organization's vice presidents to posit that "Big Data is even more important than a gaming license."

NOTE   This quote is from Bernard Marr's book *Big Data in Practice* (John Wiley and Sons, 2016).

Toward the end of the 20th century, finance and accounting departments tried to formalize and standardize the value of data as well as intellectual capital as distinct items in the financial statement of an organization. The standards never really caught on, which is one of the reasons why, despite the pleas to treat data as an asset, for most organizations, data is not recorded on a balance sheet. Treating data as an asset can be difficult when the data is not financially managed as an asset. If nothing else, Caesars bankruptcy documents demonstrated that data could be sensibly valued and established as a tangible asset.

The lack of ability to treat data as a formal asset can often mean that an organization ends up treating data as though it is something fragile. Being regarded as fragile has the drawback that the item is not touched for fear of breaking it.

Data is intrinsic to every business. Because data is so essential, organizations are paying greater attention to machine learning and AI. Advanced analytics, specifically AI, is providing a gateway for opening up data to reach its full potential as an organizational resource. But there is an issue that needs to be addressed. The very thing that makes the data appealing is also its bane.

Used in concert, the schema-less-write and the ability to dump and amass large volumes of data regardless of the quality and the utility can all too easily become orthogonal to managing data as an asset. Above all, the bane is to not know what is even there.

A significant data zone for advanced analytics and AI by the data scientist is the exploration and discovery data zone. The zone does not mean or imply that all that can be explored or discovered can be pragmatically explored and discovered. Appropriately managed, the exploration and discovery data zone should be a harvesting zone because what can be known is known. Data zones and the data asset can be paradoxical if inadequately managed and inadequately governed.

As previously mentioned several times in this book, data is inert. Data is not self-organizing. Data is not self-aware. Data is not aware of its utility and purpose. Data has no understanding of itself. Unaided, data doesn't do anything. Data requires something else in order to have utility. That something else may be a program, a machine, or even a person. But even before the data can be used by a computer program or a machine learning model, the data must be reconsidered as to how concepts are represented and also reconsidered as to what it really means to use data as a long-term asset. Volatility takes away from the value of an asset, and the pressure for organizations to constantly change places a burden on how the organization seeks to create and manage data.

The value of data is independent of the underlying technology that provides persistence or supports access through analytics and AI.

TIME IS AN INTANGIBLE ASSET

A large majority of asset types are physical and tangible. Data is a physical and tangible business asset. A tangible asset is often easier to value than its counterpart, an intangible asset. An intangible asset is typically devoid of a physical presence. An example is intellectual property, such as trademarks and licensing agreements. You'll have certain rights to your intellectual property, and others cannot copy it.

The value of data can be enhanced through the use of AI by using AI to help determine the use of time along with any other model scores. Time can, therefore, be applied as an intangible asset. It's one thing to know you need to action on something as soon as possible, but it's far more powerful to know precisely when it's the right time to perform an action.

You can derive insights, you can aid decision-making, and you can action or set in motion—all of which can be accentuated or discounted through timing. Whether for preventative purposes or for planning purposes, *time* allows an insight, a decision, and the execution of an action to occur at its optimal point—saving costs, optimizing resources, and mitigating risks.

Polyglot Persistence

The term *polyglot* refers to the ability to converse in more than one language. Polyglot is also associated with the use of data topologies, where organizations may choose to use different database technologies in each of the data zones. The phrase *polyglot persistence* is the formal term that is used to address a variety of different data technologies for a variety of types of data that need to be processed and analyzed. Hybrid Transaction/Analytical Processing (HTAP) is an example of another type of database that provides persistence and adds to the cadre of polyglot persistence.

Coined by Gartner in 2014, HTAP allows for the provision of analytics without always having to rely on data synchronization. Hybrid transaction/analytical processing is the means to use data to innovate via greater situational awareness and improved business agility. In analytics, HTAP can transcend all aspects of a data topology.

NOTE   For more information on HTAP, see www.gartner.com/doc/2657815/
hybrid-transactionanalytical-processing-foster-opportunities.

Through the use of HTAP technology, data does not have to move from operational databases to another data zone for the purpose of performing analytics. With HTAP, the transactional data is readily available for analytics at the time of creation. By using HTAP, any drill-down mechanisms from the analytic aggregates always point to the real data: the source data. An analytical data zone is typically a copy of the data from its native source. HTAP can eliminate the need in many circumstances to make a copy just for analytical purposes.

Also, managing data generated from Internet of Things (IoT) sensors is one of the biggest challenges of deploying IoT systems. Traditional on-premise or cloud-based IoT systems are challenged by the large-scale, heterogeneity, and high latencies experienced in some cloud ecosystems. One approach for managing this type of big data is to decentralize applications, management, and data analytics by using the network to provide a distributed and federated compute model. This approach is known as *fog computing*. Another derivation is *mist computing*, which attempts to move most of the analytical processing to the edge.

As with HTAP, fog and mist computing demonstrate the need to perform analytics outside of a dedicated analytical data zone. Creating an information architecture to support all forms of analytics from descriptive to predictive, from diagnostic to prescriptive, and from cognitive to AI requires that architecture support a broader ecosystem of data. Across cloud, fog, and mist computing with supporting analytics, a single data zone is unlikely to meet all of the needs of an organization and provide the necessary levels of resilience that many organizations can demand.

Analytics can be performed on data that is inflight and between its source and its target data zone destinations. By using open source technologies such as Edgent or Spark or other technologies such as IBM's Streams, analytics can be performed on transient data. Transient data belongs neither to the source data zone nor to the target data zone and must be accounted for in an information architecture for AI and other forms of advanced analytics.

By using a mixture of database technologies, an organization can seek to uncover a solution that is better adept at fitting its data, without unnecessarily augmenting the data to fit a particular solution, and further complement the preparation work that would be performed by a data scientist.

Within an information architecture, this is addressed by moving the analytical processes closer to the data rather than moving the data closer to the analytics. Whether a database is HTAP, relational, key/value pair, graph, time series, or based on a JavaScript Object Notation (JSON) data store, the organization's data estate is growing in complexity.

A data estate reframes the view that data is no longer just a byproduct or the happenstance of a business function. As mentioned in Chapter 8, "Valuing Data with Statistical Analysis and Enabling Meaningful Access," a data estate is a collection of data storage locations that natively occur across the data topography of cloud, fog, and mist computing.

Document databases that use JSON can be very versatile for both unstructured and structured data. The recursive nature of JSON readily allows for embedding subdocuments and variable-length lists. Additionally, relational styled rows can be stored in a JSON document. Graph databases are useful for managing relationships in data. A graph database can capture relations and can hold label information for each edge and for each vertex. JSON documents can often be used as well to store vertex and edge type data.

A multimodel database combines the capabilities of a document data store, a key/value pair data store, and a graph database. A multimodel database can often accommodate different data models with less operational overhead. Like the basis for HTAP technology, having multiple data models available within a single database engine can help to address some of the challenges for using different data models at the same time. Mixing different data models within a multimodel database for a single query can increase the options for application design and performance optimization.

For example, managing data for an aircraft fleet can be considered a complex dataset. An aircraft fleet may consist of several aircraft where each aircraft is comprised of hundreds of thousands of parts. Each part may be associated with various subassemblies or subcomponents, and each subcomponent can be placed into an overall hierarchy of related parts.

For optimal fleet maintenance, the organization may have to store a variety of data at different levels of the part hierarchy. Examples include part or component names, serial numbers, manufacturer information, maintenance intervals, maintenance dates, information about subcontractors, links to manuals and documentation, contact persons, warranty and service contract information, and so on. This kind of data hierarchy can be a natural fit for a graph database because the graph database can manage the relations between the different data points, including the information required on each edge and vertex.

To prepare for building a machine learning model, a data scientist might choose to use a graph database to research aspects for the inclusion of features by better understanding the parts associated with a given subassembly. The data scientist might want to do this by performing a parts explosion or a parts implosion request.

Alternatively, the data scientist might look into features associated with parts such that if a given part were to break, what other components of the aircraft contain the same part, and does the part have an identified maintenance procedure? But the data scientist might struggle to use the graph database to research features for which parts of an aircraft need to have maintenance performed within the next 10 days.

If the graph data were stored as a JSON document, associating arbitrary data across the vertices and edges, the data scientist might more readily resolve an inquiry into parts requiring maintenance within the next 10 days by using a document query.

Choosing which database to use within a data zone is to contemplate the varieties of questions that need to be addressed and the ability to address those questions in a personalized manner that is suited to the job or role of the user. Single-model data stores, as well as multimodel stores, need to be considered. All databases tend to have strengths and some weaknesses. For example, an independent graph database may not be able to implement a secondary index on the vertex data.

Overall, the aircraft fleet maintenance example is not a unique business problem. The zone maps, data flows, and data topographies of the data topology complement the approach to polyglot persistence, mostly because polyglot persistence can address the need to provide personalization by using the task at hand to the right data model.

Providing real-time polyglot data access for data scientists is part of self-service analytics. Self-service analytics can also be extended to other business users. Accomplishing self-service requires the right blend of database technology and the right data model or schema. Again, this is where personalization comes into being because an organization does not have to provision a single canonical model that everyone is forced to use.

Referencing the oil analogy from Chapter 8, generating value from oil has always been relatively complex as oil involves retrieval, transportation, refinement, and distribution. Deriving value from oil requires research, design, and operational sophistication. As such, oil needs a supporting infrastructure to help realize the value from the market.

Deriving value from data can also require a similar investment in infrastructure: the data estate. A *data estate* is simply the infrastructure to help companies systematically manage the data within the information architecture and data topology. A data estate spans the data topography, namely, the cloud, the fog, and the mist computing layers. Developing the data estate is even more fundamental to an organization when understanding the volume of data and the complexities associated with what the data conveys.

The exploding volume and speed of data growth brings several challenges that should be addressed by an information architecture that includes the complexity associated with growing clusters, overall storage, and data movement.

Leverage or value from the data can often be inextricably tied to the maturity and robustness of the underlying data infrastructure such that an information architecture should also capture how an organization is going to improve infrastructures and introduce data management as service.

An information architecture must begin to address the operational costs of a data topology, provide for elasticity and flexible capacity models, ensure diverse workloads can be accommodated, and indicate how scaling needs can be satisfied. To address all of these facets, a grounding in the understanding of data needs to exist. Whereas the previous chapter looked at aspects of statistical literacy, data literacy is also requisite.

MODELS DEPLOYED AS MICROSERVICES

Microservices are built around specific business capabilities and follow a path of decomposition to provide discrete sets of services. Docker is an example of an open source container tool that can help with building and running microservices. But, when it comes to deploying microservices as containers, another aspect that you must keep in mind is the management of the individual containers.

When using microservices, you'll want to run multiple containers across multiple machines, and you'll need to manage these efficiently. The process of starting the appropriate containers at the right time, making them interoperate with each other, handling storage and memory considerations, and recovering from failed containers or hardware requires an orchestration platform tool such as Kubernetes. The orchestration allows the containers to work together and to reduce operational management burdens.

Data scientists can leverage microservices and containers to deploy the models they build. Here are a few reasons why it makes sense to deploy AI models as microservices:

- Large monolithic applications are inherently more challenging to understand than a microservice.

- Microservices can be focused on singular business functions, making it easier for development resources to understand a small set of functions rather than an entire application.

- As microservices can be deployed into their own container, microservices can be independently scaled.

- Microservices can be exposed to both internal and external applications without having to move the code.

- Well-defined interfaces mean that data can be easily accessed.

- Containers provide built-in mechanisms for external and distributed data access.

- Vendor or technology lock-in can be avoided and also allows data scientists to choose whatever languages and tools they want to use. Deploying models as microservices with an API endpoint, data scientists and AI programmers can write models in different frameworks such as Tensorflow, PyTorch, and Keras, without worrying about compatibility across the technology stack.

- Microservices accommodate the deployment of new versions in parallel and independent of other microservices. MLOps can be leveraged in the deployment of machine learning applications.

- Deployments can occur across the topography: cloud, fog, or mist nodes. Using on-premise nodes can mitigate data privacy concerns.

- AI models that do specific functions, such as named entity recognition or information extraction, etc., can be independently developed, updated, and deployed.

Benefiting from Data Literacy

When you look at the sky, you're likely to see clouds. If the outdoors are not readily accessible, Figure 9-2 shows a picture of the sky with clouds. But what color are the clouds? Perhaps the first color that immediately came to mind was white. But take a closer look: the clouds contain different shades, and in reality, cloud colors include shades of various blues, grays, and subtle pinks (in a gray-scale figure, the clouds would simply appear in numerous shades of gray).

Figure 9-2: What color are clouds?

In many situations, the data that an organization chooses to digitize can lose nuance and fail to accurately simulate the real world in a precise manner. In Chapter 3, "Framing Part II: Considerations for Working with Data and AI," Figure 3-7 included a picture of a *gray-looking* green E-Type Jaguar. But what does *green* really mean?

First, green can be examined as a thing, an object. As a thing, green has properties. Those properties are hue, saturation, lightness, and temperature.

- *Hues* are dependent on the wavelength of light being reflected or produced.

- *Saturation* refers to the purity or intensity of a given hue. One hundred percent saturation means that there are no additional grays in the hue. The color is pure. When the saturation is at 0 percent, the hue shows as a medium gray. The higher the saturation percentage, the brighter the color appears.

- *Lightness* is a measure of the relative degree of black or white that has been mixed with a given hue. Adding white makes the color lighter by creating tints. Adding black makes the color darker by creating shades. A color can be made to seem lighter by placing the color next to a darker color.

- *Temperature* is a color's perceived warmth or coolness. Red, orange, and yellow are warmer colors. Cooler colors are green, blue, and violet.

However, green is not always an object. Green can itself be a property. Take the Jaguar in Figure 3-7 as an example. The color of the Jaguar is green—green is the color property of the car. Therefore, depending on the context, green can be a thing, or green can be a property. But then again, green can also elicit behaviors. Depending on environmental conditions, green can expand or contract: *green* can move. Defining what something actually *is* often comes from context, but in the real world, context can also shift.

Let's apply the example of green to the question "What is a person?" From one angle, a person is a thing, an object. In the green example, green had properties: hue, saturation, lightness, and temperature. Likewise, a person has properties too: a name, a date of birth, a height, a weight, and so on.

In the same way that green was the property of a car, a person can also be regarded as being the property of something. For instance, a person can be a property of a family and also a household; an employer; a certain community of interest, such as the town they live in or a particular store where they shop; and so on.

The color green was also described as being able to exhibit behaviors by expanding or contracting based on heat. A person can certainly have behaviors, as well. Happy, sad, erratic, depressed, manic, running, and skipping are just a few of the infinite number of behaviors that can be outwardly or inwardly present. All too often, when a system digitizes a person, so much of the *figurative* color is lost or never captured at all.

In Figure 9-3, how many of the objects, properties, and behaviors would ever be digitized? While an organization captures a lot of information, far more information is never captured.

Figure 9-3: Digitization misses more data than is actually collected.

Understanding a Topic

The Structure of Observed Learning Outcomes (SOLO) taxonomy is a model that is used to describe the levels of increasing complexity in understanding a subject. SOLO was initially developed by educational psychologists John Biggs and Kevin Collis. The interpretation of SOLO can also be applied to aid data literacy.

The model consists of five levels of understanding:

- **Prestructural:** The task is not attacked appropriately. An individual has not really been understood to the point and uses an approach that is far too simple.

- **Unistructural:** An individual focuses on only one relevant aspect.

- **Multistructural:** An individual chooses to focus on several relevant aspects, but they are treated independently and in an additive manner. Assessment at this level is primarily quantitative.

- **Relational:** Different aspects have become integrated into a coherent whole. Being at this level is a demonstration that the individual has attained an adequate understanding.

- **Extended abstract:** The individual can take a previous integrated whole and conceptualize the outcome at a higher level of abstraction, generalized to establish a new topic or area.

The term *data literacy* can be taken to mean the following:

- Being able to demonstrate an understanding of what data means, including how to read graphs and charts appropriately, and being able to draw the correct conclusions from data and recognizing when data is being used in misleading or in an inappropriate way (Carlson, J. R.; et. al. "Determining Data Information Literacy Needs: A Study of Students and Research Faculty." *Libraries Faculty and Staff Scholarship and Research*, 2011).

- An emphasis on the extensive use of data for information and decision-making. The use of data includes knowledge of what the data represents. The understanding exists as to how data is collected, analyzed, visualized, and shared. There needs to be an understanding of how data can be applied for either the benefit or the detriment of an outcome within the cultural context of security and privacy (Crusoe, D. "Data Literacy defined pro populo." *The Journal of Community Informatics*, 2016).

- Competence in finding, manipulating, managing, and interpreting data, including not just numbers but also text and images. Data skills must become an integral aspect of every business function and activity (Harris, J. "Data Is Useless Without the Skills to Analyze It." *Harvard Business Review*, 2012).

Skillsets

Data literacy is associated with statistical literacy and information literacy. Statistical literacy was covered in Chapter 8 and can be defined as an "ability to read and interpret summary statistics in the everyday media: in graphs, tables, statements, and essays." A data-literate person should be able to:

- Determine the extent of the information needed.

- Access required information effectively and efficiently.

- Evaluate the information and the sources of information critically.

- Incorporate selected information into one's personal knowledge base.

- Use information effectively to accomplish a specific purpose.

- Understand the economic, legal, and social issues surrounding the use of information, and access and use information ethically and legally.

NOTE   For a discussion of data literacy, see Milo Schield's Chapter 11, "Assessing Statistical Literacy: Take CARE," in *Assessment Methods in Statistical Education: An International Perspective* (Wiley, 2010).

The capabilities of a data-literate person are discussed in "Information Literacy Competency Standards for Higher Education," American Library Association.

```
2000 (alair.ala.org/bitstream/handle/11213/7668/ACRL%20
Information%20Literacy%20Competency%20Standards%20for%20
Higher%20Education.pdf).
```

A hierarchy of critical thinking skills can evolve such that data literacy can be a requisite for statistical literacy, and statistical literacy is, in turn, required for information literacy. Skills for developing literacy in data, statistics, and information can be grouped around core skills, math skills, thinking skills, communication skills, IT skills, and business acumen.

Each of these skills is essential for the data scientist and the citizen data scientist. Many of the skills apply to those who practice analytics in general. Furthermore, the following skills are essential in pursuing AI.

- Core skills
  - Think critically
  - Solve problems
  - Manipulate data
  - Think analytically
  - Make privacy choices
  - Think computationally
  - Familiarity with software
  - Understand data lifecycles
  - Cognizant with data security
  - Formulate productive questions
  - Adhere to ethical and legal rules
  - Knowledge of research methods
  - Knowledge of statistical methods
  - Create contextual data implications
  - Competent with visualization design
  - Make inferences from nonrandom sampled data
  - Think synthetically (being able to view the big picture)
- Math skills
  - Algorithms
  - Statistics
  - Statistical methods

- Thinking skills
  - Analytical thinking
  - Computational thinking
  - Problem-solving
  - Synthetic thinking
  - Critical thinking
  - Research methods
  - Scientific method
- Communication skills
  - Writing
  - Visualization
  - Visualization design
- IT skills
  - Data management
  - Data manipulation
  - Data modeling
  - Data structures
  - Databases
  - Computer programming
  - Database programming
  - Unstructured data
- Business skills especially
  - Domain/field knowledge

It's All Metadata

Fundamentally, metadata can be distilled to mean *data about data*. Invariably, the majority, if not all, of the business data that is collected by an organization is *about* something. As businesses use data to represent something that has transpired in the realm of conducting business, data can be viewed as being descriptive of something, and, realistically, that makes all data metadata. To that end, both data and information can both be regarded as being metadata.

Gaps in an attained level of data literacy can be identified in organizations that claim they are data rich and information poor, an acronym known as DRIP. DRIP is a reflection of the direct utility that an organization is able to realize from its data. DRIP is not about an insufficiency in data as a raw material, but a direct reflection of an inability to consistently consume data, as a raw material, in a meaningful and beneficial manner.

Human fallibility has been associated with ignorance and ineptitude— ignorance is having limited knowledge or understanding, and ineptitude in knowing that knowledge exists but failing to appropriately apply that knowledge.

> **NOTE**   Human fallibility is discussed by Samuel Gorovitz and Alasdair MacIntyre in "Toward a Theory of Medical Fallibility," *The Hastings Center Report*, vol. 5, no. 6, 1975.

Throughout this book, the use of curated data stores has been mentioned as a means to provide personalized or hyper-personalized data stores for users and data scientists. The ability to create specialized data and to provide data for specialized uses to promote efficiency and effectiveness has been mentioned as an essential aspect of how a data topology can assist with driving value. The creation of dedicated data zones to provision highly curated data is desirable and technically feasible.

Specialization and personalized data stores can be directly aligned to help mitigate human fallibility associated with ignorance and ineptitude. Coupled with the software and technology to aid in the gathering, analysis, and retrieval of information, personalization can serve to benefit the organization and serve to help promote data literacy.

Other previously discussed themes are relevant to data literacy, such as the data-information-knowledge-wisdom hierarchy that is used to progressively show additive value by placing the use of organized data and information into context; the six interrogatives to help holistically explore how to understand a given topic; and that data is inert and cannot self-organize, self-understand, or self-value, such that without a computer program, a model, or a means to present itself to a user, data will not accomplish anything.

> **NOTE**   The six interrogatives are what, how, where, who, when, and why.

In the example of exploring the color green, whether as an object, as a property, or by the color's behaviors, all of the data is essentially metadata. The data is about something in the real world and of interest to the business. As such, that really makes all business data or business information meta.

The Right Data, in the Right Context, with the Right Interface

The discussion of the visual representation of data at NASA's Mission Control Center in Chapter 1, "Climbing the AI Ladder," helped to reveal the data literacy principle that not all modern analytical data needs to be presented in a graphical format. Depending on the context, both highly visual graphics and text can be needed by specialists to resolve an issue, uncover insights, and drive actions. Other principles covered data democratization, but as not all data is created equal and data security and data privacy are essential, only a controlled subset of the organization's information can be effectively democratized and shared.

In a poem by William Stafford titled "An argument against the empirical method," the only line in the poem reads, "Some haystacks don't even have any needle." The implication is that while preparing data for modeling and AI, extrapolation and interpolation cannot always make up for missing information. This principle was illustrated in Figure 9-3.

> **NOTE** Dunning's poem appears in *Some Haystacks Don't Even Have Any Needle and Other Complete Modern Poems* (Lothrop Lee & Shepard, 1969).

The Greek word *aponia* is used to mean the absence of pain and was regarded by the Epicureans to be the height of bodily pleasure (`en.wikipedia.org/wiki/Aponia`). They also believed that the goal of human life is happiness. Aponia directly speaks to the principle of fairness within machine learning and AI that not only are there ethical and moral implications associated with the use of advanced analytics, but that data scientists and the organization at large should actively seek to remove bias from models and business practices through explainability.

The right data, in the right context, with the right interface, along with the data being served in the right place, can be distilled as the data being *fit for purpose*. As expressed in the preceding chapters, the needs of each individual within the organization should lead to the recognition that multiple instantiations of the data are required to fully maximize the effectiveness of each employee. As discussed in Chapter 3, hyper-personalization of the employee and not just of the customer should be an organizational goal for handling data.

ASCERTAINING CONTEXT

How are you with foreign languages? Any guesses as to which language this might be written?

Un petit d'un petit

S'étonne aux Halles

Un petit d'un petit

Ah! degrés te fallent

Indolent qui ne sort cesse

Indolent qui ne se mène

> *Qu'importe un petit*
>
> *Tout gai de Reguennes.*
>
> Van Rooten, Luis d'Antin. *Mots D'heures: Gousses,*
> *Rames: The D'antin Manuscript.* Viking, 1967.
>
> **French? Correct. . .but, more specifically, yes and no!**
> **The words are actually intended to be heard as English words. While the wording**
> **has been written to be pronounced using the French language, the words themselves**
> **were selected for their homophonic qualities. For example, in French, *un petit d'un***
> ***petit* loosely means "a child of a child" in English. But, when *un petit d'un petit* is read**
> **(sounded) aloud, the words will be heard as the opening to a nursery rhyme: Humpty**
> **Dumpty. *S'étonne aux Halles* can mean "is surprised at the market". . .but will be heard**
> **as "sat on a wall."**
> **In data literacy, establishing or determining context is first and foremost.**

Summary

This chapter addressed the frequency of change in the business world and how the adoption of hard-coded practices can have a continual impact on computer programs, database design, and machine learning model development. That effort was required in data-related practices to avoid IT departments being a bottleneck or negatively impacting the functioning of the organization. Ultimately, data is an asset, and decisions should not be made that could serve to undermine the asset.

Different technologies can be applied to leverage the asset. Using one of every available technology is not a recommended approach to building an information architecture. Organizations should instead seek to map an appropriate technology to each need to promote the efficiency and effectiveness of the organization.

In driving insights within an organization, having proficiency in data—being data literate—is of significant benefit. Part of being data literate is understanding what data is at hand and understanding what data is not captured. That balance can help serve to put insights into perspective and help to drive an appropriate action.

The final chapter is about applying the numerous concepts in the book toward the formulation of an information architecture for AI.

A Journey's End: An IA for AI

*"Some principal characteristics of the Information Age are extreme
complexity and extreme rates of change."*

—Clive Finkelstein

Enterprise Architecture for Integration

While the number and variety of use cases for artificial intelligence (AI) can be safely *predicted* at ∞, the ideas expressed in this book can successfully be applied to address extreme situations, whether in business, military defense, counter-intelligence, child safety, or *deep space*.

Today, space agencies believe they have a good handle on things up to an altitude of 2000 km above the planet—the ceiling height of low earth orbit (LEO). The International Space Station, for example, operates within LEO. Above that altitude, less and less is known, especially about the long-term impact of deep space on the human body. For instance, within LEO, some astronauts experience a syndrome known as *visual impairment intracranial pressure* (VIIP), which negatively impacts the astronaut's ability to see properly. While technological advancements now allow astronauts to carry a single pair of glasses with an adjustable prescription (a dialable lens), the precise causes behind the syndrome are not fully understood. If we don't understand everything that occurs within LEO, moving into deep space for longer-term travel certainly can pose an additional set of health risks.

Imagine that you're part of a team tasked with planning to take an astronaut to Mars, a journey filled with actual unknown unknowns. Each unknown that manifests itself might need some form of remediation that needs to be addressed in near real time, but sending and receiving a message to the spaceship (including any code changes) could take over six minutes—and that's if the communication signal traveled at the speed of light.

A weekly development *sprint* would likely prove impractical for all but minor cases. Even CI/CD approaches could be a stretch in terms of latency. That said, many of the techniques that have been described in this book can be used for adaptive deployment solutions as well as agile ones. In deep space, where lives would be continually at risk and the ability to respond must occur within an incredibly short window, the use of machine learning models that can be trained with minimal data or function on unsupervised learning would be essential. The use of data zones and data topographies along with data models that avoid hard-coding can provide for the flexible and timely responses necessary to keep the astronauts alive and such a mission on track.

This chapter serves to pull together a series of techniques that can be used for both normal use cases as well as extreme ones, with the necessary considerations for composing an information architecture to support the activities associated with model development and deployment with AI. The information architecture required for AI needs to incorporate a data topology and a highly distributed computing environment. Smarter data science initiatives understand that data-intensive AI deployments must be able to support the real-time event-driven business needs that are often required when operationally infusing AI as a means to improve the effectiveness and performance of an organization.

Development Efforts for AI

Traditional software engineering practices rely on functional decompositions to identify the scope of each computer program that needs to be written. Expected program behaviors for each program are designed into every given solution. Any deviation from the expected behavior of a computer program is, by definition, a software defect. The power of an AI model inherently lies in the ability of the model to learn and incrementally adapt without the need for a traditional computer program.

An AI model is not engineered in the traditional sense of system design. AI models are set to learn via complex neural networks with no guarantees as to the precise functional operation. The organization's data is used to help the models determine how they should behave. In this regard, data has become a new way to create a specification.

Testing a system using traditional verification techniques is not likely to work as well with AI, since there are no hard and fast rules for what must occur. Models are, by nature, pattern-based and not rules-based. Added complexity comes from the statistical nature of machine learning algorithms that can select outputs for a given input based on calculated confidence levels versus the deterministic methods that are used by traditional rule-based systems.

The personalization of outputs produced by AI models that can match specific user needs can introduce further challenges over traditional software engineering practices. The correctness of the output may be decided by the subjectivity of the business user looking at the outcome. Furthermore, traditional user acceptance tests can appear to be impractical—as traditional tests have been based on the consistency of rule-based outcomes and AI's pattern-based outcome may not yield an identical outcome each and every time.

The traditional means to recognize a defect can change with the use of AI. Unintended model consequences such as bias and other emergent behaviors may need to play out in production and not in a controlled test environment. With AI, continuous learning can manifest as a series of behavioral changes that occur over time within a system.

While traditional software systems paid attention to usability, reliability, and operational performance, AI systems often require an intensive and continual effort to focus on trust. *Trust* is a topic that can cover a range of areas that include human oversight, robustness, data privacy, fairness, ethics, transparency, and accountability.

Machine learning models are likely to be built using machine learning libraries with little attention paid to traditional techniques associated with software engineering practices. The variability associated with AI places a renewed emphasis on the need for an information architecture that can serve as a means to impose aspects of predictability for a solution that includes models whose results are not in and of themselves predictable, in other words, how an information architecture is a singular enabler for smarter data science.

The broader view of developing machine learning applications includes other activities beyond the development of the model itself. Also required are activities such as data preparation; building, training, and testing a model; DevOps/MLOps and DataOps; as well as all deployment and production monitoring activities related to AI.

Data preparation activities can often consume upward of 70 percent of the effort related to model development. For AI models and AI-infused applications, appropriate efforts to perform data preparation are required as a means to help avoid unintended bias and to help ensure fairness and trust. Feature extraction is a critical task in the data preparation process, which can help remove redundant data dimensions, unwanted noise, and other properties that can otherwise degrade model performance.

Building, training, and testing a model are required activities toward producing the best model that can meet the perceived requirements from your organization's available data. In practice, data scientists are likely to leverage various frameworks such as TensorFlow, PyTorch, and Scikit-Learn when the models are actually created. Each type of framework can provide some tooling to help support the coding process. However, if and when a model does not produce any identifiable errors, the model may still not be suitable for the intended deployed purpose.

Another important core activity in the building of a machine learning model is the separation of the training data from the validation data. The separation is required to help adequately evaluate the model's ability to generalize. Cross-validation is a practice that data scientists often follow to help with model validation. As a rule of thumb, approximately 70 percent of the available data is set aside for model training purposes, and the remaining 30 percent is set aside for model validation. Debugging an AI model can be complex since the model's behavior cannot ultimately be based on the inferred code and the training data.

When a machine learning model is deemed ready, the model can be infused into a software application. The technique of using black-box testing can help to evaluate whether the model is good enough for deployment. The use of black-box testing is to know the output or the outcome, but not to explicitly reveal how the output or the outcome was determined.

MLOps and DataOps activities also need to keep the model and training data versions synchronized so that any future changes to the model can be adequately tracked. Overall, AI development can be considered different from that of traditional software development because:

- Managing the AI data lifecycle can be more challenging when compared with other software engineering efforts that do not include machine learning.

- Model creation and reuse can require different skillsets that may not be directly comparable to other skillsets that participate in traditional software projects.

- AI components can be more challenging to manage than traditional software assets due to the difficulty in isolating inappropriate, undesirable, or erroneous behaviors.

If, for example, an AI model was built to identify objects in an image, a generative adversarial network (GAN) model could be used. Generative modeling involves the use of a model to generate new examples that could plausibly come from an existing distribution of samples. The new examples could include generated images that are similar but specifically different from a dataset of existing images.

A GAN model is a generative model that is trained using two neural network models. One of the models is known as the *generator model* and learns how to generate new plausible samples. The other model is known as the *discriminator* and learns to differentiate between generated examples and real examples.

Based on the results of testing with training datasets that include images, the accuracy of identifying a given object within the image would yield a given probability. When the model is ready for deployment, the accuracy might be found to be significantly less than during the training phase. The disparity is probably associated with drift. *Data drift* denotes a change in the data distribution during deployment as compared to the distribution of data that was used during the training phase of the model.

How quickly drift can be detected is impacted by the following:

- The data that is used in the learning process can have a high number of dimensions. Finding the difference between the learning data and the production data's distribution can be difficult to identify.

- At deployment time, the data is typically not labeled. Direct measurements of the model's performance may not be possible.

- Experimental design can require advanced sequential test analysis to help retain statistical power, the absence of which can make repeated measurements tricky to achieve.

Avoiding data drift issues can require a high degree of engineering. In the model building process, maintaining a clear separation of training data and validation data is necessary, even though the training data and the validation data can be sampled from the same distribution. Careful selection of black-box test data is critical so that the data can best reflect the data that is expected at the time of deployment.

Traditional software development has mature processes to capture and persist critical artifacts such as requirements, designs, code versions, test cases, deployment data, and so on. By contrast, the process used for developing models may not permit the permanent storage of the training data as a critical artifact.

In practice, the restriction may be due to large datasets that are required for training, limited data access, or licensing terms that prohibit the data from being used beyond the training period.

Data can also vary over time, which can make the preservation of data less relevant for use later. If capturing and preserving all the data that is necessary for training and testing a model is impractical, the ability to reproduce or post-audit the models may be impeded.

Data preparation is an activity that can be underrated in the efforts to produce a model. Data preparation holds the key to a more reliable model building regimen and can affect the final predictive accuracy more so than the actual modeling. Like modeling, data preparation can also contain parameters that are subject to tuning. Data preparation must be understood as a process that must be optimized, cross-validated, and deployed jointly with data modeling to ensure proper applicability.

The development of essential elements for an information architecture must be able to address the data preparation, model development, and xOps practices over time to ensure integrity and viability.

RETRAINING

How often should a model be retrained? You'll need to consider how you would determine your new training set. You might consider answering the question with a standard IT response: *it depends*. But, then again, on what exactly would it depend?

First, the data itself could be used to inform you. For example, if your company provides a type of subscription or renewal for its offerings, the degree of customer attrition from what is expected can indicate that the model is not adequately predicting the dissatisfied individuals or cohorts. If the company's offerings are seasonally based, it wouldn't make sense to retrain the model too frequently, because the model won't have access to a sizable set of new training data and you may have to wait until the following season to determine which customers did not re-up (because they had churned). In this case, the retraining would be performed periodically.

On the other hand, quickly changing production data might require that you retrain weekly or even daily. For distributions that vary more slowly over time, you might need to retrain the models each month or potentially on an annual basis.

Ideally, the use of monitoring metrics would allow you to automate processes to address data drift. By tracking diagnostics, model retraining can be triggered automatically when live data is diverging from the diagnostic results associated with the training data. With this approach, you'll need to determine a divergent threshold to trigger the model retraining. If the threshold is too low, you'll risk retraining the model too often, which can result in higher operating costs associated with consumed compute cycles. If the threshold is too high, you'll risk not retraining often enough, which would mean relying on suboptimal models in production for a period of time.

Complications can also arise because you'll need to determine how much new training data needs to be collected to represent the latest state of the world. Even if the data is changing, there may not be much point in retraining the model if the new training data is too small.

If your model operates in an environment that could be used in an adversarial manner—meaning that the transactions are susceptible to fraud or misuse—and the ability to detect fraud is paramount, incrementally retraining the model based on the availability of new training data rather than a specific periodic cycle would likely be advantageous.

Essential Elements: Cloud-Based Computing, Data, and Analytics

An information architecture for AI is framed around three essential elements. The elements are cloud, data, and analytics. (As an element, the word *cloud* is used in the broader sense of *cloud enablement* rather than a specific type of cloud.) The three elements are also critical to achieving any organizational goal that contributes toward digital transformation. Cloud, data, and analytic elements can overlap and intersect with each other. The intersections serve to indicate capabilities that would need to be provided to ensure a robust implementation.

For example, the intersections can illuminate cross-element operational needs for interoperability, governance, security, and workload balancing.

Earlier chapters in this book have mentioned that not all data is created equal. Similarly, inequality applies to clouds and to analytics—in that not all clouds and not all machine learning models are created equal.

Figure 10-1 shows an overarching cloud topography. The topography is tightly aligned to the data topography specified with the data topology presented in earlier chapters. (The data topology incorporated a zone map, data flows, and the data topography.) The three elements of the cloud topography are cloud computing, fog computing, and mist computing.

Each element shares a common set of facets: the inclusion of hardware, the ability to run software, the accessibility to a communications network, and the means to store information. All elements of the cloud topography can be provisioned either through a public provider, through a private provider, or be self-provided.

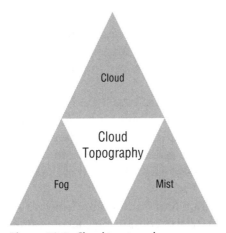

Figure 10-1: Cloud topography

A *public cloud provider* offers computing services over the public Internet. Examples of public cloud providers include Amazon Web Services, Google Cloud Platform, Microsoft Azure, and IBM Cloud. Typically, a public cloud provider can save an organization from having to purchase or license their own hardware and application infrastructures. Additionally, a public cloud provider can often take on the responsibility to manage and maintain a given environment on behalf of an organization.

Through the use of a public cloud, some software products can be deployed faster than when an organization uses traditional on-premise infrastructures. Invariably, a public cloud provider caters to higher levels of elasticity and scalability to satisfy the organization's resource needs during times of peak demand. A public cloud provider is typically associated with the cloud element in the cloud topography.

A *private cloud provider* offers computing services to select users, often a single organization, instead of the general public. The computing services are typically made available over the public Internet or through a private internal network. Private cloud computing can provide organizations with some of the benefits associated with a public cloud, such as self-service, scalability, and elasticity, without the burden of having to share certain infrastructural resources.

Additional controls and customization are also advantages for using a private cloud provider over the use of dedicated resources from computing infrastructures hosted by an organization's own data center. Private clouds can also provide improvements in the level of security and privacy through a combination of the organization's own firewalls with a private cloud-hosted firewall. The use of a private cloud provider would typically require an organization to maintain the same technical staffing levels that would have been necessary with the use of a traditional data center.

Two cloud service models that are commonly used with a private cloud include *infrastructure as a service* (IaaS) and *platform as a service* (PaaS). IaaS is designed to allow an organization to use infrastructure resources such as compute, network, and storage as a service. PaaS is designed to let an organization deliver everything from a relatively simple standalone cloud-based application to a complex enterprise system.

Private clouds, when combined with public clouds, establish a hybrid cloud solution. A *hybrid cloud* can often support the means to cloud burst. With cloud bursting, an organization can seek to scale computing services to a public cloud when the computing demand increases beyond the thresholds of the private cloud. A private cloud provider can be associated with two of the three cloud topography elements: the cloud and the fog.

Self-provided is provisioned by the organization and traditionally involves an on-premise data center. Due to the advent of portable computing such as autonomous vehicles, laptop computing, and smart devices such as tablets and mobile telephones, many self-provided computing capabilities are distributed outside of the physical data center. Self-provided capabilities are often distributed to the elements fog and mist within the cloud topography model.

The elements in the cloud topography infer a hierarchy of capability in terms of the amount of computing power, the elasticity in the possible number of execution nodes, and the overall capacity to store data for on-demand use. Understanding the differences and the benefits is critical for the development of the information architecture.

The topography elements cloud, fog, and mist represent classes of computing and not a given number of instances that may ultimately be deployed or accessible. Each deployed instance is considered a node. Physically, an organization may choose to implement zero, one, or more cloud nodes; zero, one, or more fog nodes; and zero, one, or more mist nodes.

Mist nodes can number into the tens of thousands—perhaps millions. An IoT sensor is not, by itself, regarded as a mist node. However, should the sensor be directly attached to compute, network, and storage capabilities, then the IoT sensor could participate as a recognized mist node. In a retail store, a hand-held smart device used for physical inventory control could participate as one of the mist nodes.

A retailer, for example, may choose to use a cloud node to help with managing order replenishment functions and a fog node in an organization's primary data center to run a campaign management function. The retailer may also choose to set up each of their stores with a dedicated micro data center to act as independent fog nodes. As each store, in this example, acts as a fog node, each store can operationally function as an independent entity in the case of a network outage. The ability to function independently provides a degree of operational resiliency. In this example, the primary data center and the stores are all representative of different fog nodes. The key tenancy across the cloud topography is to be able to operate in a disconnected mode. Operating in a disconnected mode is to indicate that some level of business continuity can be provided even when there is a network outage.

The ability to run AI models locally is an aspect that should be taken into consideration when constructing an information architecture. Local is contextual to where a model runs and can be independently applied to each node type.

A disconnected cloud is local for the models that run on that cloud without the need to pull or distribute data beyond the one cloud. A fog is local if the models that run on the fog node do not need to interoperate or depend on other nodes to perform a score, etc. A mist is local to the models that run on that one smart device so long as there is not a need for additional inbound or outbound data to be transmitted.

The following are the general characteristics of cloud, fog, and mist:

- Cloud
    - Regional or global
    - Managed
    - Virtual
    - Bare metal
    - One or more data centers
    - Scalable and elastic
    - Unlimited storage

- Fog
  - Localization
  - Low-latency
  - Dedicated
  - A single data center
  - Restricted scalability and elasticity
  - Restricted storage
- Mist
  - Edge
  - Ultra-localization
  - Personal computing
  - Little or no scalability or elasticity
  - Limited storage

While consideration can be given for each node to operate in a disconnected mode, a deployment can further consider peer-to-peer communications across each node type: across clouds, across fogs, and across mists. Peer-to-peer communication is separate from that of cloud to fog connectivity, fog to mist connectivity, and cloud to mist connectivity.

Comprehensive enterprise-grade deployments can be achieved and configured to cater to disparate and high-demand workloads with infused AI capabilities inside of business applications. A potential use of the fog node is to assign this type of node with a traditional enterprise data center. The data center is often referred to as on-premise or *on-prem* computing.

On-prem computing may include the use of mainframe computing, such as an IBM Z series computer that has the ability to provide complete data encryption on all data at rest and inflight. On-prem computing may include other server types such as those that use IBM's Power-based chips or even smaller servers that are based on x86 or Nvidia chipsets. (x86 is a family of instruction set architectures that are based on Intel's 8086 microprocessor.)

Servers that are deployed on-premise, whether as a single server or in a cluster, can be reviewed for horizontal and vertical scaling. But at any given point in time, there are likely to be physical limits as to the degree of scalability that can be achieved. The aspect of a physical and known limitation is the primary characteristic that distinguishes a fog node from a cloud node.

The availability of storage in the cloud, fog, and mist is critical to AI in terms of data inputs and model outputs. Figure 10-2 shows the cloud topography juxtaposed between the inherent compute capabilities and the storage capabilities required for advanced analytics.

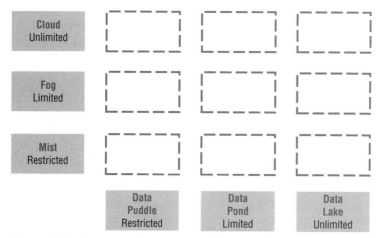

Figure 10-2: Compute and storage capabilities

RESILIENCY

When designing solutions that will be infused with AI capabilities, we'll typically start out approaching this like any other effort and think about the work in terms of a set of *happy day* use cases. A happy day use case is a set of functions that operate without exceptions or abnormal conditions.

The initial work on an AI model may also ignore some operational needs and any considerations that exist for purposes of resiliency. Potentially, we may begin to think about resiliency only once the model has been infused and its system is nearing its rollout to production. Historically, resiliency for non-AI-based applications was limited to aspects of fault tolerance and to systems with a mission-critical designation. But nowadays, all system types should function on demand whenever they are needed.

Ordinarily, we may put off addressing worst-case use cases and begin to think about such efforts only after the *happy day MVP scenarios* have been adequately addressed and, then, only if time and budgets allow.

Designing for resilience isn't just about helping to ensure business continuity by preparing for higher-level system demands, outages, failures, or disasters. Resilience also means that we need to mentally shift how we even think about business strategy and collaboration: changing our mind-set so that resilience is built in from the bottom up and not bolted on as an afterthought and weaving resilience into everything from minor functional-level decisions to major topological decisions.

By ignoring the not so happy scenarios (or edge cases), we can inadvertently destabilize our business operations. When edge cases are taken into account early on, infused AI applications will operate with less fragility. Avoiding operational blind spots would create AI solutions that are more robust and, ultimately, more valuable. Interoperability across the cloud, fog, and mist layers can be used to create a resilient system and allow for continuity for all use cases, from happy day scenarios to worst-case scenarios.

Because of the black-box nature involved with many machine learning–based processes, extra attention needs to be given for AI-infused applications as legacy-styled resilience efforts may have necessitated some level of human intervention. It'll be essential to understand the following:

- Whether or not an AI-infused system is able to make decisions with regards to resilience and that are consistent with the organization's needs.

- How the organization's resilience-based policies, processes, and procedures are propagated to an AI-infused system.

- If an AI-infused system has determined a more effective process or procedure that benefits resilience, are feedback loops in place? How will changes be tracked?

While training people on policies, processes, and procedures is critical to establishing resilience for the enterprise, AI-infused systems will be trained differently. As previously discussed, machine learning can require large datasets that can exceed the capability of employees to reasonably review. Other risks exist in the vulnerability of ML training data to result in bias, corruption, or contamination. Assessing impacts on resilience requires understanding answers to the following:

- How are expected behaviors baselined?

- How is adequate training ensured?

- How is the need for retraining determined?

- How are protections established to ensure safe operating conditions?

- How is performance affected for edge cases?

As an AI-infused system is an intelligent decision-maker, accurately measuring that continuity is enabled and not further compromised from resiliency efforts goes hand in hand when designing for resiliency.

Intersections: Compute Capacity and Storage Capacity

In Figure 10-2, the compute capabilities associated with cloud, fog, and mist computing are shown along the y-axis, and the candidate storage capabilities—the data lake, the data pond, and the data puddle—are shown along the x-axis. The compute capabilities of the cloud are labeled as being unrestricted. The compute capabilities for the fog are marked as being limited, while the mist capabilities are labeled as being restricted. While there are physical limits associated with each public cloud provider or private cloud provider, a single organization is unlikely to press those limits. Therefore, from the perspective of the organization, the limits are labeled as unrestricted.

The fog is restricted in the sense that an organization's data center cannot organically grow without addressing a number of constraints. The constraints are associated with locational limits, floor space limits, and power consumption limits. As such, the fog node is regarded as being limited. The mist is viewed as being restricted because many smart devices cannot be expanded beyond their purchased configurations.

The storage capabilities follow a similar hierarchical pattern to the compute capabilities. Here the data lake is considered unrestricted, as the lake is primarily associated with the storage capabilities coming from the cloud. A data pond has limited storage as the data pond is primarily associated with the storage capabilities of the fog. The data puddle is restricted and is primarily associated with the storage capabilities of the mist.

Each axis has representations for unrestricted, limited, and restricted capabilities. For the unrestricted compute power of the cloud, the cloud is capable of spanning more than one organizationally sized data center. The storage for the cloud can be very large and possibly exceed one brontobyte. (One brontobyte is 1,237,940,039,285,380,274,899,124,224 bytes.) The processing power of the cloud is able to run as many containers as necessary for a cloud-native application.

The limited compute power of the fog can be expressed as being equivalent to one data center, while the storage for the fog is likely to be less than one exabyte. (One exabyte is 1,152,921,504,606,846,976 bytes.) The processing power of the fog is able to run a reasonable or *limited* number of containers that might be necessary for a cloud-native-styled application.

The restricted compute power of the mist can be expressed as being less than one data center, while the storage for the mist is likely to be less than ten terabytes. (Ten terabytes are 10,099,511,627,776 bytes.) The processing power of the mist is only a few containers for a cloud-native-styled application.

The capacity of storage for the cloud, fog, or mist is independent of whether the data is held in a transient or persistent state. Transient capacity is often data that is being held in memory or data that is inflight. Persistent capacity is typically data that is held on recoverable media and is *at rest*.

The primary intersections between the nodes and the storage form natural use cases. These use cases are as follows:

- Cloud ⇨ data lake
- Fog ⇨ data pond
- Mist ⇨ data puddle

The secondary intersections between the nodes and the storage form alternative use cases. The alternative use cases are as follows:

- Fog ⇨ data lake
- Mist ⇨ data pond

The tertiary intersections between the nodes and the storage form possible but ill-suited use cases. These use cases include the following:

- Cloud ⇨ data pond
- Cloud ⇨ data puddle
- Fog ⇨ data puddle

An intersection that does not meaningfully work in any capacity between the nodes and the storage is as follows:

- Mist ⇨ data lake

Each node is often focused on various aspects of an ability to scale, the ability to provide elasticity, and the ability to offer resilience, continuity, and security. Each node is capable of accentuating one or more of these aspects. The cloud node maximizes scalability and elasticity. The fog node maximizes security, while the mist node maximizes resilience. Along with the areas of focus lies an ability to run certain types of AI models. This ability has some fundamental distinctions that relate to the intensity of the analytics.

SUSTAIN

One way to view the distinction between data management and data governance is the act of sustainment. Developing enterprise solutions for a multicloud deployment that encompasses the cloud, fog, and mist, and pushing out data to data stores in the lake, pond, and puddle, you can get into a numbers game. The sheer number of objects to manage appears overwhelming and daunting, leading to a result that is inherently (and potentially unnecessarily) complex and, therefore, not sustainable—a situation that could easily implode on itself.

From a data management perspective, it can be easy to deploy multitudes of data stores, different database technologies, and even containerized databases. Data management doesn't necessarily need to be a coordinated effort, whereby multiple development squads can create data assets or zones as and when required to support their tasks at hand.

From the viewpoint of the enterprise, rogue efforts (teams that work independently and that are not ordered to follow any established internal IT protocols) or efforts involving large numbers are not beneficial to long-term viability. Data governance can step in and be the enterprise vehicle to ensure data remains a sustainable asset. A data governance initiative should ensure that no data asset ever goes unaccounted, regardless of the situation or circumstance by which it came into being. A data governance practice that is all-encompassing can keep a complex data environment sustainable by ensuring that all data assets are registered, cataloged, and discoverable. Generating data lineage and data provenance become imperatives toward reaching sustainment.

Ultimately, all multicloud deployments will result in a complex data estate. Sustainment should be considered a vital part of a data governance program.

Analytic Intensity

The analytic intensity that is shown in Figure 10-3 is based on the ability to provision computer power and on having access to large data stores (whether transient or persistent) for a given model to act upon. A mist node is not going to have, nor is the mist intended to have, the same computing power or the same ability to locally store extremely large data stores as the cloud. Therefore, the analytical intensity is naturally lighter in weight, especially when directly compared to other fog and cloud nodes.

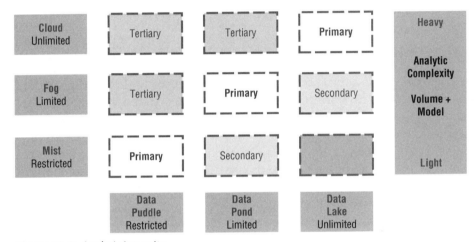

Figure 10-3: Analytic intensity

A fog node can achieve moderate analytic intensity, and a cloud node can achieve a level of heavy and complex analytic intensity for running AI models.

When any of the nodes are planned to be interoperative, the intensity can be reevaluated. For the purposes of the information architecture, the analytic intensity is viewed as a single node provisioning the data and running the AI model.

xPU ACCELERATION

Beyond software-based algorithm optimization to handle AI workloads, specialized hardware and processors are being developed to accelerate throughput. In addition to the traditional central processing unit (CPU) and newer chips such as the graphics processing unit (GPU) and tensor processing unit (TPU) chips, other xPUs now exist either as proprietary chip types or as a general chip category. Here are some examples:

- **APU:** An accelerated processing unit integrates CPUs and GPUs on the same die.

- **BPU:** A brain processing unit is a proprietary low-latency AI chip to detect objects.

- **DPU:** Deep learning processing units are designed for efficiently processing workloads for convolutional neural networks (CNNs) and recurrent neural networks (RNNs).

- **EPU:** The emotion processing unit can be used with various avatars to control body language and facial expressions.

- **IPU:** An intelligence processing unit is designed to accommodate a broad range of AI workloads.

- **NPU:** Neural processing units are designed to accelerate prediction, image classification, and object detection.

Interoperability Across the Elements

For an organization sensitive to network latencies, multiple cloud providers might be leveraged for performing cloud computing. An organization is likely to choose a provider's cloud zones that are located nearer to its operational locations to reduce latency times. For other organizations, multiple cloud providers might be used to keep the processing of data isolated within a political or country border for regulatory purposes. Still, other organizations might elect to use multiple cloud providers to force an additional layer of workload distribution across the application portfolio.

The fog compute node can take on multiple characteristics. The use of a traditional on-premise data center to support all back-office operations is one such characteristic. A larger organization ordinarily uses multiple data centers that are configured to take on the workload of another data center should an outage of some type arise. Each data center would be an independent fog node with regard to an information architecture. Depending on the industry and the needs of an organization, additional fog computing nodes may be established.

A hospital system with hospitals throughout a country might choose to have a fog node located within each hospital or leverage a regional setup to support several hospitals that have a geographical proximity. An oil and gas company might choose to have a fog node located on each oil rig; a shipping company might decide to have a fog node located on each tanker or cargo ship. A university might choose to have a fog node on each campus; a manufacturer might want to have a fog node in each plant; a retailer, in each store; and a government might elect to provide each agency or ministry with its own fog computing nodes.

In many instances, a fog node may make use of a private Long-Term Evolution (LTE) network for wireless broadband communication. Private networks can help support remote locations and may provide higher degrees of resilience.

The mist compute node is the lightest node of the three elements. The mist node typically represents the most restriction in terms of compute processing capabilities. As previously stated, a mist node can be a smart device such as a tablet computer or a mobile telephone handset. Additionally, a mist node might be the computing power located in the trunk of a police car. A passenger vehicle might be a mist node and able to operate in peer-to-peer relationships with other vehicles through a vehicle area network (VAN).

Indeed, an autonomous vehicle would be a mist node and must be able to unequivocally operate in a disconnected mode. Mist nodes that can participate in a wireless fifth-generation (5G) network are likely to play an increasing role in taking on distributed workload across the elements. The massive capacity provided by 5G networks means that many more machines, objects, and devices can also be simultaneously interconnected. 5G is designed to support high giga-byte per second transfer rates and provide for ultra-low latency.

> **NOTE** The other mobile network generations are 1G, 2G, 3G, and 4G. The first-generation wireless networks were limited to just providing analog voice capabilities. 2G provided digital voice through a channel access method for radio communication technologies where several transmitters could send information simultaneously over a single communication channel. 3G ushered in the expanded use of mobile devices through an access standard that could support the sending of voice, data, and signal data between mobile phones and cell sites. 4G LTE paved the way for making mobile Internet computing possible.

In a hierarchical communication flow, the mist compute nodes can provide data to the fog node or directly to the cloud node. In turn, the fog compute node can provide data to the cloud node.

The communication flows for advanced configurations can be more elaborate by providing for the following:

- Bidirectional communication flows
- Peer-to-peer communication flows

Figure 10-4 shows all of the communication flows. The complexity to instantiate each flow can be significant when taking into account data governance, data security, data privacy, and the overall orchestration of the distributed workload. But, being able to deploy AI models to operate singularly or in ensemble patterns across the distributed nodes and close to the data can provide unbridled deployment opportunities and can be expressed through the information architecture.

> **NOTE** Ensemble models are used in machine learning to combine the decisions from multiple models together to improve the overall performance. Multiple techniques exist for establishing a final prediction from the machine learning models, but some of the most popular techniques include the most popular prediction and an average prediction. The most popular prediction or the max voting method is often used for classification problems. With max voting, multiple models are used to

make predictions for each data point, and each prediction is considered to be a vote. The prediction that is used by the majority of the models is then used for the final prediction. With averaging, multiple predictions are also made for each data point. To make the final prediction, an average of all the predictions from all the models is taken and used. Averaging can be used for making predictions in regression problems or while calculating probabilities for classification problems.

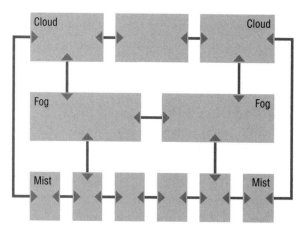

Figure 10-4: Communication flows

The ability to communicate peer-to-peer means that network traffic is not forced to unnecessarily traverse the communication map in a rigid up and down manner. Because all three elements (cloud, fog, and mist) have compute capability, predictions, scores, or signals from AI models can be transmitted without having to transmit individual data points unnecessarily.

A mist node could collect sensor readings and continuously run a model on each data point. Only when necessary would the mist need to send a score or a signal to the cloud or the fog. Additionally, the compute capability of the mist means that various data points can be aggregated prior to any transmission to reduce network traffic, or alternatively, all of the data points can be communicated with either in real time or via a planned lag to avoid peak communication times.

The flexibility in the paradigm should allow for quicker business decisions. In all likelihood, those business decisions are going to be automated decisions where the ability to react close to real time can bode well for an organization and create significant advantages in terms of competitiveness, cost savings, or improved safety.

The fog may be used to correlate data from multiple mist nodes for decision-making based on predictions, and the cloud may correlate data points from multiple fog nodes for decision-making that may be more diagnostic in nature.

The machine learning models at each node are reflective of the computing power, storage capabilities, and any inherent latencies. Each model is optimized to the node, and the node is reflective of the context for which the prediction is sought.

The overall topography is deliberately highly distributed. But individual application or system needs within the topography can certainly be centralized to an appropriate node. Not every application needs to scale, and not every application needs elastic computing; some workloads can be highly predictable and stable. For machine learning, the key is to tailor the models to fit the node.

Overall, the communication across the nodes is to foster interoperability and to foster ensemble modeling where predictions from other distributed nodes might be highly relevant in decision-making. The counter aspect of interoperability is to understand what is needed to provide resilience. Balancing the two provides for many options to support real-time, near real-time, and batch needs for machine learning in all application types.

By architecting the communication paths, the actual flight paths provide areas of interest to exploit machine learning in terms of activities for preflight, inflight, and postflight predictions.

A USE CASE

Several special weapons and tactics (SWAT) teams have been deployed to investigate a series of buildings that are spread out in different areas of the city. Handheld devices have been included as part of their equipment. The handhelds are mist nodes due to their ability to provide compute, storage, and connectivity. To aid the SWAT teams, a mobile command center has been deployed with the onboard compute capabilities participating as a fog node to connect with the mist nodes using a private 5G network. A separate commercial 5G network is being used to connect the fog node to a cloud node.

The SWAT teams are using bodycams to capture video processed by the handhelds—a haptic vibration will alert an officer to look at the handheld device. Under a kitchen sink in one of the buildings, a bottle of MEKP (an over-the-counter product that can be used to make a resin for things like jewelry) is detected. The detected object is shared with the other peer-level mist nodes. Within the next 30 seconds, a second SWAT team processes the image of a bottle of hydrogen peroxide in a bathroom medicine cabinet. Subsequently, each mist node executes a recipe algorithm to determine what other household items, or otherwise, could provide additional ingredients for constructing an explosive.

If the building occupants are working together, they could be distributing chemicals for nefarious actions to various locations until they are ready to combine them. Additionally, the fog node is further sharing the information in real time with the cloud node to determine whether other watch-list groups or incidents have used similar chemical recipes to disrupt society.

Performing image processing in real time and correlating results from a single-user mist node and across multiuser mist nodes, along with the ability to perform analytics for recipes, serves to showcase an ability to exploit the use of AI across the data topology.

Data Pipeline Flight Paths: Preflight, Inflight, Postflight

The preflight, inflight, and postflight flightpaths give an indication of when a machine learning model can be initiated relative to the flow of data. Three flights are identified as follows:

- **Preflight:** Predictions in the split moment before the flow begins
- **Inflight:** Predictions that occur during the flow and while the data is still regarded as being transient between a start point and an endpoint
- **Postflight:** Predictions that occur after the flow ends

At each flight stage lies the opportunity to perform machine learning and the means to predict or trigger an appropriate signal (see Figure 10-5). Preflight data, or source data, may be in-memory or persistent data. A preflight prediction might seek to understand the quality of the source data and potentially interpolate any missing values prior to sending the data. A preflight model may also determine that transmitting data is unwarranted and hold back the data.

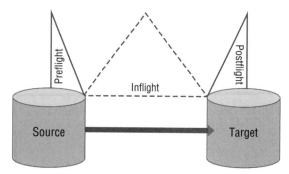

Figure 10-5: Flight paths for model execution

Inflight prediction occurs while the data is transient between begin and endpoints. Inflight prediction offers closer to real-time prediction and decision-making. Most IoT data is streamed, and IoT data is a prime candidate to have inflight predictions infused into the transferring of data. Inflight prediction can allow a model to uncover potential anomalies in the data so that other processing events can be triggered in a timely manner. Inflight prediction also accommodates proactive business decision-making.

Postflight prediction occurs at the target. The target may be in-memory or persistent data. Postflight data affords the most comprehensive models but at a potential cost of latency.

At each flight stage, data can be correlated with other data to extend features that are used with machine learning. Depending on the technology used for inflight processing, the data may be multicast to many targets. For example, a fog node can multicast to mist nodes, or a fog node can multicast to each cloud node. Multicasting is the distribution of data that occurs simultaneously to multiple endpoints and is not serialized.

The flights can occur across the cloud, fog, and mist nodes as well as within the cloud, fog, or mist. Therefore, the flight paths can be interzonal or intrazonal. The types of data held in each node place a different impact on data management.

A USE CASE (CONTINUED)

In preflight, the image of the household item is classified by a model. During an inflight streaming process, the classified image is included in a proximity-based analysis to determine likely outlets where the noncontraband chemical could have been purchased. In postflight, machine learning is performed to identify other terrorist events that have involved the same or similar products.

Data Management for the Data Puddle, Data Pond, and Data Lake

Data management within the data topology can include operational data stores as well as other data stores to encompass advanced analytics such as the data puddle, the data pond, and the data lake. The puddle, pond, and lake have discrete analytic uses and can support discrete capabilities.

The data puddle is characterized by the predominant use of in-memory and flash storage media. Data tends to be raw sensor data, and the machine learning models tend to be primitive in nature and are also restricted by the availability of data to make certain predictions or assertions.

The data pond is characterized by the ability to handle raw sensor data, structured data, and limited unstructured data. The machine learning models are broader when compared to the data puddle. Improved storage capability accommodates reasonable amounts of historical data.

The data lake is characterized by the ability to handle any data type and provide meaningful and contextual data to a mixed and broad set of end-user needs and machine needs, too. The data lake can also address the needs of *delta lakes* that seek to provide alternative levels of data consistency. The machine learning capabilities extend to all forms of advanced analytics, including predictive, diagnostic, prescriptive, sensemaking, cognitive, augmented intelligence, and AI.

NOTE   Traditional databases were extolled for their ability to support ACID transactions. ACID is an acronym for atomicity, consistency, isolation, and durability. ACID databases ensured that there would never be any discrepancies in the data values seen across users or applications. A delta lake is an open source storage layer that provides ACID transactions for data lakes.

For a manufacturer, examples of data that may feed the mist's data puddle include the following: localized ambient temperature, localized humidity, roller speeds, thermal images, vibration (seismic) activity, acoustic sound waves, identifiers and parts associated with an assembly or a subassembly, an operator, a shift, measures that may be taken in time increments (e.g., every second), measures that may be taken in length increments (e.g., every 30 centimeters/one foot), the recording of a transaction, etc.

Examples of data that may be used to feed the fog's data pond for a manufacturer include data sent from mist compute nodes, ambient temperature outside a manufacturing plant, humidity outside a manufacturing plant, lighting conditions, manufacturing schedule for material and resources, motion detection, etc.

A manufacturer may use the cloud's data lake for data sent from mist and fog compute nodes, bills of lading, bills of material, maintenance reports for plant machinery, warranty claims against shipped products, etc.

Conversely, a social services agency might use the data puddle to predict activities during a site visit, and the data pond may be used to perform predictions during regular intake or eligibility processes. The data lake may be used to predict citizen outcomes by performing longitudinal assessments.

In viewing the needs of an organization, the machine learning models may be accompanied by descriptive analytics as well, but all analytics need to be placed within the context of the organizational needs, the content of the data, and the needs of the user or machine.

A POTENTIAL BABEL FISH

Across the data topology, deployed systems need to represent accurate and precise implementations of business requirements. Data management policies and standards by themselves are not always sufficient to reliably produce consistent outcomes. Historically, mis- or nonalignment of data across different implementations has been a point of significant friction. In the book *The Hitchhiker's Guide to the Galaxy* (Douglas Adams, Harmony Books, 1980), the Babel fish was used as a practical universal translator to avoid *friction* in communication.

Today, machine learning infused data catalogs can be used as a surrogate Babel fish to aid alignment and to compensate for misalignment and actively accommodate tolerance. Conformity in how data is preserved is not always possible and, if possible, not always practical. Accommodating inconsistencies without allowing for them to be disruptive is to the benefit of the enterprise.

Driving Action: Context, Content, and Decision-Makers

Harold Leavitt's 1964 paper, "Applied Organization Change in Industry," introduced a four-part model for interactions within an organization.

- **Structure:** How people are organized
- **Tasks:** How people perform their work
- **People:** The individuals who are tasked to perform work
- **Technology:** Tools that people use to conduct work

Nowadays, the model is commonly condensed into three parts: people, process, and technology. How people should perform their work and what work they should perform are still critical organizational questions. With increased levels of automation through AI, machines can be added to the people aspect so that people can be further generalized and recast as decision-makers. The generalization of decision-maker, therefore, refers to either a person or a machine. Decision-making is an activity that can be collaborative between people, between machines, or between people and machines.

Processes help decision-makers work better. Processes define and standardize work, preventing people from reinventing the wheel every time a task is begun and allowing for machines to work in a predictable manner.

Technology can help decision-makers work faster and smarter. Business outcomes need to be accomplished in a manner that is faster, more efficient, and better than with an older version of the technology. But questions can arise about the need to become faster, to be more efficient, to be better.

If organizations are not fast enough, additional automation from machine learning should be sought. Machines would then act as the decision-maker and be further supported by processes and technology. If organizations are not sufficiently efficient, then seeking the means to optimize tasks and processes can further be explored—processes would need to leverage additional utility from any decision-makers as well as technology. If organizations are not being innovative and creating new value (being better), then rethinking the use of technology along the lines of hyper-distributed computing models using cloud, fog, and mist computing can provide new opportunities—technology becomes the means to provide new methods for processes and decision-makers.

While broader IT themes can be aligned to decision-makers, processes, and technology, data-centric discussions around machine learning can be centered on the topics of context and content, as well as decision-makers. As shown in Figure 10-6, context, content, and decision-makers are used to help drive prediction, automation, and optimization for data-intensive work activities.

- **Context:** Alignment of machine learning with business goals, funding, politics, culture, technology, resources, and constraints

- **Content:** Subject-matter objectives, document and data types, volume, existing structure, governance, and ownership

- **Decision-makers:** Audience, collaboration, tasks, needs, information-seeking behavior, and experience

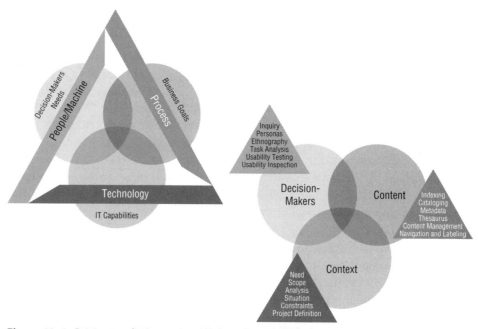

Figure 10-6: Driving prediction, automation, and optimization

While the use of a given technology and any newly adopted business processes are all susceptible to future change, the context-content-decision-makers paradigm is sufficiently acute to be directly associated with a given point in time. As such, while an outcome is within the bounds of reasonableness, the outcome itself may be something that is not repeated in the same way. This is an inherent by-product of using continuous learning with machine learning, addressed earlier in this chapter.

The basis for using machine learning is that it provides an ability to identify and react to patterns and not rules. While a pattern may span time, a pattern may alternatively be anchored to a single point in time.

Content is highly volatile in terms of accumulated knowledge. The discussion of statistics in Chapter 8, "Valuing Data with Statistical Analysis and Enabling Meaningful Access," included differences between a sample set and a population set. While a population is always complete at a given moment in time, the population set in many business scenarios is subject to an impending change.

The content associated with a given point in time is not likely to be the same as the content associated with a different point in time. Aspects of past, present, and future provide for a shifting lens. What is the future becomes the now, and the now becomes the past. The content relative to the past, present, and future is time-oriented to a single point in time. Past, present, and future impact context too. What a cohort or a given individual is likely to do (the future) is quite different than what a cohort or a given individual has done (the past). The situation is further compounded by what a given cohort or a given individual is currently doing (the present).

Context is attributable to a task at hand and frames the rationale for gathering content and even sets the validity of participation by decision-makers. While people-process-technology looks at addressing decisions over time, context-content-decision-makers look at addressing a decision for a point in time. Even if a decision were to change over time, the ability to ensure that a decision is appropriate for a point in time is critical.

EXPLAINABLE AI

In Chapter 6, "Addressing Operational Disciplines on the AI Ladder," we mentioned several algorithms that can be used to help understand model behavior, including LIME and MACEM. And, earlier in this chapter, we discussed the difficulty of isolating inappropriate or erroneous behaviors in AI. Monitoring technology that uses algorithms such as LIME and MACEM includes H2O.ai's Machine Learning Interpretability within its H2O Driverless AI and IBM's OpenScale to provide insight into critically monitoring point-in-time aspects of machine learning.

For example, OpenScale can operate across an AI application's lifecycle, from build to run to manage. OpenScale provides a runtime for performance monitoring for accuracy and fairness in the outcomes of machine learning. Logs are automatically recorded for every payload of data that is processed by the model and enables traceability of all decisions and predictions and full data and model lineage. This logging data improves audit and compliance reporting.

By generating real-time alerts if an accuracy score falls below an acceptable threshold, OpenScale can help an organization ensure that data scientists and operations personnel are immediately notified should the model begin to drift. Detecting drift early can reduce the risk of unknowingly using an unreliable model to make decisions.

With OpenScale, users can query any business transaction and obtain an explanation as to how the model arrived at a given recommendation. OpenScale can inform the business in language that a line-of-business user can readily follow. OpenScale also uses contrastive techniques to explain model behavior in the vicinity of the target data point, identifying feature weighting of the least and most important features used for a given decision. OpenScale can be applied to any zone within the data topology that exercises machine learning.

Keep It Simple

When building and deploying a data topology, remember that the data topology is likely to evolve over time. Working to overcome any inherent weaknesses associated with your data topology should be part of a long-term plan for success. First and foremost is an understanding of whether a data topology is being represented within your organization as a concept or part of a fleshed-out information architecture.

The data zones must be able to support over-time and point-in-time needs, which means that the data must be well organized and be to practical extents immutable so that scenarios can be reconstructed—for which OpenScale can be meaningfully leveraged.

Although sensitive data, data privacy, and data security can all be addressed in the context of an information architecture, these topics can still be challenging for a comprehensive enterprise deployment. An aspect of establishing a leaf-level data zone is to focus on simplifying data sensitivity, data privacy, data security, and even data governance at the expense of adding another copy of the data that may on the surface appear redundant or a replica. Simplification is also complementary to providing a hyper-personalized dataset to support the needs of any decision-maker (person or machine).

Consider a raw data zone that contains both sales data and human resource data. In most situations, it would be reasonable to expect that a sales analyst would want to consume only sales data and not the human resource data. On the other hand, a human resource analyst is likely to solely focus on the human resource data. In terms of the two analysts, their activities are not heavily intermixed or interlocked.

However, when combining human resource data with sales data to track employee performance, there could be a valid reason to comingle the data. Comingled or correlated data is likely to be highly sensitive, requiring additional controls. How best to apply security for any correlated data would remain an important task to resolve, especially as the correlated data may flow into and across other data zones. Separating data into data zones that can be overlaid with straightforward security profiles can aid protection and also mean that machine learning models only consume relevant features.

Transitive closure was initially discussed in Chapter 8 with the Eminem example. The issue of transitive closure is how the use of nondemocratized data can pose significant security challenges. Transitive closure could come into a situation where multiple tables or datasets need to be accessed and, depending upon the privileges of what data can be visible and by whom, means that any activity associated with data discovery can equate to a scenario of data vulnerability. See Figure 10-7.

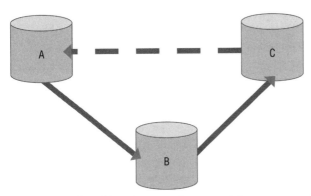

Figure 10-7: Transitive closure and access privileges

In Figure 10-7, if the data from dataset A can be matched against data from dataset B, which in turn can be matched against the data in dataset C, then A and C can be asserted to be equivalent even if the matching logic is insufficient to yield a direct match against datasets A and C.

If a user does not have permission to see the data in dataset B, should that user be allowed to know that A and C have equivalency, especially if the outcome is advantageous to the organization? Beyond securing access privileges to the datasets, the privileges would need to carry through into any indexing technology.

Within the context of machine learning, machine learning is a subfunction of all the possible functions that consume data to achieve an outcome. Ultimately, the data zones need to be placed in the frame of context, content, and decision-makers.

Before trying to understand the data in the context of an information architecture, a formal approach for establishing a data topology must be set in place. The purpose of each data zone should be deliberate and should not be construed as being arbitrary. The use of data zones should serve to foster a sense of simplicity within the overall information architecture.

A data topology is a method and approach for classifying and clustering data coupled with all the essential data flows exposed. The resulting outcome from a data topology must attempt to create a zone map that is sustainable over time and one that should be unaffected by the continuous change of data characteristics that come from volume, variety, velocity, veracity, and perceived value. Any continuous change should not result in the loss of affinity between content and context. Protecting affinity may require the need to silo certain aspects of the data.

ALTERNATIVES TO COMPLEX DATA SECURITY PROFILES

Scoring a machine learning model occurs in real time, in a batch cycle, or as the result of an event being triggered. Calculating a score ahead of time in a batch process can be a useful alternative for handling real-time scoring needs for high volumes of data. Data can be collected over a designated period of time—such as a day or an hour—and then processed as a single batch.

Beyond the traditional use for batch processing, a batch scoring process can be used to simplify data security. The batch process is singularly authenticated or accessed for permission to execute, rather than authenticating each individual user. If a situation exists where each user is allowed to consume only a very specific subset of data within a common data store, data policies could require a complex data security implementation that could inadvertently result in a vulnerability.

In addition, a model may use features for which a user would not ordinarily be granted access. The user may have permission to see the score, but not the other features. A batch scoring process can provide for an effective remediation in simplifying data security where permissions are not granted at the data store level but on combinations of data elements.

The Silo Is Dead; Long Live the Silo

Mentioning a data silo in negative terms is likely to be received with cheers. *The dastardly silo, a blight to progress and momentum. Bah humbug!*

In the nomenclature of a data topology, data is literally organized as silos. However, unlike the negative silo, the silos of the data topology are intended for planned interoperability through design and not by happenstance. The human body can be used analogously (see the sidebar "The Body as a Myriad of Silos") to highlight the positive aspects of establishing specialized silos that are designed with interoperability in mind.

Each nonleaf zone and leaf-level zone in the data topology promotes a level of purposeful isolation, redundancy, and duplication. Zones are directly used to promote agility and flexibility—for the business and for IT developers—but are established at the expense of creating silos. Silos are also paramount to the ideas behind managing a data value chain: keeping the raw data zone separate from the refined data zone and separate from personalized data zones.

Singularly, the means to address and apply interoperability, a concept that is manifest through the data flows of the data topology, is what can separate good silos from bad silos. Silos are often thought of as being in a closed environment that cannot readily participate with anything that is external. But if a silo is deliberately designed to foster accessibility through integration or interoperability, the silo can become a technique of leverage and a tangible asset. Only when interoperability with data is a core discipline can an organization become agile in more than just name.

On a diagram, a data flow is normally illustrated as a line. Potentially, the line is also given an arrowhead to indicate a direction. Literally, mastering lines is one of the keys to successfully establishing and deploying an information architecture. A diagram is likely to contain more lines than any other graphical symbol, so mastering how each line can be supported is an imperative for any squad. For example, even a traditionally styled high-level conceptual diagram, as shown in Figure 10-8, contains more lines than the other symbols. In an actual deployment, you'll find the actual number of lines will significantly grow.

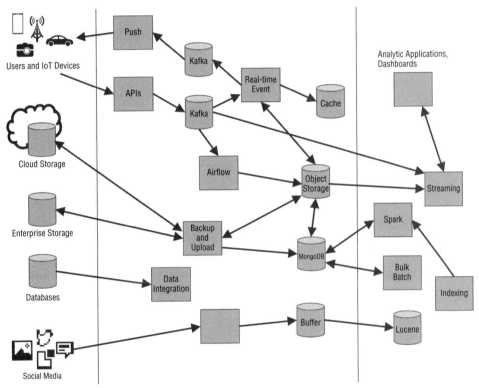

Figure 10-8: A proliferation of lines serves to highlight the need for line management as a formal discipline.

A line is likely to hold true even if the underlying technology or data payloads are subject to change, so line mastering must include the use of agile and adaptive processes. For simplicity within a data topology and an information architecture, separate diagrams should be used to decompose any line. By removing technology overlays from lines, you can start to create diagrams that are more stable over time.

Commonly, lines across a data topology or information architecture may use a disparate set of technologies. For example, you may decide to use Change Data Capture technologies to move committed business transactions, streaming technologies for IoT feeds, event queues, message queues, bulk loads, micro-batches, and even software products such as Apache Spark, Apache Kafka, Apache Nifi, IBM Streams, IBM DataStage, and so on.

> **NOTE**   With the exception of IBM DataStage, these products were defined in Chapter 5, "A Look Forward on Analytics: Not Everything Can Be a Nail." DataStage is an ETL-styled product that can move data in batches or in real time.

The design and creation of data silos—if planned, managed, and interoperable—will provide you with a corporate advantage and not a disadvantage for your information architecture. Realistically, the advantage is predicated on your mastering the lines that connect each silo: the data pipelines and flows whether preflight, inflight, or postflight. Understanding the data flows begins with building a taxonomy for the data topology.

THE BODY AS A MYRIAD OF SILOS

From the outside, we humans look like a singularity. Our oneness is equivalent to an operational enterprise. But, delving below the outer shell, the skin, we can clearly see that our enterprise is actually made up of many siloed systems. These siloed systems include the nervous system, digestive system, respiratory system, the skeleton, the circulatory system, etc.

Each system has a predesignated purpose, and much of our flexibility and ability to perform is entirely based on the fact that we are comprised of silos. The silos also provide for enhanced recovery. In many situations, we can self-heal as not all problems result in a systemic, single point of failure. We can break a bone, and the breakage is isolated—not everything gets broken.

The one thing that our personal silos do exceptionally well is interoperate. Anything can be poorly designed, but silos are an answer to flexibility, performance, and recovery.

Taxonomy: Organizing Data Zones

A data topology for an information architecture can be expressed via a *taxonomy*. The root layer expresses the scope and boundary of the data topology. Multiple roots can exist within an enterprise or the ecosystem of the enterprise. When multiple root zones exist, a meta-zone model can be established to describe the intent and purpose of each of the multiple root zones. This can be especially useful if there are any overlaps between root zones.

The ecosystem of an enterprise may include outside partners and stakeholders and their respective enterprises. Establishing a root zone from the ecosystem perspective can provide for a broader holistic view of the data that the organization needs and can use to achieve higher levels of benefit.

Associated with the data topology root is a definition of the scope and the intended boundary. The root zone should be absent of any physical data store. The root zone is an aggregate zone. The root establishes the theoretical limit of knowledge for the analytical environment and models: the boundary of what is knowable.

The root zone is not limited to the natural boundary of the organization. The root zone can indeed encompass all operational, nonoperational, and analytical data zones but can fully encompass the enterprise. Additionally, the root zone can encompass the ecosystem that may include vendors, partners, etc.

The root zone can also contain any other type of data that can be identified and zoned, such as third-party data, social media, weather data, etc. What is knowable is critical to building a fully featured model.

In Figure 10-9, styles A and B reflect alternative representations and show the use of establishing a subzone. Below the root zone in style A are six different nonleaf zones: weather (from an outside source), operational data (internally sourced), a data lake, two data ponds, and a data puddle. Style B clusters the data lake, the data ponds, and the data puddle below a common nonleaf zone for analytics. The lake, ponds, and puddle are now subzones of the analytics nonleaf zone. Overall, style A and style B both reflect zone maps.

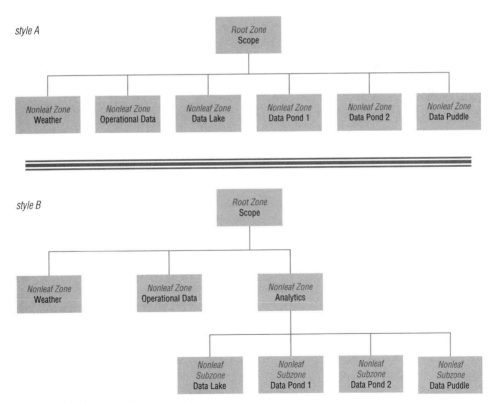

Figure 10-9: Taxonomic representation

Figure 5-11 in Chapter 5 showed a third style for representing zones that used a box-in-box style to represent the root zone and nonleaf zones. The hierarchical style and the box-in-box styles can be intermixed.

As virtualized access services or technologies may be used within a zone map, Figure 10-10 illustrates a dashed-line grouping technique that can be especially useful when the subzones are known to exist in different locations or they make use of multiple technologies.

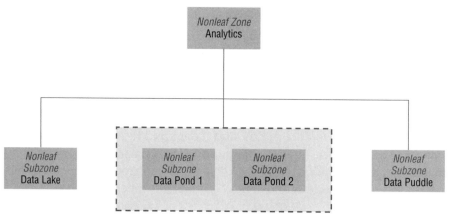

Figure 10-10: Virtualized data zones

The two data ponds in Figure 10-10 are likely to exist in separate fog nodes, but the data scientist might be interested to know that the information architecture has been established with a virtualization capability so that both ponds can be accessed as a singularity for data science activities.

As stated, the leaf zone should be the zone that identifies a specific instantiation of data. Leaves should be established to help drive simplicity in managing data. Reasons to establish an independent leaf zone can include ensuring privacy, providing security, offering personalization, addressing democracy, adding curation, incorporating ingestion, improving refinement, provisioning sandboxes, establishing exploration and discovery, etc.

Other zones may be created for distinct types of data, such as video, audio, and images. Persisted videos may have a series of complex security requirements for viewing. For example, a video of a hospitalized patient may reveal the patient's name and date of birth on a visible wristband and serve to violate specific medical regulations. Here separate zones can be established to simplify security with one zone set to incorporate videos without identifiable personal information and a different zone for videos that contain personally identifiable information. Deep learning can be used to determine whether a video contains identifiable information and route inflight videos to the correct leaf zone.

The dashed-line technique can further delineate hybrid cloud and multicloud approaches to data management, where data is also kept physically separated to address regulatory or compliance needs.

The use of data zones should result from a deliberate thought process to develop a cohesive classification approach based on subject areas for managing data in an information architecture. The number and type of data zones should be aligned to the business and be defined in a manner that illustrates how business value is to be derived.

Aligning a data zone to value can help eliminate any arbitrary data storage. All data stores should have an identified owner in the unified data governance function. The following is a list of criteria to help determine when to use subzones within a zone:

- A leaf-level data zone is easier to manage if there is only one underlying technology.

- To avoid complicated security models or a high mixture of redacted/obfuscated data with nonredacted/obfuscated data, consider the creation of separate subzones.

- Storing duplicate or redundant data is not an issue if managed, and the data governance facility provides the appropriate level of visibility.

- Data sharing is not the driving force in decision-making for a data zone. Any opportunity for data sharing is a derivative of a zone map. Therefore, decision-making precedes data sharing in zonal decisions.

- The impetus behind the creation of a data zone is to ultimately provide a user with the wealth of information needed to carry out their analytic responsibilities with a means that is as simple as possible.

- Users should be grouped into communities of interest to ascertain like needs and data sharing opportunities.

- A community of interest is permitted to contain only a single decision-maker.

- Each data zone should be aligned to one or more communities of interest.

- A community of interest may exclusively contain internal users, external users, or machines.

- Subzones can be created to work with or workaround firewall issues.

- Any data is subject to levels of granularity and representation.

- Subzones can be created to accommodate the needs of granularity or representation.

- All data flows to populate a data zone must be predetermined to minimize any side effects and to avoid undesirable outcomes.

- Not all data is created equal, and not all data zones are created equal. So, apply a zone toward a fit-for-purpose paradigm.

- Zones represent an area of specialization.

- Always strive for holistic (overall) simplicity.

All leaf zones must be instantiated in some capacity and fit into an overall platform or solution.

THE BODY AS A MYRIAD OF SILOS: SPECIALIZATION

Each silo within the human body is designed to perform a limited, but highly specialized, set of functions. One silo doesn't try to do the work of another silo. The renal system, for example, doesn't jump in and perform the tasks associated with the immune system. The zones in the topology should be designed to complement specialized business functions and not cause specialized business functions to become less adaptable.

Capabilities for an Open Platform

An information architecture (IA) for AI is ultimately an aggregation of integrated (cohesive and associative) artifacts. The information architecture consists of a number of models, one of which is the data topology and includes the zone maps and data flows.

In developing solutions using machine learning, the practice is not defined solely by a series of algorithms that conform to a given syntax. For example, the following code snippet is just one aspect of a machine learning activity that needs to be addressed by a data scientist and other IT and business professionals responsible for managing a production environment:

```
#apply a light gradient boost model
import lightgbm as lgb
train_data = lgb.Dataset(x_train, label=y_train)
#define parameters
params = {'learning_rate':0.001}
model = lgb.train(params, train_data, 100)
y_pred = model.predict(x_test)
for i in range(0,185):
    if y_pred[i] >= 0.5:
    y_pred[i] = 1
else:
    y_pred[i] = 0
```

Machine learning can involve many activities, including the following:

- Data preparation
  - Ingesting data

- ▪ Exploring data
- ▪ Cleansing data
- ▪ Model development
  - ▪ Engineer features
  - ▪ Train
  - ▪ Tune and test
- ▪ Deployment
  - ▪ Publish
  - ▪ Consume
  - ▪ Monitor

The activities listed previously culminate in the following tenets:

- ▪ **Accessibility:** Data is ready for consumption by machine learning models.

- ▪ **Trustworthiness:** Higher levels of data quality are being realized, data provenance has been added to all data assets, and all AI outcomes can be adequately explained. AI is not regarded as a black-box event.

- ▪ **Resiliency:** An AI environment can operate and perform at scale and is always available.

- ▪ **Measurability:** All activity can be monitored and measured.

- ▪ **Promoting innovation through evolution:** Outcomes are delivered, and the outcomes continually serve to provide a positive impact on the business.

A deployed solution or platform for an information architecture that supports AI should probably be unified around open source assets with a philosophy of embracing hybrid data management. For a modern environment that leverages cloud, fog, or mist computing, a solution should also seek to take advantage of a microservices-based architecture for additional agility and scalability. An open source solution also means that many capability extensions can be incorporated without the need to scrap and rework major portions of the solution.

Core capabilities of a given platform would provide an affinity to the AI ladder that was outlined earlier in the book, namely, the means to collect, organize, analyze, and infuse data for purposes of providing business benefit through AI.

- ▪ Collect data of any type regardless of where the data is physically sourced.

- ▪ Organize data into trusted and curated digital assets that are business-aligned.

- ▪ Analyze data in smarter ways with machine learning and deep learning.

A deployed solution should also be able to augment AI with additional analytic capabilities so as to provide the means to develop complete insight for any decision-maker. Analytic capabilities should address the following:

- Descriptive analytics
- Diagnostic analytics
- Predictive analytics
- Prescriptive analytics
- Sensemaking
- Machine learning models
- Deep learning models

AI itself is an aggregate analytic capability that consists of one or more of the following characteristics:

- Deep learning
- Predictive analytics
- Machine learning
- Translation
- Classification and clustering
- Information extraction
- Natural language processing
- Speech to text
- Text to speech
- Expert systems
- Planning, scheduling, and optimization
- Robotics
- Image recognition
- Machine vision

A deployment in support of AI should include the following:

- Hybrid data management to manage multiple data store technologies
- Unified data governance to ensure planning, oversight, and control over the management of data in the data topology
- Relationships to schema designs, though not the schema designs themselves
- The identification of all technologies involved in exercising the data flows and managing transient and persistent data

- The identification of all technologies involved in providing a secured environment that can ensure privacy and confidentially, inhibit unauthorized access, and provide for logging and auditing of all activities

- The policies and standards to control the analytic environment

- The identification of tools to support all analytics, including self-service tools

- The means to catalog all assets for purposes of discovery as separate from other data governance provisions

- Guidance as to acceptable data quality for purposes of reducing the risk associated with decision-making as a result of cultivating insights

Other areas of a deployment should incorporate the following:

- Search engines
- Cognitive classification
- Inference engines
- File retrieval
- Data discovery
- Data retrieval
- Naming conventions
- Indexing methods
- Registries
- Ontologies
- Taxonomies
- Vocabularies for metadata management
- Data standards
- Middleware
- Data vaults
- Format standards
- Change control

As your organization begins to accelerate its transformations to predict and reshape future business outcomes, attention will gravitate toward higher-value work. The need to automate experiences through AI will grow ever more critical. To implement AI successfully, across an open platform, the platform should help with supporting the data topology to address data complexity, aid with applying collaborative data science, and foster trustworthiness in the outcome from each and every model, every time.

Summary

The Ladder to AI is a progressive concept toward smarter data science by helping organizations understand that they cannot leapfrog reasonable practices for basic and advanced data analytics by going directly to AI. IA for AI is a progressive architecture to build out analytic capabilities that include AI and deep learning. In essence, there is a deep sense that one reaches the ability to enact AI through a prescriptive journey: *a journey to AI*.

Some organizations might be tempted to rush into AI before reaching a critical mass of automated processes and mastering structured analytics. IA for AI is a means to avoid impenetrable black-box systems, cumbersome cloud computational clusters, and a vast plethora of redundant open source toolkits.

By building on a good analytic foothold, organizations should be able to make breakthroughs in complex and critical areas by layering in AI capabilities. But without basic automation, strategic visions for solving complex problems could prove to be elusive. Only after processes critical to achieving an efficient ingestion and data distribution (data flows) mechanism exist can AI be used to yield insights that all organizations are likely to demand.

Organizations do not need to build a repository of pure golden records or establish a definitive and declarative source of truth. Absolute precision in data accuracy is not a de facto standard; the diligent avoidance of fixable data garbage, however, should be a requirement. A schema-less-write approach to data management should not be an excuse for organizational laziness in the data management of an analytical environment within an information architecture.

AI is useful for analyzing a wide set of data and for incorporating diverse data sources such as social media, call center notes, images, open-ended surveys, videos, and electronic body language. The better the data is organized, the quicker an organization can realize value. The use of AI can beget organizational change, and an organization must remain ready and able to change in order to maintain relevance.

Successful organizations on the AI ladder do not skip the basics and understand the need to invest the time, money, and energy to be prepared with sufficiently automated and structured data analytics to maximize the benefit of AI.

This chapter discussed some of the challenges with the software development lifecycle for developing machine learning models, especially in terms of testing models. IBM's OpenScale can assist with testing and evaluating the performance and explainability of a model in production.

For developing an information architecture for AI, a backdrop for a heavily distributed architecture was discussed that involved cloud, fog, and mist computing. Incorporating a rich deployment capability into the information architecture means that applications infused with AI can provide capabilities for systems of engagement and aid in IoT applications for real-time event processing that harnesses machine learning.

Correlating analytical environments to the capabilities of the cloud, fog, and mist maps additional opportunities for an information architecture to bring AI closer to the data. The distributed computing model provides a means to introduce resiliency and continuity into an information architecture while still providing AI-infused competences. The flight paths further offer insight as to when to use AI to act on data.

Data management and the methodical use of siloed data stores can help to maximize the opportunity to serve data in a meaningful way to users across any specialized need that may arise. Provisioning data to users should use the most appropriate database technology, whether that is a graph database, a relational database, a document store, and so on.

The taxonomy for organizing data zones also showed how to address virtualization and federation. Pulling everything together is the need for a technology platform that supports collecting, organizing, analyzing, and infusing AI models with data and applications together.

The journey toward *smarter data science* incorporates the need to establish an information architecture for artificial intelligence—an IA for AI. For your organization to begin *succeeding with enterprise-grade data and AI projects*, multicloud deployment models with cloud, fog, and mist computing will be essential. By following the prescriptive approach outlined by the AI ladder, organizations can be prescriptive in their model deployments. As data is digitized, it means that a copy can be taken without the fear of loss or degradation. Organizations need to take advantage of the fact that copying data doesn't suffer from a generational loss to provision data in a meaningful and manageable way across a zone map—though applying a transformation or exercising a compression algorithm might result in some data loss.

Change is an inevitable consequence of life for people and for organizations. While change cannot be avoided, how we set ourselves up to respond to change can be premeditated. Many aspects of our organizational IT work can be designed to be adaptive in nature, rather than continuously reworked, reintegrated, and redeployed. Creating zones for a data topology should allow for adaptation as much as possible. So too should our work in designing data assets and machine learning models. Embracing the notion of the silo as being paramount to addressing specialization within the organization is critical, as well as becoming knowledgeable in all aspects of data for business use.

Glossary of Terms

This appendix contains a list of acronyms, abbreviations, and initials used throughout this book.

The first column in this table indicates whether the second column is an acronym (A), abbreviation (Ab), or initialism (I).

I	3NF	Third Normal Form
I	5G	Fifth Generation (of Cellular Networking)
I	AGI	Artificial General Intelligence
I	AI	Artificial Intelligence
I	AKA	Also Known As
I	AML	Anti-Money Laundering
I	AMQP	Advanced Message Queuing Protocol
I	API	Application Programming Interface
I	APU	Accelerated Processing Unit
I	BCBS	Basel Committee on Banking Supervision
I	BI	Business Intelligence
A	BLOB	Binary Large Object
I	BME	Biomedical Engineer

I	BPU	Brain Processing Unit
I	CDC	Centers for Disease Control and Prevention
I	CFO	Chief Financial Officer
I	CI/CD	Continuous Integration and Continuous Delivery
A	CLOB	Character Large Object
I	CNN	Convolutional Neural Network
A	COP	Conditions of Participation
I	CPA	Certified Public Accountant
I	CPU	Central Processing Unit
A	DAG	Directed Acyclic Graph
I	Db2	Database 2
I	DBA	Database Administrator
I	DBMS	Database Management System
I	DDL	Data Definition Language
I	DDW	Departmental Data Warehouse
I	DIKW	Data, Information, Knowledge, Wisdom
I	DMZ	Demilitarized Zone
I	DNA	Deoxyribonucleic Acid
I	DPU	Deep Learning Processing Unit
Ab	Dr.	Doctor
A	DRIP	Data Rich, Information Poor
I	DVD	Digital Versatile Disc
A	EBCDIC	Extended Binary Coded Decimal Interchange Code
I	EDW	Enterprise Data Warehouse
I	EKG	Electrocardiogram
I	ELT	Extract, Load, and Transform
I	EPU	Emotion Processing Unit
I	ETL	Extract, Transform, and Load
I	EUR	Euro
A	FAQ	Frequently Asked Question
A	GAN	Generative Adversarial Networks
I	GBP	Great Britain Pound

I	GDPR	General Data Protection Regulation
I	GPS	Global Positioning System
I	GPU	Graphics Processing Unit
I	HDFS	Hadoop Distributed File System
A	HIPAA	Health Insurance Portability and Accountability Act
A	HTAP	Hybrid Transaction/Analytical Processing
I	HTTP	Hypertext Transfer Protocol
I	IA	Information Architecture
I	IaaS	Infrastructure as a Service
I	IBM	International Business Machines Corporation
I	ID	Identifier
Ab	III	The Third
I	IMF	International Monetary Fund
I	IoT	Internet of Things
I	IPU	Intelligence Processing Unit
I	IRS	Internal Revenue Service
A	ISO	International Standards Organization
I	IT	Information Technology
I	JDBC	Java Database Connectivity
I	JFK	John F. Kennedy International Airport
I	JMS	Java Message Service
A	JPEG	Joint Photographic Experts Group
A	JPG	Joint Photographic Experts Group
Ab	Jr.	Junior
A	JSON	JavaScript Object Notation
I	KBE	Knight Commander of the Most Excellent Order of the British Empire
I	KPI	Key Performance Indicator
I	KYC	Know Your Customer
I	LCV	Lifetime Customer Value
A	LEO	Low Earth Orbit
I	LGA	LaGuardia Airport
A	LIME	Locally Interpretable Model-Agnostic Explanations

I	LTE	Long-Term Evolution
A	MACEM	Model Agnostic Contrastive Explanations Method
I	MDP	Minimum Desirable Product
I	MEKP	Methyl Ethyl Ketone Peroxide
I	ML	Machine Learning
I	MMF	Minimum Marketable Feature
I	MMP	Minimum Marketable Product
I	MMR	Minimum Marketable Release
Ab	Mr.	Mister
Ab	Mrs.	Missus
I	MVOT	Multiple Versions of the Truth
I	MVP	Minimally Viable Product
A	NAS	Network Attached Storage
A	NASA	National Aeronautics and Space Administration
I	NFS	Network File System
A	NoSQL	Not Only Structured Query Language or Non-Structured Query Language
I	NPU	Neural Processing Unit
I	NY	New York
I	NYC	New York City
I	ODS	Operational Data Store
I	OLTP	Online Transaction Processing
A	OSAPI	Ownership, Stability, Abstraction, Performance, Interfaced
A	OSHA	Occupational Safety and Health Administration
A	PaaS	Platform as a Service
Ab	Ph.D.	Doctor of Philosophy
I	PHI	Protected Health Information
I	PII	Personally Identifiable Information
I	QA	Quality Assurance
I	RDA	Return on Data Assets
A	RESTful	Representational State Transfer
I	RNN	Recurrent Neural Networks

I	ROA	Return on Assets
I	ROI	Return on Investment
A	SaaS	Storage as a Service or Software as a Service
I	SAE	Society of Automotive Engineers
A	SAN	Storage Area Network
I	SLA	Service Level Agreement
A	SOLO	Structure of Observed Learning Outcomes
I	SQL	Structured Query Language
Ab.	Sr.	Senior
I	SVC	Salvadoran Colón
I	SVOT	Single Version of the Truth
A	SWAT	Special Weapons and Tactics
I	TPU	Tensor Processing Unit
I	U.S.	United States of America
I	USD	United States Dollar
I	UX	User Experience
A	VAN	Vehicle Area Network
A	VIIP	Visual Impairment Intracranial Pressure
A	VIN	Vehicle Identification Number
Ab	WK	Week
I	XBD	European Unit of Account 17
I	XDR	Special Drawing Rights
I	XPT	Platinum
I	XML	eXtensible Markup Language
I	XTS	Code Reserved for Testing
I	XXX	No Currency
A	YARN	Yet Another Resource Negotiator

Index